SPECTRUM

Reading

Grade 4

Frank Schaffer Publications®

Spectrum is an imprint of Frank Schaffer Publications.

Send all inquiries to:
Frank Schaffer Publications
8720 Orion Place
Columbus, Ohio 43240-2111

Spectrum Reading—grade 4

ISBN 0-7696-3864-3

4 5 6 POH 11 10 09 08

Index of Skills

Reading Grade 4

Numerals indicate the exercise pages on which these skills appear.

Vocabulary Skills

Reading Skills

Study Skills

Table of Contents

A Morning in Maine

What would you like to see if you traveled to Maine?

1 "Cameron!" called Grandpa. "Are you awake yet? It's almost eight o'clock. We're wasting the day!" Grandpa stood in the doorway. He wore faded blue jeans, a checkered shirt, and a big grin.

2 "Grandpa," groaned Cameron, "it's the first day of my vacation. I never get up this early when I'm on vacation."

3 "That's because you don't live in Maine," replied Grandpa, opening the shutters and letting the sun spill across the bed. "There is so much to do here that you won't want to miss a thing. Besides, I'm making blueberry pancakes. If you don't get up soon, they may not last."

4 "Okay. The pancakes convinced me, Grandpa," said Cameron, swinging his legs out of bed.

5 "I had a feeling they might," Grandpa chuckled.

6 Over blueberry pancakes with warm maple syrup, Cameron and Grandpa discussed their plans for the day. "I'd like to do some exploring this morning," said Cameron, taking a gulp of milk. "Does that path next to the cabin go straight down to the beach? And how do you get to that little island with the pine trees? Do you think we could catch some fish for dinner?"

7 Grandpa laughed. "I thought there were a few things you might want to do today instead of sleep. Why don't we go for a walk on the beach after breakfast? Later, we can go fishing on the island."

8 "Sounds good to me," said Cameron excitedly.

9 Cameron and Grandpa did the dishes. Then, they put on some old sneakers and followed the sandy path to the beach. The air felt crisp and warm. There was not a cloud in the sky.

10 Cameron was a few steps ahead of his grandfather. He stopped to look at a pool of water that had formed between some rocks. "Look at this, Grandpa!" shouted Cameron. "It's like a miniature ocean."

11 Cameron crouched down to get a better look. Grandpa peered over his shoulder. "There are so many little creatures in there," Cameron said. "How did they get there?"

12 "It's a tide pool, Cameron," said Grandpa. "You'll see them all along this beach. They are my favorite thing to look for on my morning walks. You see, when the tide goes out, water gets caught in shallow pools. It's a pretty neat way to see a little slice of ocean life."

13 Cameron nodded. "This is very cool," he said. "If we had stuff like this at home, I might actually want to get up early. I have a feeling this is going to be a great vacation!"

NAME ______________________

Vocabulary Skills

Write the words from the story that have the meanings below.

1. changed someone's mind

   ______________________ Par. 4

2. talked about

   ______________________ Par. 6

3. very small

   ______________________ Par. 10

4. ocean water that moves in and out several times a day

   ______________________ Par. 12

5. not deep

   ______________________ Par. 12

A **synonym** is a word with the same or nearly the same meaning as another word. Find a synonym in the story for each of the words below.

6. laughed ______________________ Par. 5
7. swallow ______________________ Par. 6
8. several ______________________ Par. 10
9. yelled ______________________ Par. 10

A **prefix** is a group of letters added to the beginning of a word to change its meaning. The prefix **pre-** means *before*. For example, *preheat* means *to heat before*. Add **pre** to each word below. Then, use each new word in a sentence.

10. _______view ______________________

    ____

11. _______pay ______________________

    ____

12. _______wash ______________________

    ____

Reading Skills

Write **T** before the sentences that are true. Write **F** before the sentences that are false.

1. _____ Cameron is visiting his grandpa in Massachusetts.
2. _____ Cameron wakes up before Grandpa does.
3. _____ Grandpa makes blueberry pancakes for breakfast.
4. _____ Cameron and Grandpa plan to go fishing in the afternoon.
5. _____ Cameron and Grandpa have to drive to get to the beach.
6. _____ Grandpa finds the tide pool before Cameron does.
7. Name one thing Cameron wants to do when he goes exploring.

   ____

Study Skills

Guide words are printed at the top of each page in a dictionary. The guide word at the left is the first word on the page. The guide word at the right is the last word on the page. Check each word that could be found on a page having the guide words shown in dark print.

1. **crate—crib**

   _____ crayon _____ cringe _____ create

2. **mile—mix**

   _____ minus _____ minute
   _____ microphone

3. **paint—park**

   _____ paste _____ packet _____ pants

A Slice of Ocean Life

What do you think you might see in a tide pool?

1 You might think that the ocean is the only place in nature to find sea creatures. But if you visit the beaches of the northeast United States, you might get to see all kinds of ocean life in the miniature worlds of tide pools.

2 Tide pools form when the tide goes out and ocean water is trapped in rocky hollows near the shore. Many different types of plants and animals live in these pools. The one thing they have in common is that they must be strong. It is not easy to survive in an environment that changes often.

3 High-level pools are shallow. They are the most difficult types of pools for animals to live in. The sun causes some of the water in these shallow pools to evaporate, or dry up. That makes the water even saltier than the ocean. On the other hand, when there is a lot of rain, high-level pools lose much of their saltiness. This can also be hard for sea creatures to survive.

4 Some animals have shells that keep them from drying out in the sun. A barnacle has a soft, slippery body that is covered with a hard shell made of tiny plates. Barnacles attach themselves to rocks. When sea water washes over them, barnacles open up their plates. They use their legs to trap small bits of food from the water.

5 It is a bit easier for sea creatures to live in mid-level tide pools. The water is deeper there. The tide washes over them several times a day, so they do not become too dry. Creatures like the starfish and the sea urchin live in mid-level pools. Their sticky tube feet help them cling to rocks. This keeps them from being pulled out to sea by big waves.

6 Sea anemones, which look like seaweed, also live in mid-level tide pools. An animal that gets stung by the tentacles of a sea anemone finds out very quickly that it is not a plant.

7 Low-level tide pools often contain forests of kelp, a type of brown seaweed. The kelp provides a home or serves as food for many types of sea animals, such as small fish, worms, crabs, sponges, and sea urchins. Ocean animals are not the only ones who find a good use for kelp. People use it as an ingredient in ice cream.

8 The next time you have a chance to stroll along the ocean shore, be sure to keep your eyes open. You just might get to peek through a window into the world of underwater animals.

NAME ______________________

Vocabulary Skills

Write the words from the article that have the meanings below.

1. to stay alive

______________________ Par. 2

2. area around you; surroundings

______________________ Par. 2

3. to catch or capture

______________________ Par. 4

4. gives or offers

______________________ Par. 7

5. to look

______________________ Par. 8

Read each word below. Then, write the letter of its synonym on the line beside the word.

6. _____ difficult	a. totally
7. _____ completely	b. walk
8. _____ usually	c. hard
9. _____ stroll	d. often

A word that means the opposite of another word is an **antonym**. Find an antonym in the story for each of the words below.

10. huge ______________________ Par. 1

11. slowly ______________________ Par. 6

12. few ______________________ Par. 7

The prefix **non-** means *not*. For example, *nontoxic* means *not toxic*. Add **non** to each word below. Then, use each new word in a sentence.

13. _______sense ______________________

____

14. _______stop ______________________

____

15. _______swimmer ______________________

____

Reading Skills

Circle the word that best completes each sentence and write it on the line.

1. Plants and animals must be ______________ to survive in a tide pool.

   weak   large   strong

2. When water dries up, it ______________.

   evaporates   dies   melts

3. Starfish and sea urchins have sticky ______________.

   backs   eyes   feet

4. Which type of tide pool is most difficult for animals to live in?

   ____

5. What is one way humans use kelp?

   ____

6. Check the reason the author probably wrote this story.

   _____ to entertain the reader

   _____ to give some facts about tide pools

   _____ to teach people about ocean tides

Grandpa's Light Show

What would you think if you saw colored lights moving across the night sky?

1 Cameron and Grandpa were preparing for Cameron's parents to arrive for the weekend. First, they opened all the windows so the cabin would smell like the fresh ocean air. Grandpa did three loads of laundry, and Cameron helped him hang the sheets to dry on the clothesline. Then, they picked two buckets of blueberries. "Enough to turn our fingers and our tongues blue!" said Grandpa.

2 It was just before dinnertime when Cameron's parents arrived. They were exhausted from their long drive and ready to relax.

3 "Wait until you see what we have planned for dinner," said Cameron, hugging his parents. He gave them only a few minutes to change their clothes and unpack before he led them down the path to the beach. Grandpa had already started a small fire in the fire pit.

4 "I had no idea you two were such good fishermen and cooks!" said Mom when she sampled the fish and the roasted corn. "This tastes wonderful! It reminds me of summers in Maine when I was a girl," she said, smiling and patting Grandpa on the knee.

5 "It gets even better, I hear," said Dad. "When's dessert?"

6 Mom, Dad, Grandpa, and Cameron were eating their blueberry sundaes on the porch when streaks of green, yellow, and purple shot across the sky.

7 "Did you see that?" shouted Cameron, jumping out of his chair. "What do you think that was? It looked like it could have been a spaceship or something!"

8 Mom began to laugh. "That," she said, "was the perfect ending to a perfect day."

9 "Those are the northern lights, Cameron," said Grandpa. "I'm so glad you got a chance to see them. Spring and fall are usually a much better time than summer to see them in Maine."

10 "Look, there they go again," said Dad, pointing to a flickering of pink and pale green light over the water.

11 "But what are they?" asked Cameron.

12 "I guess you could call them a colored light show in the night sky," said Grandpa. "You can only see them in the parts of the world that have high latitudes, which means the areas are closer to the poles. Tonight is a perfect night to see the northern lights because it is clear and moonless."

13 Cameron sat back down in his chair and picked up his bowl of ice cream. "Grandpa, I think I just might have to move to Maine. There is definitely too much to see here on just one vacation!"

NAME ____________________

Vocabulary Skills

Write the words from the story that have the meanings below.

1. getting ready

________________________ Par. 1

2. very tired

________________________ Par. 2

3. take it easy; unwind

________________________ Par. 2

4. tried; tasted

________________________ Par. 4

5. most of the time

________________________ Par. 9

Check the meaning of the underlined word in each sentence.

6. Cameron and Grandpa <u>picked</u> two buckets of blueberries.

_____ chose

_____ gathered

7. Cameron thought the northern lights <u>looked</u> like a spaceship in the sky.

_____ appeared

_____ stared

8. You can see the northern lights in parts of the world that are closer to the <u>poles</u>.

_____ long, thin sticks

_____ the most northern and southern ends of Earth

The prefix **mis-** means *badly*. For example, *misspell* means *to spell badly*. Add **mis** to each word below. Then, write the meaning of the new word.

9. _______behave ____________________

10. _______match ____________________

11. _______count ____________________

12. _______understand ____________________

13. _______use ____________________

Reading Skills

Write **C** before the groups of words that describe Cameron and **G** before the groups of words that describe Grandpa.

1. _____ said that spring and fall are better times for seeing the northern lights

2. _____ thought the northern lights were a spaceship

3. _____ started a fire in the fire pit on the beach

4. _____ wants to move to Maine

5. _____ said blueberries would turn their fingers blue

Write **T** before the sentences that are true. Write **F** before the sentences that are false.

6. _____ Cameron and Grandpa bought some blueberries at the store.

7. _____ Grandpa picked up Cameron's parents at the airport.

8. _____ Dinner reminds Mom of summers in Maine when she was little.

9. _____ Grandpa has never seen the northern lights before.

10. _____ The northern lights are usually seen only in places with high latitudes.

11. Name one thing Cameron and Grandpa do to prepare for Cameron's parents.

____

____

Mysterious Lights

What do you think causes the northern lights?

1 Many years ago, people who saw waves of color dance across the sky at night were frightened. Some groups of people made up legends to explain what today is known as the northern lights, or *aurora borealis* (uh-ROAR-uh bore-ee-A-LUSS). Aurora was the Roman goddess of dawn, or early morning. The word *boreal* means *north* in Latin, so *aurora borealis* means *northern lights*.

2 The sun gives off particles that are filled with energy. Large groups of these particles travel together. They are called *solar wind*. The particles travel through space at hundreds of miles per second. Even traveling that fast, it still takes several days for the particles to reach Earth. When the solar wind gets close to Earth, it moves toward the two magnetic poles, the North Pole and the South Pole.

3 When the solar particles get close to Earth, they become trapped in Earth's atmosphere. They collide, or run into, gases in the atmosphere. The energy that is made in that collision creates light. When lots of these collisions happen at the same time, northern lights can be seen from Earth. The northern lights are harmless, but it can be frightening to see the sky fill with flashing colored lights if you do not know what they are.

4 As far as scientists can tell, the northern lights do not make any sounds that people on Earth can hear. Even so, if you live in a place where the northern lights can be seen, you might notice problems with your television, radio, or cell phone every once in a while. The energy created by solar wind in the Earth's atmosphere can get in the way of sound waves and pictures that travel through the air to your TV or radio.

5 The northern lights are truly amazing, especially the first time you see them. Even in the highest latitudes, the lowest section of the lights are still 40 miles above Earth. The northern lights stretch up about six hundred miles into the atmosphere. Imagine what a light show you would see if you were an astronaut looking down on the northern lights from space.

NAME ______________________

Vocabulary Skills

Read each word below. Then, write the letter of its antonym on the line beside the word.

1.	_____ dangerous	**a.**	creates
2.	_____ destroys	**b.**	closer
3.	_____ apart	**c.**	harmless
4.	_____ farther	**d.**	separate
5.	_____ collide	**e.**	together

Think of the meaning of the prefix in each word. Then, write the meaning of the word.

6. precook ______________________

7. nonfiction ______________________

8. misspell ______________________

9. nonsense ______________________

10. preschool ______________________

Reading Skills

Circle the word that best completes each sentence and write it on the line.

1. Some people made up ____________ to explain the lights they saw in the sky.

paintings legends experiments

2. Solar particles and ____________ collide in Earth's atmosphere to create the northern lights.

gases light ice

3. Scientists do not think the northern lights make any ____________.

explosions steam sounds

4. In Roman myths, who was Aurora?

____

5. Toward which two areas of Earth does solar wind move?

____

6. About how far away from Earth is the lowest section of the northern lights?

____

7. Check the sentence that best states the main idea of the selection.

_____ The northern lights are amazing the first time you see them.

_____ Collisions of solar particles create lights in the night sky.

_____ The northern lights are also called *aurora borealis*.

Study Skills

An **outline** is used to put ideas in order. It shows the important facts in a story. Use the facts from paragraph 1 to complete Part I. Use the facts from paragraph 3 to complete Part II.

I. Northern lights in history

A. People saw moving colors in sky and were frightened

B. ______________________

C. Aurora was Roman goddess of dawn

II. How northern lights are created

A. Solar particles get trapped in Earth's atmosphere

B. ______________________

C. Energy from collision creates light

D. When lots of collisions happen at once, northern lights can be seen

The Land of the Northern Lights

What legends have you heard that explain something in nature?

1 Many years ago, there lived a Wabanaki chief. He had only one child, a son. The chief often worried about his son. He did not see the boy run and play with other children in the village. Still, the boy would disappear for hours at a time. His parents were never quite sure where he would go.

2 One day, the chief saw his son follow a milky white path up into the sky. The chief followed his son on the path but lost sight of him when he arrived in strange and unfamiliar country.

3 "Where am I?" the chief wondered aloud as he stood looking around the strange land where everything was lit by a dim white light.

4 An old man with wrinkled skin and kind eyes heard the chief. "You are in the Land of the Northern Lights," replied the old man.

5 "But how did I get here?" asked the chief. "Where has my son gone?"

6 The old man placed his hand on the chief's shoulder. "You came here the same way I did," he said. "You followed the trail of the Milky Way. Your son comes often to play with our children."

7 "Please take me to him," said the chief.

8 The two men walked along until they came to a group of braves playing ball. The chief had never seen children playing ball before. He watched excitedly as they ran and laughed and tossed the ball through the air. Each brave wore a belt made of a rainbow. As they leaped and ran after the ball, lights in the colors of the rainbow swirled around them.

9 For a few moments, the chief could only watch as the children chased the ball and threw it in the air. Shimmering lights in blue, green, red, gold, and purple danced across the milky white sky. The brightest lights came from the chief's son, who moved quickly and easily among the other braves.

10 When the game had ended, the boy noticed his father watching him. "You are not angry with me, are you?" he asked the chief.

11 "No, I am not angry," answered the chief, putting one arm around the boy's shoulder. "But it is time to go back to our village now. Perhaps you can teach the children to play the games you have played here."

12 The old man sent two large birds to carry the chief and his son along the path of the Milky Way to their village. From that day on, whenever the chief and his son saw the northern lights, they thought of the children laughing and playing ball in the sky, the colors from their rainbow belts swirling around them.

NAME ______________________

Vocabulary Skills

Write the words from the story that have the meanings below.

1. small town

______________________ Par. 1

2. not known

______________________ Par. 2

3. not bright

______________________ Par. 3

4. threw

______________________ Par. 8

5. jumped

______________________ Par. 8

6. twinkling

______________________ Par. 9

In each row, circle the three words that belong together.

7. years days path minutes
8. leaped jumped hopped quickly
9. hand shoe shoulder arm

The prefixes **im-** and **in-** mean *not.* For example, *impossible* means *not possible. Inexact* means *not exact.* The prefix **im-** is usually used before words that begin with *b, m,* or *p.* The prefix **in-** is usually used before words that begin with other letters. Add **im** or **in** to each word below. Then, write the meaning of the new word.

10. ________expensive ______________________
11. ________perfect ______________________
12. ________correct ______________________

Reading Skills

1. Number the events below from **1** to **5** to show the order in which they happened in the story.

_____ Whenever the chief and his son saw the northern lights, they thought of the children playing ball.

_____ The chief and the old man watched the braves play ball.

_____ The boy's parents were worried about him.

_____ The boy asked the chief if he was angry.

_____ The boy followed the trail of the Milky Way.

2. The boy's parents were worried about him because ______________________.

3. How did the boy and the chief get to the Land of the Northern Lights?

____

____

4. What were the belts the braves wore made of?

____

____

5. What do you think the boy taught the children in the Wabanaki village when he got home?

____

____

____

____

A Mancala Morning

Have you ever played a game from another country?

1 On Saturday morning, Madison and her friends Drew and Kiona were planning to go for a bike ride. They were waiting for Malaika, the high school exchange student from Africa who was staying with Madison's family.

2 Madison, Drew, and Kiona had a snack while they waited for Malaika to come home from the library. Madison was just pouring some popcorn into a big bowl when she heard a rumble of thunder.

3 "Uh-oh," said Drew, looking out the kitchen window. The sky was turning darker, and the wind blew dry leaves across the backyard. "It looks like today might not be the best day for a bike ride."

4 Suddenly, the front door slammed. Malaika came inside and put down her backpack. Her hair was ruffled from the wind. Tiny drops of rain dotted her glasses.

5 "Hi, Malaika!" called Madison. "What's it like outside?"

6 "It looks like a big storm is rolling in," said Malaika, wiping her glasses on the corner of her shirt.

7 Madison sighed. "Now we have nothing to do this afternoon," she said. "I really wanted to go for a bike ride. It's going to start getting cold out soon. This might have been the last weekend to ride until spring!"

8 Malaika laughed. "My brothers, sisters, and I never had bikes," she said, "but we still had plenty of things to keep us occupied on rainy days. Have you ever played the African game called *Mancala*?"

9 "I've never heard of it," said Madison, shaking her head.

10 "I haven't either," added Kiona.

11 "I played that at camp last year," said Drew. "It was one of the games in our game room. But how can we play without a board?"

12 "I know just the thing," said Malaika. "All we need is an egg carton, some dried beans, and some markers."

13 Madison and Drew gathered the materials. Then, Malaika and Kiona put red dots on 24 beans and green dots on the other 24 beans.

14 "Now what?" asked Kiona.

15 "Well, we need to have two teams. Since Drew and I have both played before, we'll be on different teams. What should we name the teams?"

16 "Let's see," said Kiona. "Drew and I will be the Mancala All-Stars." She grinned. "As long as you can be all-stars without having won anything yet."

17 "Malaika and I will be the 5Ms," said Madison. "That stands for Madison and Malaika the Marvelous Mancala Masters!"

18 "Are you ready to learn the rules and play the first game?" asked Malaika.

19 "Sure," said Kiona. "I can't wait to earn our name."

20 "Not if we can help it!" shouted Madison and Malaika together.

NAME ______________________

Vocabulary Skills

Write the words from the story that have the meanings below.

1. closed loudly

_________________________ Par. 4

2. lots; many

_________________________ Par. 8

3. busy

_________________________ Par. 8

4. collected or brought together

_________________________ Par. 13

A word that means the opposite of another word is an **antonym**. Write the pair of antonyms from each sentence.

5. Madison worried it would get cold soon, and she wouldn't be able to ride her bike until warm weather came again.

_____________ _____________

6. Malaika and her siblings never had bikes, but they always found fun things to do.

_____________ _____________

7. One team will use the right side of the egg carton, and the other team will use the left.

_____________ _____________

When you add an apostrophe (') and the letter **s** to a singular noun, it shows that a person or thing owns something. Write the possessive form of each word in parentheses.

8. _____________ family is hosting an exchange student. (Madison)

9. There were spots of rain on _____________ glasses. (Malaika)

10. The _____________ color grew darker and darker. (sky)

11. The _____________ goal is to win the game. (team)

12. The _____________ rules are easy to explain. (game)

Reading Skills

A **fact** is something that can be proven to be true. An **opinion** is what a person believes. It may or may not be true. Write **F** before the sentences that are facts. Write **O** before the sentences that are opinions.

1. _____ Madison's friends are named Drew and Kiona.
2. _____ Thunderstorms are exciting.
3. _____ Madison put some popcorn in a bowl.
4. _____ Drew doesn't know how they will play Mancala without a board.
5. _____ Drew and Kiona will win the game.
6. _____ Mancala All-Stars is a great name for the winning team.
7. Check the sentence that best states the main idea of the story.

   _____ Madison gets bored when it rains.

   _____ On a rainy afternoon, Malaika teaches some friends how to play an African game.

   _____ Malaika tells her friends about her life in Africa.

8. Where did Drew learn how to play Mancala?

____

9. What does the team name the *5Ms* stand for?

____

It's All a Game

What are some of your favorite games to play?

1 Games from all around the world can be fun and simple to play. Some of the games might be similar to ones you have played many times before. Others may be new to you. The one thing you can be sure of is that you will enjoy getting a glimpse of how children in countries around the world like to play.

2 Many countries have a version of the game of jacks. In the United States, it is played with a small rubber ball and 15 star-shaped metal pieces. The object of the game is to pick up a certain number of jacks in one hand on the first bounce of the ball. There are many variations of this game. In Brazil, it is called *Cinco Marias*, or Five Marias, and it is played with pebbles instead of jacks. Smooth, flat stones and two to four players are all you need to play.

3 Another interesting game is the Chinese tangram. It is a puzzle that has been enjoyed in China for more than two hundred years. It might appear to be a simple game, but it is more complex than it seems. You begin with a square of paper that has been divided into seven pieces: five triangles, a square, and a rhombus. The goal is to make as many pictures as possible using the pieces. You can make pictures of animals, people, objects, or things in nature. It is possible to make more than 1,500 images with the seven pieces in a tangram!

4 Have you ever seen a group of people kicking around a small, colorful footbag? *Takraw* is a popular game in Thailand. Traditionally, the ball was made of rattan, or a hard, basketlike material. Today, the ball is usually made of hard plastic. The players stand in a group and try to pass the ball back and forth to one another without allowing it to touch the ground. Does this sound too simple? The trick to the game is that you can use only your head, shoulders, feet, and legs, not your arms or hands.

5 The next time you get together with your friends to play a game, think about trying a game from another country. You might find something familiar, or you might find a brand-new pastime.

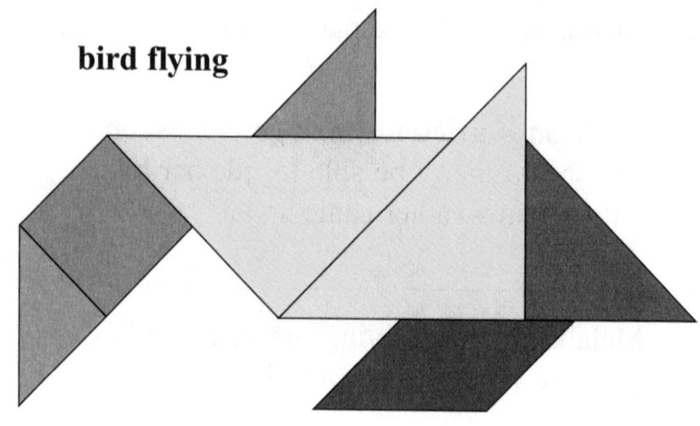

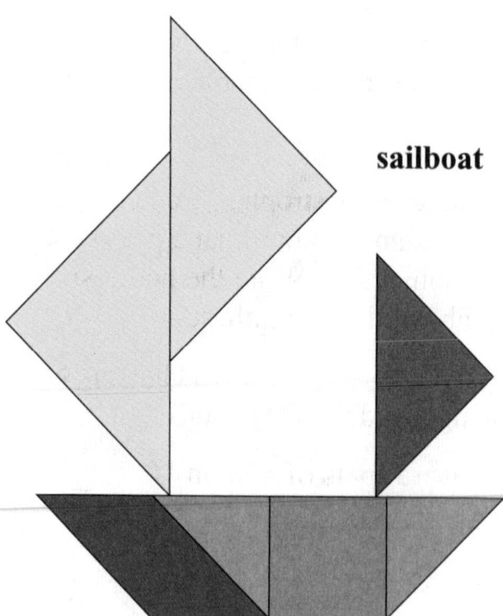

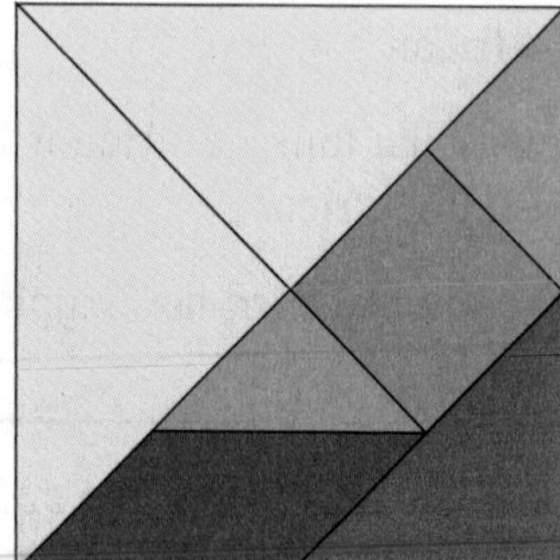

Square cut into the seven shapes needed for Chinese tangrams.

NAME ______________________

Vocabulary Skills

Write the words from the article that have the meanings below.

1. a quick look

_____________________ Par. 1

2. to seem

_____________________ Par. 3

3. complicated; not simple

_____________________ Par. 3

4. as it has been done in the past

_____________________ Par. 4

5. a pleasant way of spending time

_____________________ Par. 5

A **synonym** is a word with the same or nearly the same meaning as another word. Find a synonym in the article for each of the words below.

6. easy _____________________ Par. 1

7. goal _____________________ Par. 2

8. separated _____________________ Par. 3

9. letting _____________________ Par. 4

Underline the word with a prefix in each sentence. Then, write the meaning of the underlined word on the line.

10. Do not forget to preheat the oven when you make the pizza.

____

11. We took a nonstop flight from Cleveland to New York.

____

12. The tickets we bought last week were inexpensive.

____

Reading Skills

Circle the word that best completes each sentence and write it on the line.

1. The Chinese tangram is _______________ than it seems.

   easier older harder

2. In the past, the *takraw* ball was usually made of _______________.

   plastic rubber rattan

3. You cannot use your _______________ to hit the ball in *takraw*.

   feet shoulders hands

4. Check the sentence that best states the main idea of the story.

   _____ *Takraw* is a popular game in Thailand.

   _____ The Chinese tangram puzzle is not as easy as it may seem.

   _____ It can be fun and interesting to play games from all around the world.

5. How many shapes is the paper divided into in tangram?

   ____

6. What rule of the game makes *takraw* difficult to play?

   ____

Write **J** before the words that describe the United States' version of the game of jacks. Write **T** before the words that describe Chinese tangram.

7. _____ played with metal pieces

8. _____ possible to make more than 1,500 images

9. _____ begins with a square divided into seven shapes

10. _____ exists in many variations

Birthday Breakfast

Have you ever made a surprise meal for someone?

1 "Malaika!" whispered Madison into the early morning darkness. Malaika rolled over in her bed, but she didn't wake up. "Malaika!" whispered Madison again, this time gently shaking the girl's shoulder. "Are you awake?"

2 "What's wrong, Madison?" asked Malaika sitting straight up in bed.

3 "Nothing. Today is Mom's birthday. Dad and I are going to make her a surprise breakfast of pancakes and eggs. Do you want to help?"

4 Malaika stretched and grinned. "I would love to help, Madison. I've never made pancakes before, and I don't think I've ever eaten American-style eggs. Besides, your mom definitely deserves a birthday surprise!"

5 "Great!" said Madison. "We'll meet you downstairs in about 15 minutes."

6 When Malaika joined Madison in the kitchen, she was assembling the breakfast ingredients. Madison was still wearing her favorite pink pajamas. Her fuzzy white slippers peeked out below her pajama pants like two small rabbits. Dad was dressed for the day, but he didn't look quite awake yet. He sat at the kitchen table sipping coffee from a large mug.

7 "Malaika, I need your help. Dad and I are both terrible at cracking eggs without getting the shells in the batter. Can you break the eggs?"

8 "Sure, Madison. I can even show you how I do it. You just have to give the egg a good crack on the side of the bowl. If you do it too lightly, you have to tap the egg several times. Then, the shell cracks into small pieces," said Malaika.

9 Dad nodded. "That's what Madison's mom always tells us, but we just don't seem to have the touch."

10 "I'm going to try it this time, Dad," said Madison.

11 Madison successfully cracked the eggs into the pan. "I did it!" she cheered.

12 "Shhhh!" said Dad and Malaika.

13 "Oops," said Madison. "I forgot Mom was still sleeping."

14 The rest of the preparation went smoothly. Malaika flipped pancakes while Dad squeezed fresh orange juice and Madison scrambled the eggs. At the last minute, Madison grabbed a fake flower from an arrangement in the living room. She added it to Mom's breakfast tray.

15 "That's what I call a team effort," said Dad. Madison and Malaika agreed.

16 "This will be the best eggshell-free birthday breakfast Mom ever had!" said Madison.

NAME ___________________________

Vocabulary Skills

A word that sounds the same as another word but has a different spelling and meaning is a **homophone**. Circle the homophone that correctly completes each sentence below and write it on the line.

1. Madison asks Malaika if she ______________ like to help make breakfast. (would, wood)
2. Dad and Madison think it is hard to ______________ eggs. (brake, break)
3. Madison uses a ______________ from the arrangement in the living room. (flour, flower)

A **compound word** is a word made by combining two smaller words. For example, *lighthouse* is made of the words *light* and *house.* Underline the compound word in each sentence. Then, write the two words that make up each compound.

4. Our dog likes to play in the backyard.

   ______________ ______________

5. I would love to own a sailboat one day.

   ______________ ______________

6. Don't forget to bring sunscreen to the beach!

   ______________ ______________

7. I have to do my homework before I can go to the park.

   ______________ ______________

Reading Skills

Write **T** before the sentences that are true. Write **F** before the sentences that are false.

1. _____ Madison wakes up Malaika because she is hungry.
2. _____ Madison's favorite pajamas are pink.
3. _____ Malaika has not made pancakes before.
4. _____ Mom helps everyone make pancakes and eggs for breakfast.
5. Do you think Madison will ask Dad and Malaika to help her the next time she wants to plan a surprise? Why or why not?

   ____

   ____

6. Madison and her dad don't like cracking eggs because ______________________.

Circle the word that best completes each sentence and write it on the line.

7. Madison's idea for making a surprise breakfast was a ______________.

   mistake success failure

8. Dad thinks that he, Madison, and Malaika work well as a ______________.

   team business surprise

Study Skills

Circle each word that could be found on a dictionary page having the guide words shown in dark print.

1. **artist—attic**

   anteater argument ask

2. **deer—doughnut**

   distant deep dodge

3. **star—supper**

   soap stand sunny

4. **warn—wicker**

   windy whine wag

Plenty of Pancakes

Have you ever followed a recipe before?

Before you begin:

- Never use the stove without an adult's supervision.
- Always remember to keep the handle of the skillet turned in so you cannot accidentally bump into it.
- Be sure to wash your hands with soap and hot water after you touch the raw eggs.

Perfect Pancakes

1 cup flour
1 tablespoon sugar
2 teaspoons baking soda
$\frac{1}{4}$ teaspoon salt
1 egg
1 cup milk
2 tablespoons oil

1 Here are some other things you will need: a measuring cup, a teaspoon, a tablespoon, a small bowl, a medium-sized bowl, a wooden spoon, cooking spray, a skillet, a spatula, AND a big appetite.

2 First, mix together the dry ingredients in a medium-sized bowl. Then, mix the milk, egg, and oil together in a small bowl. Make a well, or hole, in the middle of the dry ingredients. Pour the egg mixture into the well. Stir the batter only until it is moist. It should still look lumpy. (If you stir it too long, the pancakes will be tough instead of fluffy.)

3 Coat a skillet with cooking spray and heat it over a medium heat. When the skillet is hot, pour in enough batter to make a circle about the size of your fist. Then, tilt the skillet slightly to let the batter spread out and form a bigger circle.

4 When the edges turn light brown and start to bubble, use a spatula to flip the pancake.

5 Serve the pancakes with butter and warm maple syrup. This recipe makes about 8–10 pancakes.

Banana Akara
(African Banana Fritters)

6 very ripe bananas
1 cup flour
$\frac{1}{4}$ cup granulated sugar
$\frac{1}{4}$ cup water
1 teaspoon nutmeg

6 Here are some other things you will need: a measuring cup, a teaspoon, a fork, a small bowl, a large bowl, cooking spray, a skillet, and a spatula.

7 Peel the bananas, and place them in the large bowl. Mash the bananas with a fork. Then, add the flour and stir until blended.

8 Mix together the water and sugar in a small bowl to make a syrup. Then, add the nutmeg to the syrup. Add the syrup to the banana mixture, and mix well. If it is thicker than pancake batter, add a bit more water.

9 Coat a skillet with cooking spray, and heat it over a medium heat. When the skillet is hot, pour in a small amount of the mixture.

10 Use a spatula to turn the fritter when the edges begin to turn golden brown. This recipe makes about 24 small banana fritters.

NAME ______________________

Vocabulary Skills

Write the words from the recipes that have the meanings below.

1. frying pan

______________________ Par. 1

2. damp or slightly wet

______________________ Par. 2

3. to turn slightly so something slopes or slants

______________________ Par. 3

4. a wet mixture used in cooking

______________________ Par. 3

Underline the prefix in each word for numbers 5–8. Then, complete each sentence with one of the words.

5. misuse
6. preview
7. nonfiction
8. incomplete
9. Kahlil used a ______________ book about dinosaurs to write his report.
10. My parents wanted to ______________ the movie before my sister and I watched it.

Reading Skills

1. Check the reason the author probably wrote this story.

_____ to show you how to become a chef

_____ to tell about how to make different types of pancakes

_____ to explain some important rules to remember when you are cooking

2. Number the sentences below to show the order in which you should do each step when you make banana akara.

_____ Mash the bananas with a fork.

_____ Flip the fritter when the edges turn brown.

_____ Coat the skillet with cooking spray.

_____ Peel the bananas.

_____ Add the nutmeg to the syrup.

3. What will happen if you stir the pancake batter for too long?

____

____

Study Skills

An **index** is located at the end of many nonfiction books. It is an alphabetical listing of all the topics in a book. You can use the index to find out where to look for information about a particular topic. Use the index below to answer the questions.

INDEX

banana fritters (akara) 16
cranberry-walnut bread 12
French toast. 9
pancakes 2
    blueberry pancakes 3
    banana-pecan pancakes 4
spice cake 21
waffles 5

1. On what page can you find a recipe for French toast?

____

2. How many pancake recipes are there in this book?

____

Ready for a New Friend

Will Estéban want to get a new dog?

1 "I'm home, Mom!" called Estéban as he tossed his backpack on the bench in the hallway. "Are we still going to the mall to buy my shoes tonight?"

2 "I almost forgot," said Mrs. Ramirez, giving Estéban a quick kiss on the top of his head. "Things were a bit chaotic at work this afternoon."

3 "No problem," Estéban replied. "Can we still go to the mall, though?"

4 "Of course we can," said Mrs. Ramirez, hunting for her keys in her purse.

5 Estéban and Mrs. Ramirez were both surprised at how quickly they found the pair of shoes Estéban was looking for. As they left the athletic store, they passed a couple walking in the opposite direction. The man walked slowly, and he gripped the leash of a red harness in his hand. At the other end of the leash was a chocolate Labrador with glossy fur and an eager, friendly face.

6 "Mom," said Estéban as they walked to the parking lot, "was that a seeing-eye dog?"

7 "Yes," replied Mrs. Ramirez. "He looked like such a good, attentive dog, didn't he?" she asked her son, smiling.

8 "Sure," said Estéban. "Are they allowed to go anywhere?"

9 "I think they can go almost anywhere people can," said Mrs. Ramirez. "That's what the dogs are there for—to help their owners do everyday things that they might need a little extra help doing."

10 "I miss Sadie," said Estéban suddenly. Sadie was the sweet-natured mutt that the Ramirez family had adopted when Estéban was just a baby. She had died nearly six months ago, but Estéban still thought of her almost every day.

11 Mrs. Ramirez unlocked the car door and gave Estéban a quick hug with one arm. "I miss her, too, sweetie," she said. "That dog had such a good heart, didn't she?"

12 Estéban nodded. "Mom, you said to tell you when I thought I might be ready to get another dog."

13 Mrs. Ramirez smiled at Estéban in the rearview mirror. "I thought you might be ready soon. How do you feel about the idea of being a foster family to a puppy that will grow up to be a seeing-eye dog?" she asked.

14 Estéban was quiet for a moment. "We'd have to give the puppy back, though, wouldn't we?"

15 "Yes, we'd only have the puppy for about a year. It would be our job to socialize her so she would get used to lots of different kinds of people and places."

16 Estéban grinned. "I think we'd be the perfect foster family for a puppy," he said.

17 "Let's talk about it with your dad tonight," Mrs. Ramirez said. "Then, maybe we can find out some more information on the Internet."

18 "We're getting a puppy!" said Estéban to himself, leaning back in his seat. "There will be so much to teach her!"

NAME ________________________________

Vocabulary Skills

Write the words from the story that have the meanings below.

1. in a state of great confusion

   ______________________________ Par. 2

2. something that fits around an animal's upper body

   ______________________________ Par. 5

3. alert; giving a lot of attention to

   ______________________________ Par. 7

4. abruptly; all at once

   ______________________________ Par. 10

5. to train to be well-adjusted and easy to be around

   ______________________________ Par. 15

In each row, circle the words that belong together.

6. tossed threw used flung
7. common ordinary unusual everyday
8. wonder tell inform explain
9. shiny dry glossy sleek

When you add an apostrophe (') and the letter **s** to a singular noun, it shows that a person or thing owns something. Write the possessive form of each word in parentheses on the line.

10. ______________ mother took him to the mall to buy new shoes. (Estéban)
11. A ______________ foster family will keep the puppy for about a year. (puppy)
12. A seeing-eye ______________ job is to help a blind person get around more easily. (dog)

Reading Skills

1. Number the events below in the order in which they happened in the story.

   _____ Mrs. Ramirez asked Estéban if he would be interested in fostering a puppy.

   _____ Estéban said that he missed Sadie.

   _____ Mrs. Ramirez looked for her keys in her purse.

   _____ Estéban saw a man with a seeing-eye dog at the mall.

   _____ Estéban and Mrs. Ramirez went to the mall.

2. Estéban and his mother went to the mall because ______________________________.

3. Who is Sadie?

   ____

   ____

4. Why would the Ramirez family only have a foster puppy for about a year?

   ____

   ____

5. A **summary** is a short sentence that tells the most important facts about a topic. Check the sentence below that is the best summary for paragraph 5.

   _____ The chocolate Labrador wore a red harness.

   _____ Estéban was interested to see a man and his seeing-eye dog at the mall.

   _____ Estéban found the shoes he wanted.

A Big Decision

What would it be like to foster a puppy?

1 On the first day of classes, the Ramirez family arrived early at the Seeing-Eye Dog Center. They were going to learn about being a foster family for a puppy.

2 "Okay, group," said Mr. Crockett. "I think we're ready to begin." He was a tall man with a graying beard. "How many of you are here tonight because you might like to foster one of our puppies?"

3 About half the people in the group raised their hands. Mr. Crockett nodded. "First of all, you should know how happy we are to have you here. Fostering a puppy is very important work. I think you'll find it very satisfying, but it is also quite demanding."

4 "What do you think some of your responsibilities will be?" Mr. Crockett asked.

5 Estéban raised his hand. "Well, I think it will be our job to make sure the puppy gets used to being around people. We'll have to take her to lots of different places, like shopping malls and ball games."

6 "That's right," said Mr. Crockett. "You should try to expose your puppy to things like crowds, the sounds of traffic, riding in cars or on buses, and other animals. That way she won't grow up to be a dog who gets frightened or startled easily."

7 A teenage girl with curly light brown hair sat across the room from Estéban. She rested one hand lightly on the back of a golden retriever who sat beside her chair. "This is Mitzi," she said, patting the dog on her side. "We've had her for about nine months. When you get your puppies, you have to be ready to spend a lot of time with them. They might feel lonely at first. Most of them have never been away from the other pups in the litter until they come to live with you. The first couple of nights we had Mitzi, I actually slept in a sleeping bag on the floor so I could be near her. It made her feel safe and comfortable."

8 The girl chuckled. "I don't recommend more than a couple of nights on the floor, though." She grinned and rubbed her back at the memory.

9 "What questions do you have so far?" asked Mr. Crockett as he looked around the circle.

10 "How can you give up the puppies after a whole year?" asked Estéban. "Don't they feel like part of your family by then?" This is what had worried him most about the idea of fostering.

11 Mr. Crockett nodded. "I can't tell you that it isn't hard," he said. "My family and I have fostered seven dogs over the years, and we loved every one of them. You just need to remember how important these dogs will be to their new companions. They really help open up the world to people who are blind. If you can remember what a gift seeing-eye dogs are, it becomes a little easier to say good-bye."

12 As the meeting ended, Mr. and Mrs. Ramirez turned to Estéban. "What do you think?" asked Mr. Ramirez. "Is this something we can handle? It will be a big responsibility."

13 Estéban looked at his dad. "I know we can do it, Dad. I can't wait to meet our puppy."

NAME ____________________

Vocabulary Skills

Write the words from the story that have the meanings below.

1. to take care of temporarily

_______________ Par. 2

2. fulfilling

_______________ Par. 3

3. to show

_______________ Par. 6

4. friends

_______________ Par. 11

A word that sounds the same as another word but has a different spelling and meaning is a **homophone**. Circle the homophone that correctly completes each sentence below.

5. The Ramirez family (made, maid) the decision to foster a puppy.
6. They will (rays, raise) the puppy for about a year.
7. A puppy will wag its (tale, tail) to show that it is happy.
8. The teenage girl patted Mitzi on her (side, sighed).
9. A puppy with large (pause, paws) will probably grow up to be a big dog.

Underline the compound word in each sentence. Then, write the two words that make up each compound.

10. There is a new playground at the park near my house.

_______________ _______________

11. The small, red farmhouse sat at the edge of the field.

_______________ _______________

Reading Skills

1. Puppies may feel lonely at first because _______________.
2. Why does a foster family need to expose a puppy to lots of different things?

____

____

3. Why does Estéban feel worried about giving up a puppy after a year?

____

____

4. Do you think Mr. Crockett will foster more seeing-eye puppies in the future? Why or why not?

____

____

5. Check the words that describe Estéban.

_____ responsible

_____ kind

_____ competitive

_____ funny

_____ thoughtful

6. Write **F** before sentences that are facts. Write **O** before sentences that are opinions.

_____ About half the people at the meeting are thinking about fostering a puppy.

_____ Fostering puppies is an enjoyable way to spend time.

_____ Estéban and his parents will be a good foster family.

_____ The girl sitting across from Estéban has curly hair.

Not Just Monkeying Around

Do you think that animals other than dogs can be trained to help people?

1 Have you ever heard of Monkey College? Who do you think goes to school there? If you said monkeys, you were right. Dogs are not the only animals that can be trained to help people. Helping Hands, an organization in Cambridge, Massachusetts, trains capuchin monkeys to be companions and helpers for people in wheelchairs who cannot move their arms or legs.

2 More than 20 years ago, Dr. M. J. Willard was working with a person who had recently become paralyzed. She thought that a monkey might be able to help her patient with some basic household chores. Dr. Willard was right. Not only can monkeys be trained to help people, they are also wonderful companions.

3 Capuchin monkeys are found in the wild in South Central America. They are about the size of a small cat and can live to be nearly 40 years old. They are very intelligent. They are also known for being friendly and good with their hands. Capuchin monkeys have opposable thumbs, which means they can use their hands much in the way that people do.

4 Everyday tasks, like turning on a light, putting something in the microwave, or pressing *play* on a CD player, can be difficult for someone who cannot use his or her arms and legs. Capuchin monkeys can easily perform these tasks. This allows their owners more freedom. They can accomplish things on their own and can live independently.

5 The monkeys and their owners become friends and learn to depend on each other. Some owners say the monkeys are almost like children to them. The monkeys can be mischievous and sometimes like to play tricks on their owners. This is especially true of young monkeys. Mostly, though, they like to please their owners. They like the treats they receive when they do a good job, and they like to be praised. Capuchin monkeys also love the affection they get from their companions. They love to snuggle, too.

6 Helping Hands matches people with disabilities to monkey companions who can help them. But the close friendships between the monkeys and their owners happen all on their own.

NAME ______________________________

Vocabulary Skills

Check the meaning of the underlined word in each sentence.

1. Helping Hands <u>trains</u> capuchin monkeys.

   _____ groups of railroad cars

   _____ teaches or instructs

2. A Helping Hands monkey is more than just a <u>pet</u> for its new owner.

   _____ a tame animal that lives with a person

   _____ to stroke or touch lightly

3. In the <u>wild</u>, capuchin monkeys spend a lot of time playing in the trees.

   _____ out of control

   _____ a natural area; wilderness

Fill in the blanks below with the possessive form of the word in parentheses.

4. A _______________ opposable thumbs allow it to use its hands for many things. (monkey)

5. The _______________ friendship with his or her monkey is often very strong. (owner)

6. People with disabilities are often amused by their _______________ actions. (companions)

7. _______________ experiment was quite a success! (Dr. Willard)

Reading Skills

1. Check the sentence that best states the main idea of the story.

   _____ Monkeys are fun to have as pets.

   _____ Monkeys can be trained to help people with disabilities.

   _____ Monkeys can be mischievous.

2. Name two reasons why monkeys are good at helping humans.

   ____

   ____

3. Where is Helping Hands located?

   ____

4. Where do capuchin monkeys live in the wild?

   ____

Write **T** before the sentences that are true. Write **F** before the sentences that are false.

5. _____ Capuchin monkeys live to be about 20 years old.

6. _____ Capuchin monkeys can learn to perform many different tasks.

7. _____ Dr. Willard taught capuchin monkeys to speak.

8. _____ Most monkey owners form a strong relationship with their companions.

Study Skills

A **table of contents** is one of the first pages in a book. It shows the title and page each chapter begins on. Use the table of contents below to answer the questions.

Monkey Business
Table of Contents

Chapter 1: Types of Monkeys 2
Chapter 2: Habitat. 7
Chapter 3: Eating Habits 12
Chapter 4: Communication 15

1. What kind of information would you find on page 12?

   ____

2. On what page does the second chapter begin?

   ____

Monkey Training

What would it be like to live with a monkey?

1 It is not that rare to hear of a family who is fostering a puppy for a seeing-eye dog school. It is much more unusual to hear of a family who is fostering a capuchin monkey for the Helping Hands organization.

2 Just like puppies, young monkeys need to be socialized before they can be trained as human helpers. One difference is that monkeys live longer than dogs do. This means that a monkey's "childhood" is also longer than a dog's. They need plenty of time to play and act like children before they are ready to settle down to the serious business of training. Monkeys may spend four to six years in a foster home before they are ready to begin training. The foster families say it is almost as much work as raising a young child!

3 Once a monkey begins training, it usually takes about a year for it to learn enough tasks to be a good helper. When a monkey is learning a task, it is rewarded with a treat. If the monkey makes a mistake, it is not punished; it just does not get a treat for that task.

4 One thing that the monkeys need to learn is how to follow commands. For example, if a person wants to have the lights turned on, he or she might give the command "sun." If the owner has dropped something, he or she might say "fetch." The monkey will know just what its owner means by these commands, and it will complete the task. Then, it will often get a reward like a pat on the head or a lick of peanut butter.

5 As the monkeys get better at completing their tasks, they learn new and more difficult ones. Some monkeys can scratch an itch on their owners or even learn how to use a computer!

NAME ______________________

Vocabulary Skills

Write the words from the article that have the meanings below.

1. taught how to behave correctly

______________________ Par. 2

2. given something in return for a service or good behavior

______________________ Par. 3

3. an order

______________________ Par. 4

4. to finish

______________________ Par. 4

5. Write the two words in the first paragraph that are synonyms.

__________ __________

6. Write the two words in the third paragraph that are antonyms.

__________ __________

Find an antonym in the article for each word below.

7. similarity ______________________ Par. 2
8. seldom ______________________ Par. 4
9. simple ______________________ Par. 5

The suffix **-less** can mean *to be without.* For example, *useless* means *to be without use.* Add **less** to each base word below. Then, use each new word in a sentence.

10. worth__________ ______________________

____

11. pain__________ ______________________

____

Reading Skills

1. Does a dog or a monkey have a longer "childhood"?

____

2. Name two tasks the article says that a monkey can do for a person.

____

____

3. How long do monkeys spend in a foster home before they begin their training?

____

4. Why do you think it is more common for people to foster dogs than monkeys?

____

____

5. Check the phrase that best describes the author's purpose.

_____ to compare different types of monkeys

_____ to share information about how companion monkeys are trained

_____ to convince the reader to get a monkey as a pet

6. Check the sentence below that is the best summary for paragraph 2.

_____ Monkeys have a longer life span than dogs.

_____ Monkeys need time to grow up before they can be socialized as human helpers.

Soccer Summer

Have you ever attended a sports camp?

1 "Eliza, have you decided what you'd like to do during the week that Mom and I will be in California this summer?" asked Eliza's dad. He and Eliza were setting the table for dinner.

2 "Well," said Eliza, "I'd rather go to California with you and Mom."

3 "I know, Eliza. We wish you could come with us, too. But it's just going to be so busy with all the meetings we have to go to that you wouldn't have any fun. Actually, I'd trade places with you in a second," said Dad with a big grin. "You don't think Mom would notice if I went to horseback riding camp or soccer camp, do you?" he joked.

4 Eliza laughed. "I'm pretty sure she'd notice, Dad. I guess that if I can't go with you and Mom, I'd like to go to soccer camp. Madeline is going, so at least I'll know someone, even if I'm not very quick on the field."

5 "Eliza, I think you'll do just fine," said Dad. "I know it's a little scary to go to a new place and meet so many new people. I think you'll be glad you did it, though," he said, resting his hand on her shoulder. "Besides, I've seen you play soccer. You're more talented than you think you are."

6 When Eliza and Madeline arrived at camp, they were happy to see that two girls from their class were also enrolled. "Now it feels a little more like home," said Eliza happily.

7 On the first day of camp, the counselors had the girls choose teams. Eliza was surprised that she was chosen as captain of her team, the Quick Kickers. That afternoon, the girls practiced several drills. Eliza was the first one done with each task the counselors assigned. She did her best to cheer on her teammates as they completed the course.

8 At the end of the first practice, a shy girl named Annie approached Eliza. "I just wanted to say thanks for helping us stay focused out there," said Annie. "I was really nervous about coming to camp, but you made me feel so comfortable and motivated."

9 Eliza couldn't help laughing. "Oh, Annie," she said, "I was probably even more nervous than you were!"

NAME ______________________________

Vocabulary Skills

Write the words from the story that have the meanings below.

1. good at something

______________________________ Par. 5

2. signed-up for

______________________________ Par. 6

3. leaders; supervisors at a camp

______________________________ Par. 7

4. exercises in which you learn by doing something over and over again

______________________________ Par. 7

5. excited and encouraged

______________________________ Par. 8

Read each word in the column on the left. Then, write the letter of its synonym on the line beside the word.

6.	_____ grin	**a.**	exchange
7.	_____ trade	**b.**	select
8.	_____ notice	**c.**	smile
9.	_____ choose	**d.**	observe

The suffix **-ment** can mean *the act of*. For example, *agreement* means *the act of agreeing*. Add **ment** to each base word below. Then, use each new word in a sentence.

10. excite__________ ____________________

____

11. embarrass__________ ____________________

____

12. measure__________ ____________________

____

Reading Skills

Circle the word that best completes each sentence and write it on the line.

1. Eliza finished each ______________ the counselors assigned.

   task conversation team

2. Annie talked to Eliza after the first ______________.

   lesson practice evening

3. Dad thinks Eliza is a ______________ soccer player.

   funny talented lazy

Write **B** if the sentence describes something that happens before Eliza goes to camp. Write **A** if the sentence describes something that happens after Eliza gets to camp.

4. _____ Madeline and Eliza are happy to see that two girls they know are enrolled.
5. _____ Eliza tells Annie she was nervous.
6. _____ Dad and Eliza set the table for dinner.
7. _____ Annie thanks Eliza for helping her stay focused.
8. _____ Dad tells Eliza that she'll do fine at camp.
9. Do you think Eliza will want to go to camp again next summer? Why or why not?

____

____

10. Why does Eliza tell Annie that she felt nervous?

____

____

Play Ball!

How did soccer become such a popular sport in the United States?

1 What if someone asked you to go to an association football game? Would you be interested? You might be more interested if you knew they were talking about soccer, the world's most widely played sport. Games similar to soccer were played as long as two thousand years ago in China! Modern soccer got its name from association football, a game played in England in the mid-1800s. The word *association* was shortened to *assoc*, which finally turned into *soccer*.

2 The first soccer clubs were formed in England in the 1850s. The first professional players joined in the 1880s. Soccer quickly spread across Europe and became very popular in countries such as Spain, Italy, and Germany. Soccer even spread to countries in faraway South America. People seemed to like how simple the game is. All you need to play is a ball and two goals. Everything else comes from the players. Soccer still remains incredibly popular in both Europe and South America. Professional players there are often as popular as movie stars are in the United States.

3 One of the best and most famous of these professionals is Edson Arantes do Nascimento. He is better known by his nickname, Pelé. Pelé was born in Brazil, a country in South America. With Pelé's help, Brazil won three World Cup titles from the late 1950s to the early 1970s. Today, he is still one of the all-time leading scorers in World Cup history with 12 goals. The International Olympic Committee named Pelé Soccer Player of the Century in 1999.

4 The World Cup is the worldwide soccer competition that is held every four years, once for women and once for men. More than 200 teams work hard to be chosen as one of the 32 best teams that get the honor of competing in the Men's World Cup. More than a billion people watched the 2002 match on television. The first Women's World Cup match was played in 1991 in China. Today, about 100 teams compete for just 16 spots.

5 It took longer for soccer to be accepted in the United States than it did in other places around the world. A different kind of football was already being played in this country. People were not eager to try another form. After Pelé joined the New York Cosmos in 1975, soccer became more popular in the United States. It continues to grow in popularity. Today, soccer is the second favorite sport for kids in the United States!

NAME ________________________

Vocabulary Skills

Circle the homophone that correctly completes each sentence below and write it on the line.

1. Brazil ______________ three World Cup titles. (one, won)
2. A ______________ and some goals are all you need to play a game of soccer. (ball, bawl)
3. After playing for a long time, the soccer players need to take a ______________. (brake, break)

Write a compound word using two words in each sentence.

4. A ball that you kick with your foot is a ______________.
5. Wood that is used to make a fire is ______________.
6. A yard that is near a barn is called a ______________.
7. Work that you do at home is ____________.
8. A bell that you ring at someone's door is a ______________.

Reading Skills

1. Number the events below in the order in which they happened in the selection.

   _____ More than a billion people watched the World Cup on television.

   _____ Pelé was named Soccer Player of the Century.

   _____ The first soccer clubs were formed in England.

   _____ Games similar to soccer were played in China.

   _____ Pelé joined the New York Cosmos.

2. Check the reason the author probably wrote this story.

   _____ to tell people about the history and popularity of soccer

   _____ to explain how the game of soccer is played

   _____ to show how soccer got its name

3. Name two European countries where soccer is popular.

   ______________ ______________

4. What do you need to play a game of soccer?

   ____

5. In what country was Pelé born?

   ____

6. It took longer for soccer to be accepted in the United States because ____________
   ________________________________.

Study Skills

Use the chart below to answer the questions that follow.

World Cup Statistics

Country	Number of 1st Place Wins	Number of Games Played	Total Games Won
Brazil	4	80	53
Italy	3	66	38
France	1	41	21

1. Which country has the most first place wins? ______________
2. Which country has won a total of 21 games? ______________
3. How many World Cup games has Italy played? ______________
4. How many World Cup games has Brazil won? ______________

Quick Feet and a Big Heart

What is it like to play soccer professionally?

1 When Mia Hamm was growing up, there were not many female athletes to have as role models. Today, there are many more women in professional sports. Mia Hamm, often called the world's best all-around female soccer player, is happy to be a role model for many young athletes, both girls and boys.

2 Mariel Margaret Hamm was born in 1972 in Selma, Alabama. Her father was in the military, so she moved around a lot as a child. Mia's mother wanted her to take ballet lessons, but Mia was not interested. She wanted to take soccer lessons, instead. This turned out to be the right choice for her. Mia was just 15 years old when she became the youngest player ever to get a spot on the U. S. National Team!

3 Mia attended college at the University of North Carolina at Chapel Hill. She helped the women's soccer team there win the national championship four times in a row. When Mia graduated, her number was retired. This is a great honor for any athlete.

4 In 1991, the first Women's World Cup was held in China. At only 19 years old, Mia was the youngest member of the team, but she still helped the United States win the title.

5 In the 1996 Olympic Games in Atlanta, Georgia, Mia was proud to lead the women's team as it won a gold medal. More sports fans came to watch this game than had ever before attended a women's event. This was a good sign that women's sports were being taken more seriously in the United States. In 2004, Mia helped the U.S. team win another gold medal. She retired from the national team later that year, so the victory at the Athens Olympics was very meaningful for her.

6 During her career, Mia scored 158 goals in international competition. This makes her the leading scorer in the world among both men and women!

7 Since her retirement, Mia has had more time to devote to the charities that are important to her. In 1997, Mia's older brother Garrett died of a bone marrow disease. Mia and her brother had been very close. In his honor, Mia started the Mia Hamm Foundation to raise money to fight bone marrow disease and to support sports programs for girls. Mia also works with many other charities. She likes to help other young athletes, both boys and girls, achieve their goals.

NAME ______________________

Vocabulary Skills

Write the words from the article that have the meanings below.

1. mark of excellence

______________________ Par. 3

2. of two or more countries

______________________ Par. 6

3. to help or to supply

______________________ Par. 7

4. reach; accomplish

______________________ Par. 7

Check the meaning of the underlined word in each sentence.

5. Mia has scored many <u>goals</u> in international competition.

_____ something a person works hard for

_____ a score for driving a ball into a certain area

6. When Mia was a teenager, she won a <u>spot</u> on the U. S. National Team.

_____ a mark or stain

_____ a place; a position

The suffix **-able** can mean *capable of. Reasonable* means *capable of reason*. Add **able** to each base word below. Then, use each new word in a sentence.

7. afford_________ ______________________

____

8. teach_________ ______________________

____

9. adjust_________ ______________________

____

Reading Skills

Write **T** before the sentences that are true. Write **F** before the sentences that are false.

1. _____ Mia Hamm was born in Chapel Hill.
2. _____ Mia's brother's name was Garrett.
3. _____ Mia is happy to be a role model for young athletes.
4. _____ Mia wanted to take ballet lessons when she was younger.
5. _____ Mia helped her team win a gold medal in the 1996 and 2004 Olympics.
6. Why did Mia start the Mia Hamm Foundation?

____

____

7. Explain why Mia might enjoy being a role model for girls.

____

____

8. Why do you think Mia Hamm has been so successful in her life?

____

____

9. Check the sentence that best states the main idea of the selection.

_____ Mia Hamm liked playing soccer better than taking ballet lessons.

_____ Mia Hamm is a talented athlete and a giving person.

_____ Mia Hamm helped her college team win the national championship four times.

Soccer's Newest Star

What does it take to become a young sports star?

1 Even if you don't pay much attention to soccer, you may have heard of Freddy Adu. America has never seen another young soccer player like this amazing teenager.

2 In 1997, Emelia Adu brought her sons Freddy and Fro to America from Ghana, a country in Africa. She wanted them to have more opportunities for a good education. Freddy first learned to play soccer in Ghana when he was six years old. He often played barefoot in neighborhood games with older boys and even grown men. Freddy thinks that these games helped him develop his skills and become a better player.

3 Freddy did not play organized soccer right away when he moved to Potomac, Maryland. A classmate was amazed by Freddy's skills in a school game and took him to a local soccer tournament. Freddy met the coach, Arnold Tarzy. Tarzy was so impressed when he saw Freddy play, he asked Freddy to join the Potomac Cougars. That was the start of Freddy's soccer career.

4 Later, Freddy moved to Florida to train and play with the "under-17s," a group of male soccer players who are under 17 years old. While he was in Florida, he spent a lot of time doing schoolwork. In fact, Freddy worked so hard, he was able to finish his last three years of high school in just two years.

5 Once he had finished school, Freddy was offered a large sum of money to play for a European soccer league team. He, his coach, and his parents decided that he was too young. Instead, Freddy accepted a position with the DC United, a major league soccer team in Washington, D.C. That makes Freddy Adu the youngest major league soccer player ever!

6 People admire Freddy Adu because of his speed, his fearlessness, and his skills on the soccer field. But Freddy is also a hard worker. He has a great deal of respect for the game, his teammates, his family, and himself. The world expects great things from Freddy Adu, and it looks like he will have no trouble living up to those expectations.

NAME ______________________

Vocabulary Skills

Write the words from the article that have the meanings below.

1. a good set of circumstances; a good chance

______________________ Par. 2

2. to grow and progress

______________________ Par. 2

3. to look up to

______________________ Par. 6

4. bravery; courage

______________________ Par. 6

Circle the words in each row that belong together.

5. amazed worried surprised astonished
6. league team organization position
7. follow quick speedy rapid
8. honor admire disappoint respect

Underline the suffix in each word. Then, write the meaning of the word on the line next to it.

9. enjoyable ______________________
10. useless ______________________
11. reasonable ______________________
12. amazement ______________________

Reading Skills

1. Emelia Adu brought her sons to the United States because ______________________

______________________.

2. In what city and state did Freddy live when he first moved to the United States?

____

3. Why didn't Freddy accept the offer to play for the European soccer league team?

____

____

4. Where did Freddy first play soccer? With whom did he play?

____

____

5. Check the words that describe Freddy.

_____ hardworking

_____ fearless

_____ lazy

_____ talented

_____ bored

Write **F** before the sentences that are facts. Write **O** before the sentences that are opinions.

6. _____ Freddy Adu was born in Ghana, Africa.
7. _____ Emelia Adu made the right choice when she decided to move to America.
8. _____ Freddy is the nicest young soccer player today.
9. _____ Freddy trained with the "under-17s" in Florida.

Study Skills

Number the words in each group to put them in alphabetical order.

1.		2.	
_____	wonder	_____	excited
_____	whisper	_____	extreme
_____	whom	_____	exact

Applecreek Orchard

Have you ever picked fruit in an orchard?

1 On Friday morning, the sky was bright and clear, and the air was crisp. The school bus turned onto the gravel road that led to Tomás's uncle's apple orchard. As the bus pulled up to the small white house with green shutters, a large man with dark hair and a wide grin came outside.

2 Tomás's class got off the bus and stretched. Ms. Hallowell shook Uncle Luis's hand. "Thank you so much for allowing our class to visit your orchard," she said. "It's all they could talk about this week."

3 Uncle Luis laughed. "Well, I'm glad you could all come," he said to the class. "Are you ready to do some picking?" he asked in a booming voice.

4 "Yes!" shouted Ms. Hallowell's class.

5 "Well, hop up on the tractor bed, and remember to keep your arms and legs inside at all times," said Uncle Luis.

6 Tomás's uncle stopped the tractor at the beginning of a neat row of trees that were bursting with ripe fruit. He turned to the class. "Northern California is a wonderful place to grow apples," he said. "We have a lot of the weather they like—rainy springs, warm summers, and cool, crisp nights. Here at Applecreek Orchards, we mostly grow three varieties of apples: Granny Smith, Braeburn, and Pink Lady. Today, you'll be picking Braeburn apples. They are sweet, spicy, and crisp. They taste good raw, but they are also good for cooking."

7 "Who picks all your apples?" asked Cara, who was sitting next to Tomás.

8 "Every fall, I hire a crew to come and help me pick them. They work long days, seven days a week, just to make sure that the apples are picked at the right time," answered Uncle Luis.

9 "Once all the apples are picked, what do you do all winter?" asked Tomás's friend Kelly. "Do you get to go on vacation?"

10 Uncle Luis chuckled. "There is still a lot of work to do in the orchard during the winter. We have to grade, or assign categories, to the apples. Then, they have to be packed and shipped all around the country. We ship apples to places as far away as Florida. We also have to prune the trees. That helps them stay healthy and grow in the spring. It also lets more light reach the leaves and the apples."

11 "Whew!" said Tomás. "That sounds like a lot of work."

12 Uncle Luis nodded and handed Tomás a glossy red apple he had just picked. "Try this," he told his nephew. Tomás bit into the apple, and a bit of sweet juice ran down his chin. "What do you think?" asked Uncle Luis. "Is it worth all the hard work?"

13 Tomás's mouth was full of apple, so all he could do was nod and smile.

NAME ______________________

Vocabulary Skills

Write the words from the story that have the meanings below.

1. a place where fruit trees are grown

   ______________________ Par. 1

2. window coverings often found on the outside of houses

   ______________________ Par. 1

3. a sound that is loud and deep

   ______________________ Par. 3

4. kinds or types

   ______________________ Par. 6

5. to trim or thin out

   ______________________ Par. 10

Circle the homophone that correctly completes each sentence below, and write it on the line.

6. A small ______________ ran beside the apple orchard. (creak, creek)
7. Uncle Luis had to ______________ people to help him pick the fruit. (hire, higher)
8. There was a tin ______________ next to the barn door. (pail, pale)
9. Apple trees need plenty of ______________ to produce large, sweet fruit. (reign, rain)

Write the words from the story that match the abbreviations below.

10. Fri. ______________________
11. CA ______________________
12. FL ______________________

Reading Skills

Circle the word that best completes each sentence, and write it on the line.

1. At the farm, the school bus turned onto the ______________ driveway.

   smooth concrete gravel

2. Uncle Luis's farm is in Northern ______________.

   Maine California Arkansas

3. Tomás is Ms. Hallowell's ______________.

   teacher student parent

4. Check the phrase that best describes the author's purpose.

   _____ to convince the reader to buy apples only from California orchards

   _____ to explain how to buy and run your own orchard

   _____ to tell a story about a class trip to an orchard

5. Name two types of apples Uncle Luis grows at Applecreek Orchards.

   ______________ ______________

6. Do you think Uncle Luis will take a vacation next winter? Why or why not?

   ____

   ____

   ____

To Market, to Market

What kinds of things can you find at a farmers' market?

1 "I'll see you in a couple of days!" called Tomás's mom through the car window. "If you bring some apples home with you on Sunday, I promise I'll make a pie." Tomás and his uncle waved and headed back to the house. Uncle Luis was going to start selling his apples at the local farmers' market. Tomás was spending the weekend with his uncle to help him set up the fruit stand.

2 "What's the first thing we need to do?" asked Tomás.

3 "Well, I thought we could load my truck with everything we'll need to bring with us tomorrow," answered Uncle Luis. "We'll have to leave pretty early in the morning. Your days often start before dawn when you are a farmer."

4 Tomás and Uncle Luis carried basket after basket of fresh, fragrant apples to the truck. They loaded the long folding tables and the yellow striped awning. Finally, Uncle Luis added the green and red wooden sign that said *Applecreek Orchards*.

5 "Can you think of anything we're forgetting?" Uncle Luis asked his nephew.

6 Tomás thought for a moment. "Won't you need money to make change for your customers? Also, I think we need a scale to weigh the apples."

7 "You're absolutely right, Tomás," said Uncle Luis. "This is just why I wanted your help. I have a change box in the house, and it's all ready to go, but I would have completely forgotten about bringing a scale. Good thinking!"

8 The next morning, Tomás and Uncle Luis were on the road just as the sky was beginning to turn as pink as cotton candy. They hadn't had any breakfast yet, but Uncle Luis promised Tomás that there would be plenty of choices at the farmers' market.

9 As they pulled into the town's small downtown area, Tomás could see more than a dozen vendors setting up their stands. When the truck was unloaded, Uncle Luis gave Tomás a few dollars and asked him to buy some breakfast. A few minutes later, Tomás returned with warm cinnamon buns that were frosted with a thin layer of melting sugar. He handed the money back to his uncle.

10 Uncle Luis looked surprised. "These look too good to have been free," he said. "What happened?"

11 Tomás grinned. "They wanted to trade the cinnamon rolls for a few fresh apples. It sounded like a good deal to me."

12 Uncle Luis nodded his head. "Tomás, it looks like you and I are in business together!"

NAME ______________________

Vocabulary Skills

Write the words from the story that have the meanings below.

1. the time of day just as the sun begins to rise

   ______________________ Par. 3

2. having a pleasant smell

   ______________________ Par. 4

3. the son of your brother or sister

   ______________________ Par. 5

4. twelve

   ______________________ Par. 9

5. people who sell things

   ______________________ Par. 9

Fill in the blanks below with the possessive form of the word in parentheses.

6. The ______________ cinnamon buns were warm and sweet. (baker)
7. ______________ uncle wanted to sell his apples at the market. (Tomás)
8. Tomás and Uncle Luis drove into the ______________ small downtown area. (town)
9. The ______________ market offered many different kinds of produce. (farmers)

Reading Skills

1. Why is Tomás spending the weekend with his uncle?

   ____

   ____

2. Do you think Tomás will help Uncle Luis again? Why or why not?

   ____

   ____

3. What does Tomás remind his uncle to bring to the farmers' market?

   ____

   ____

4. What does Tomás get for breakfast? What does he plan to exchange for his breakfast?

   ____

   ____

Write **T** before the phrases that describe Tomás and **L** before the phrases that describe Uncle Luis.

5. _____ forgot to load the scale into the truck
6. _____ traded apples for cinnamon buns
7. _____ said that your days often start before dawn when you are a farmer
8. _____ waved to his mom in the driveway

Study Skills

Use the information on the poster to answer the questions below.

Rocky River Organic Farm Produce	
Tomatoes	$1.95 per pound
Peppers.........	$2.00 per pound
Cucumbers	$1.25 each
Potted Herbs	$2.50 per pot or 5 pots for $10.00
Honey	$2.25 per jar

1. How much would it cost to buy two pounds of peppers? ______________
2. What costs $2.25 per jar? ______________

Bees in the Trees

How do bees help apple farmers?

1 Have you ever seen an apple tree in bloom? If you have, you know that the blooms are a delicate, pale pink that slowly fade to white. They make the air smell as sweet as honey. There is a good reason for this. Apple trees need to attract bees, and a sweet odor is just the thing to do it.

2 Bees can be picky. They do not like to fly when it is below 60 degrees outside. They also do not like being out in weather that is windy or rainy. Apple farmers know that their apples depend on bees, so many purchase bees to release into their orchards every spring. They usually release about one hive of bees per acre of orchard.

3 When the weather is good, the bees get to work. The bee collects the nectar from the apple tree's flower. As it does this, its wings brush against the pollen. When the bee flies to another flower to gather more nectar, it pollinates that flower. A bee might pollinate one type of apple blossom with the pollen from another type of apple tree. This means that a seed from a Red Delicious apple might not produce a Red Delicious tree.

4 How do owners of apple orchards get the types of trees they want? To produce a certain type of tree, apple farmers use a process called *grafting*. They take a twig, or *scion* (SIGH-un), from the parent tree and attach it to a small, young tree. The two will grow together as a single plant. The scion contains buds that will produce new twigs and leaves that are the same type as the parent tree. Because it is so easy to create new varieties of apples, nearly 7,500 different types exist around the world.

5 Growing apples was a popular hobby with some of the most famous Americans. Presidents George Washington and Thomas Jefferson were both apple growers. They even liked to trade wood from their apple trees so they could grow new varieties.

6 The next time you bite into a sweet, crisp apple, think about its long history in America and the work of the bees and the apple farmers who helped it along.

NAME ______________________________

Vocabulary Skills

Write the words from the article that have the meanings below.

1. lose brightness or color

   ______________________________ Par. 1

2. to draw to itself; to interest

   ______________________________ Par. 1

3. to buy

   ______________________________ Par. 2

4. to let go

   ______________________________ Par. 2

5. a sweet liquid found in flowers

   ______________________________ Par. 3

In each row, circle the three words that belong together.

6. bloom flower blossom honey
7. odor orchard fragrant scent
8. process nectar pollen flower
9. twig branch bee scion

Fill in the blanks below with the possessive form of the word in parentheses.

10. The apple ______________ color slowly fades to white. (blossom)
11. The ______________ wings brush against pollen when they collect nectar. (bees)
12. An ______________ seeds might not produce the same type of tree. (apple)
13. The ______________ buds will produce new twigs and leaves. (scion)

Reading Skills

Write **T** before the sentences that are true. Write **F** before the sentences that are false.

1. _____ Most apple tree blossoms are pale yellow.
2. _____ The sweet smell of the flowers attracts bees.
3. _____ Bees do not like to be out in bad weather.
4. _____ A Red Delicious apple seed will always produce a Red Delicious tree.
5. _____ There are about 3,500 varieties of apples around the world.
6. Why do apple farmers purchase bees?

   ____

7. How do bees carry pollen from one flower to another?

   ____

8. What is the name of the process apple farmers use to produce the type of apple tree they want?

   ____

9. What is a *scion*?

   ____

10. Number the following steps in the order in which they occur.

    _____ The scent of the flowers attracts bees.

    _____ The bee carries the pollen to another flower.

    _____ The bee collects nectar from the flower.

    _____ The apple tree flowers.

An Apple a Day

What kinds of foods can you make using apples?

Before you begin:

- Never use the stove without an adult's supervision.
- Always remember to keep the handle of the pan turned in so you cannot accidentally bump into it.

Homemade Applesauce

4 medium apples
$\frac{1}{2}$ cup water
$\frac{1}{4}$ cup sugar
$\frac{1}{8}$ teaspoon cinnamon
$\frac{1}{8}$ teaspoon nutmeg

1 Here are some other things you will need: a measuring cup, teaspoon, peeler, cutting board, knife, pan, wooden spoon, and a fork or potato masher.

2 First, peel the apples. Have an adult help you slice them. (You can throw away the cores.) Then, cut the apple slices into small chunks.

3 Put the apple chunks in the pan with the water. Let them simmer over a medium heat for 15 minutes. Then, stir in the sugar, cinnamon, and nutmeg.

4 When the applesauce cools, mash the chunks with a fork or a potato masher. Serve with graham crackers or a spoonful of whipped cream. Refrigerate any applesauce you do not eat.

Baked Apples

4 large apples
$\frac{1}{4}$ cup brown sugar, firmly packed
1 teaspoon cinnamon
1 teaspoon nutmeg
$\frac{1}{4}$ cup raisins
$\frac{1}{4}$ cup chopped pecans or walnuts
4 teaspoons butter
$\frac{1}{2}$ cup apple juice or cider

5 Here are some other things you will need: a measuring cup, a teaspoon, peeler, apple corer, small bowl, aluminum foil, and a baking dish.

6 Preheat the oven to 400°F.

7 Peel the apples and core them. Try not to remove the whole core. Leave a little of the core at the bottom of the apple to hold the juices. Place the apples in the baking dish.

8 Combine the brown sugar, cinnamon, nutmeg, raisins, and nuts in a small bowl. Spoon one-fourth of the mixture into the hollow core of each apple. Top each apple with 1 teaspoon of butter.

9 Pour the apple cider or juice into the baking dish. Cover the dish with foil and bake for 25 to 30 minutes. Serve warm.

NAME ______________________

Vocabulary Skills

Write the words from the selection that have the meanings below.

1. the center parts of things

   ______________________ Par. 2

2. to cook at a low boil

   ______________________ Par. 3

3. to take away

   ______________________ Par. 7

4. to mix or put together

   ______________________ Par. 8

5. a type of apple flavored drink

   ______________________ Par. 9

Check the meaning of the underlined word in each sentence.

6. You can buy caramel apples at the <u>fair</u>.

   _____ an outdoor event with games and exhibits

   _____ equal; just

7. Fresh apples should be <u>firm</u> to the touch.

   _____ a company or organization

   _____ hard; solid

8. The apple pie took <u>second</u> place in the contest.

   _____ occurring after the first

   _____ one sixtieth of a minute

Reading Skills

1. Number the directions below from **1** to **5** to show the order in which they are listed in the recipe for baked apples.

   _____ Cover the dish with foil.

   _____ Preheat the oven.

   _____ Top each apple with butter.

   _____ Peel the apples.

   _____ Spoon the mixture into the hollow core.

Circle the word that best completes each sentence, and write it on the line.

2. You should ______________ any applesauce you do not eat.

   forget refrigerate donate

3. Use a wooden spoon to ______________ in the sugar.

   whip squeeze stir

4. Spoon part of the ______________ into the hollow core.

   mixture apple cider

5. Why shouldn't you remove the whole core when you make baked apples?

   ____

   ____

6. How many ingredients do you need to make baked apples?

   ____

   ____

7. How long do you need to bake the apples?

   ____

   ____

A New Virginia Home

Have you ever gone hiking?

1 It was the first weekend that Amira and her family had spent in their new house. Amira had finished unpacking the boxes in her bedroom. On one wall of her room, she hung a map of Michigan. That was the state her family used to live in. She would miss going to visit Lake Michigan and all the fun she'd had at the beach. On another wall, Amira hung a map of Virginia, the state that was her new home.

2 Amira heard a soft tapping. She saw her father's head poke around the door. "Hi, Dad," said Amira. "What's going on?"

3 "I just wanted to see how you were doing," said Dad. "Your room is starting to look pretty good. I like the maps."

4 "Thanks," said Amira, sighing and flopping down on the bed.

5 Dad sat next to her. "Why the big sigh?" he asked.

6 "I guess I miss Michigan and my friends," said Amira. "I don't know anyone here, and there's nothing to do."

7 "There are some kids your age who live on this block, but they may be on vacation still," said Dad. "I know you'll meet people as soon as school starts next week. As far as there being nothing to do, you're in luck. I'm looking for someone to go hiking with me this afternoon." Amira's dad stood up and walked over to the map of Virginia.

8 "We were lucky to move near one of the greatest hikes in the country," he said. "Have you ever heard of the Appalachian Trail?" he asked, tracing something on the map with one finger. Amira shook her head.

9 "Well, then, I think you ought to put on your hiking boots, grab some bug spray, and come along with me," said Dad.

10 Amira sighed again, but she looked a little bit interested. "I'm pretty sure you won't regret it," said Dad. "I'll meet you downstairs in 15 minutes, okay?"

11 Amira nodded and walked to her closet to look for her hiking boots. Fifteen minutes later, Amira and her dad said good-bye to her mom and drove to the trailhead. In her backpack, Amira carried some bug spray, a water bottle, two granola bars, and two oranges. In Dad's backpack, there was a cell phone, a water bottle, a tree identification guide, sunscreen, and a camera.

12 As Amira and her dad hiked through the woods, she felt her spirits start to lift. The air smelled clean and fresh, and a slight breeze whispered through the treetops. When Dad turned around, he noticed a big grin on Amira's face.

13 "That's nice to see for a change," joked Dad.

14 "This is great," she answered. "I don't miss Michigan nearly so much right now."

NAME ______________________

Vocabulary Skills

Write the words from the story that have the meanings below.

1. a long, deep breath

   ______________________ Par. 5

2. walking for pleasure, usually in a wooded area

   ______________________ Par. 7

3. nation

   ______________________ Par. 8

4. to wish you hadn't done something

   ______________________ Par. 10

5. shows or proves what something is

   ______________________ Par. 11

An **antonym** is a word that means the opposite of another word. Find an antonym in the story for each of the words below.

6. last ______________________ Par. 1

7. far ______________________ Par. 8

8. finish ______________________ Par. 12

Write a compound word using two words in each sentence.

9. A pack that you wear on your back is called a ______________.

10. The top of a tree is called a ______________.

11. The days that come at the end of the week are called the ______________.

12. The room where you keep your bed is a ______________.

13. The head of a trail, or the place where you begin it, is called a ______________.

Reading Skills

1. Check the reason the author probably wrote this story.

   _____ to tell a story about a girl and her dad and a hike they went on

   _____ to persuade the reader to hike the Appalachian Trail

   _____ to tell the reader facts about the Appalachian Trail

2. Check the sentence below that is the best summary for paragraph 7.

   _____ Amira's dad tries to make her feel better about the move to Virginia.

   _____ Amira's dad walked over to the map of Virginia.

3. Do you think Amira will want to go hiking again? Why or why not?

   ____

   ____

4. Name three things that can be found in Amira's backpack or her dad's backpack.

   ____

   ____

5. Check the words that you think best describe Amira's dad.

   _____ athletic

   _____ cheerful

   _____ angry

   _____ shy

   _____ caring

A Long Way Home

What are some hiking trails that are near your home?

1 What is the farthest you have ever walked? Was it to a friend's house on another block or to the store in your neighborhood? Imagine walking more than two thousand miles. The Appalachian Trail stretches from Georgia to Maine. It is one long hike, but thousands of people have walked the entire trail. Three to four million people use at least part of the trail every year for much shorter hikes.

2 In the 1920s, a man named Benton MacKaye thought that people who lived in cities would like to have a place where they could spend time in nature. This idea was the start of the Appalachian Trail. The first section opened in 1923 in Bear Mountain State Park, New York. In 1925, MacKaye went to Washington, D.C. to promote his idea. The Appalachian Trail Conference, or ATC, became the organization that would design and run the trail.

3 Myron Avery was one of the most important people involved in developing the trail. During the late 1920s, he spent all of his free time discovering and mapping almost the whole trail. He also encouraged many people to help him. By 1937, the trail had grown to 2,049 miles and ran from Springer Mountain, Georgia, to Katahdin, Maine, without any gaps.

4 However, right away the trail ran into some problems. In 1938, a hurricane destroyed a large section in New England that took many years to repair. An even bigger problem was traffic. Many people wanted to drive through the countryside and forests instead of hiking. The government decided that parts of the trail would be made into scenic roads. The Appalachian Trail had to be moved.

5 While the trail was being repaired and adjusted, the first "thru-hike," a hike of the whole trail from Georgia to Maine, was completed by Earl Shaffer in 1948. This hike was covered by the news. Many more people learned of the Appalachian Trail from the reports. Shaffer hiked the whole trail again in 1965, going from Maine to Georgia this time. Then, in 1998 at the age of 79, he did it again! He became the oldest person to thru-hike.

6 Because it takes about six months to hike the trail, people cannot carry all the food and other supplies they need. To solve this problem, hikers have their friends or family mail packages to towns along the route. Hiking the whole trail is not easy. Even though almost 2,500 hikers try to do it each year, only about 450 complete it. With good reason, thru-hikers are very proud of their accomplishment.

NAME ______________________________

Vocabulary Skills

Circle the homophone that correctly completes each sentence below, and write it on the line.

1. Many people _______________ about the Appalachian Trail when it was covered in the news. (heard, herd)
2. _______________ of the reasons the trail had to be moved was an increase in traffic. (Won, One)
3. It is not that unusual to see a _______________ as you hike the Appalachian Trail. (bare, bear)

Fill in the blanks below with the possessive form of the word in parentheses.

4. Benton _______________ plan was a success. (MacKaye)
5. _______________ families may mail packages to them along the route. (Hikers)
6. The _______________ purpose is to give people a place to spend time in nature. (trail)

Reading Skills

1. Where did the first section of the Appalachian Trail open?

   ____

2. Why can't people carry all the supplies they need with them on the trail?

   ____

3. About how many people hike the entire trail each year?

   ____

Write **T** before the sentences that are true. Write **F** before the sentences that are false.

4. _____ The Appalachian Trail goes from Georgia to Ohio.
5. _____ No one has ever hiked the entire trail.
6. _____ In the 1920s, Myron Avery mapped almost the whole trail.
7. _____ Part of the original Appalachian Trail had to be moved.
8. Check the sentence that best states the main idea of the selection.

   _____ It takes about six months to hike the entire Appalachian Trail.

   _____ The Appalachian Trail, built as a natural escape from city life, is the longest trail in the country.

   _____ The Appalachian Trail stretches from Springer Mountain, Georgia, to Mt. Katahdin, Maine.

Study Skills

A **time line** shows the order in which things happened. Use the time line below to answer the questions that follow.

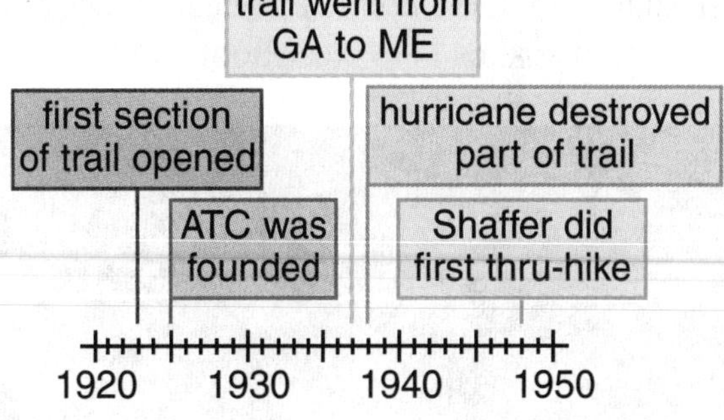

1. What happened in 1925?

   ____

2. When did a hurricane destroy part of the trail?

   ____

3. How many years after the hurricane did Shaffer complete the first thru-hike?

   ____

The Wild Side of the Trail

What kinds of wild animals do you see near your home?

1 If you ever decide to hike the Appalachian Trail, you might run into some interesting animals along the way. Hikers are often both excited and apprehensive about spotting a black bear. In some parts of the country, such as Georgia and the Great Smoky Mountains National Park, black bears have become used to humans and are no longer frightened of them. It might seem strange to you that a bear would be frightened of a human being. This fear often protects both bears and humans.

2 Most hikers do not run into a problem with bears on the trail. They just have to be sure to hang their food high in a tree at night. They also must be careful never to come between a mother bear and her cubs. A mother bear who thinks her cubs are in danger can be very aggressive.

3 Another type of animal that you might see if you hike the Appalachian Trail is a snake. There are many different kinds of snakes that live along the trail. Most of them are not poisonous, but there are poisonous copperheads and rattlesnakes in some areas. The best way to be safe around snakes is to wear boots for protection and to avoid putting your hands or feet in places you cannot see. It is also helpful to have a book that allows you to identify the animals you see.

4 The nine-banded armadillo might be one of the strangest and most unusual looking animals you could meet on the trail. The armadillo is a mammal whose name means *little man in armor* in Spanish. It has hard, bony plates that cover its head, body, and tail. Even though it is so well protected, the armadillo can also run quickly and burrow underground. It can even swim if it has to.

5 Another strange and interesting animal is the southern flying squirrel. This type of squirrel has an extra fold of skin between its front and rear legs. The skin acts as a sail or a parachute. Even though this squirrel cannot really fly, it can glide as far as 80 yards through the air, usually to get from one treetop to another.

6 If you walk quietly and look carefully, you might have a chance to see some animals that very few people ever have the opportunity to see in the wild.

NAME ______________________

Vocabulary Skills

Write the words from the article that have the meanings below.

1. feeling afraid of

______________________ Par. 1

2. forceful; quick to attack

______________________ Par. 2

3. to recognize

______________________ Par. 3

4. to dig a hole in the ground

______________________ Par. 4

5. material that catches the air and slows a fall to the ground

______________________ Par. 5

Read each word below. Then, write the letter of its synonym on the line beside the word.

6. _____ answer	**a.** find
7. _____ different	**b.** reply
8. _____ locate	**c.** complete
9. _____ finish	**d.** varied

Check the correct meaning of the underlined word.

10. The short story was <u>incomplete</u>.

_____ complete before

_____ not complete

_____ capable of completing

11. The winner of the spelling bee did not <u>misspell</u> any words.

_____ spell always

_____ spell before

_____ spell badly

12. We were excited about getting to <u>preview</u> the new movie.

_____ view before

_____ not view

_____ view badly

Reading Skills

1. Why do you think a hiker might be both excited and apprehensive about seeing a bear?

____

____

2. Why is it bad to come between a mother bear and her cubs?

____

____

3. What are two types of poisonous snakes you might see along the trail?

__________ __________

4. What does the name *armadillo* mean in Spanish?

____

____

5. Check the sentence below that is the best summary for paragraph 4.

_____ The armadillo can swim if it has to.

_____ The armadillo is a strange-looking animal that has many ways to protect itself.

A Friendly Hike

Will Sarah and Edie accomplish their goal?

1 In March of 1999, Edie and Sarah began hiking the Appalachian Trail in Georgia. Sarah was a teacher, so she and Edie thought their hike would be an interesting learning experience for students. Before they departed, they visited classrooms for two weeks. Students had the opportunity to try on a backpack to see how much weight Sarah and Edie would be carrying during the trip. Students also were able to ask Sarah and Edie questions about the trail and doing a thru-hike. Sarah and Edie planned to post photos and journal entries on the internet during the trip so that the students would be able to check on their progress.

2 Before they left, Sarah and Edie packed 18 boxes with supplies like crackers, granola bars, pasta, peanut butter, and dried fruits and vegetables. Their parents would mail the boxes to small towns along the trail so Sarah and Edie could pick them up along the way. That way, Sarah and Edie did not have to carry all their supplies with them from the beginning of the trip. Those backpacks would have been too heavy to lift.

3 Sarah and Edie met plenty of friendly hikers during their trip. People who are hiking the Appalachian Trail, or AT, often create "trail names" for themselves and their friends. That explains why Sarah and Edie met hikers with names like "Chewy" and "Baked Bean"!

4 There are many shelters along the AT. Hikers can stay there overnight, especially in times of bad weather. There are also books called *registers* at many of the shelters. Hikers can sign the books and leave notes for friends they have made who are also hiking the trail.

5 Sarah and Edie encountered all kinds of weather on their hike. They had days of beautiful clear weather, but they also hiked through rainstorms and thunderstorms. Once, they even saw thunder and lightning during a blizzard. Sometimes they hit icy spots along the trail, and sometimes the weather was so hot that they had to drink a lot of water. They did not want to become dehydrated.

6 When Sarah and Edie were in Virginia, there was a forest fire. They had to wait until it was completely out before the forest service would allow them to go back on the trail. Because of a fire in Shenandoah National Forest, they missed a 45-mile portion of the hike. Later in their trip, Sarah and Edie had someone drive them back there so that they would not miss a single mile of the AT!

7 Four and a half months after they began the hike in Georgia, Sarah and Edie completed it at Mount Katahdin in Maine. They were close friends when they began their journey and even closer when they came home. They had accomplished their goal!

NAME ______________________

Vocabulary Skills

Write the words from the article that have the meanings below.

1. left

______________________ Par. 1

2. movement toward a goal

______________________ Par. 1

3. necessary materials

______________________ Par. 2

4. experienced; ran into

______________________ Par. 5

5. extremely thirsty

______________________ Par. 5

Write the word or words from the article that match each abbreviation below.

6. GA ______________________

7. AT ______________________

8. VA ______________________

9. ME ______________________

Write a compound word using two words from each sentence.

10. Sarah and Edie visited several rooms where classes were held.

____

11. The hikers endured storms during which there was thunder.

____

12. Hikers can rest at shelters over the period of time when it is night.

____

Reading Skills

1. Why did Sarah and Edie plan to post journal entries and photos?

____

____

2. Do you think Sarah and Edie would recommend this hike to their friends? Why or why not?

____

____

3. Do you think Sarah and Edie will go hiking together again? Why or why not?

____

____

4. How long did it take Sarah and Edie to complete their hike?

____

Check the word that best completes each sentence.

5. Sarah and Edie thought their trip could be a(n) ______________ experience for students.

_____ educational _____ normal

_____ boring

6. Sarah and Edie were ______________ for the help of their families and friends.

_____ annoyed _____ entertained

_____ grateful

7. Bad weather is one ______________ of the trip that hikers have to plan for.

_____ type _____ element

_____ shelter

On the Right Track

Where could you look for animal tracks?

1 The more time Amira and Dad spent hiking the Appalachian Trail, the more Amira enjoyed living in Virginia. She and Dad had seen squirrels, chipmunks, and many types of birds on their hikes. Amira kept seeing animal tracks, but she didn't know how to identify them.

2 "Why don't we bring Mom's digital camera with us on our next hike?" suggested Dad. "Then, we can take some pictures of the tracks we've seen. When we get home, we'll go to the library and see if we can find a book that has pictures of animal tracks."

3 "That's a great idea, Dad!" said Amira excitedly. "Do you think we might find some bear tracks?" she asked.

4 Dad raised his eyebrows. "I don't think I want to get that close to a bear," he said. "Actually, you and I probably don't hike far enough into the woods to see one."

5 "Well, I still hope we find some bear tracks," said Amira.

6 That weekend, Dad and Amira drove to a section of the Appalachian Trail that they hadn't hiked before. They brought lunch with them so they could spend the whole day in the woods. As soon as they got started, Amira spotted some tiny tracks in a muddy area near a tree. Dad showed her how to use the digital camera to take a close-up picture of the tracks.

7 "Good eyes!" he commented. "I think I would have walked right past those tracks."

8 As the day went on, Amira took pictures of more and more animal tracks. She seemed to see a new set every few minutes. By the end of the day, Amira was tired and dirty, but happy.

9 When they got home, Mom was excited to hear about their adventures. She knew that Dad and Amira were looking for tracks along the trail, so she had bought a small identification guide for them.

10 "This is great, Mom!" said Amira. She began flipping through the guide until she located pictures that looked like the ones she had taken that afternoon.

11 "Did you find any matches?" asked Mom.

12 "I found a lot of matches," answered Amira. "We took pictures of chipmunk, raccoon, deer, and skunk tracks."

13 "No bears?" asked Dad.

14 "Not yet," said Amira. "But I'm going to keep looking!"

NAME ______________________________

Vocabulary Skills

Write the words from the story that have the meanings below.

1. liked

______________________________ Par. 1

2. footprints

______________________________ Par. 1

3. offered an idea

______________________________ Par. 2

4. a part or portion

______________________________ Par. 6

5. found

______________________________ Par. 10

In each row, circle the word that does not belong.

6. squirrel chipmunk tracks deer
7. photo detailed picture camera
8. rare common usual ordinary
9. identify library match prove

Reading Skills

1. Check the phrase that best describes the author's purpose.

_____ to explain where to look for bears on the Appalachian Trail

_____ to tell a story about the tracks a girl and her dad find while hiking

_____ to persuade the reader to take photos of animal tracks

2. Who do you think would rather see a bear—Amira or Dad? Why?

____

____

3. Name two types of tracks Dad and Amira found.

______________ ______________

4. Why did Dad and Amira bring lunch with them?

____

____

5. How did Amira use the identification guide?

____

____

6. Why does Dad say, "Good eyes!" to Amira?

____

____

Study Skills

The bar graph below shows the types and numbers of animal tracks that Amira found during hikes in the fall. Use the graph to answer the questions that follow.

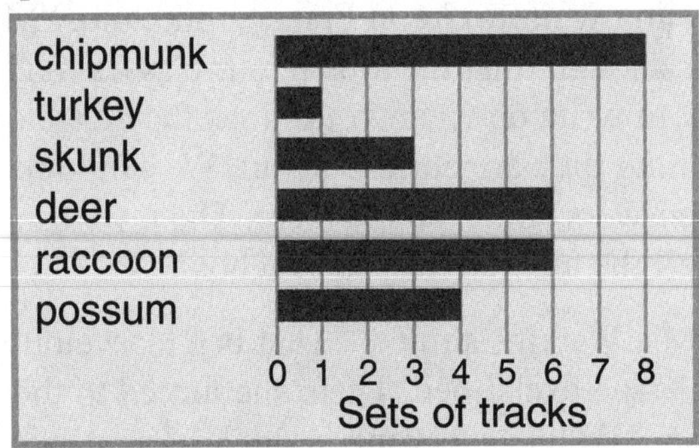

1. How many sets of deer tracks did Amira find?

____

2. Amira found the same number of tracks for two animals. What animals were they?

______________ ______________

3. What type of track did Amira find only one set of?

____

A French Connection

Have you ever traveled to another country?

1 "I'd like to have everyone's attention, please," said Ms. Watkins. The fourth- and fifth-grade students at Robert Louis Stevenson Elementary School sat in the cafeteria for a special announcement after lunch. They weren't sure why the principal wanted to talk to them or why there wasn't an assembly for the whole school.

2 Ms. Watkins cleared her throat. "Your classmates Hannah and Jack are lucky enough to have the opportunity to live in France for the next year. Mr. DiSalvo will be teaching there, and his family will be joining him. I know Hannah and Jack will miss all of you. I'm sure that the year will go quickly, and they'll have all sorts of interesting stories to share with us when they return."

3 Hannah and Jack were sitting at the same table in the cafeteria. Hannah looked excited, but Jack looked a little nervous. "Hannah, Jack, do you have anything you'd like to add?" asked Ms. Watkins.

4 Hannah nodded. "We're going to do a lot of traveling while we're in France," she said. "My mom thought that the kids in our classes might want to write down any questions they have or anything they are curious about. We can look for the answers while we are there. Then, we can e-mail the answers to you at school."

5 Ms. Watkins smiled. "That is a marvelous idea!" she exclaimed. Then, she turned to the group. "I'd like everyone to think of a question or two for Jack and Hannah. They will be leaving in two weeks. Don't forget to give your questions to them and wish them *bon voyage*!"

6 Jack turned to his sister. "What does that mean?" he asked.

7 Hannah smiled. "That's what you say to people who are going on a trip. It's the French way of wishing someone happy, safe travels."

8 A moment later, Hannah's and Jack's classmates gathered around them. They had so many questions: "Are you going to go to the top of the Eiffel Tower?", "Will you know how to speak French when you get home?", "Where will you live?", "What kinds of foods do people eat in France?"

9 Jack and Hannah looked at each other and started to laugh. "I guess we'll have our work cut out for us, won't we?" said Hannah.

NAME ______________________

Vocabulary Skills

Write the words from the story that have the meanings below.

1. something said to a large group
______________________ Par. 1
2. a group of people gathered together
______________________ Par. 1
3. worried
______________________ Par. 3
4. eager to learn
______________________ Par. 4
5. said with surprise or excitement
______________________ Par. 5

Find an antonym in the story for each of the words below.

6. part ______________________ Par. 1
7. boring ______________________ Par. 2
8. terrible ______________________ Par. 5
9. remember ______________________ Par. 5

Underline the suffix in each word. Then, write the meaning of the word on the line next to it.

10. comfortable ______________________
11. development ______________________
12. thoughtless ______________________

Reading Skills

1. What does the phrase *bon voyage* mean?
____
____
2. Why will the DiSalvos be moving to France for a year?
____
____
3. Why do you think Jack feels nervous?
____
____
4. How will Jack and Hannah send answers to their classmates' questions?
____

Write **T** before the sentences that are true. Write **F** before the sentences that are false.

5. _____ Hannah and Jack go to Robert Frost Elementary School.
6. _____ The DiSalvos are moving to France for two years.
7. _____ Jack doesn't know what *bon voyage* means.
8. _____ The students are gathered in the gym.

Study Skills

Look at the dictionary entry below. Then, answer the questions that follow.

pen *(noun)* 1. a fenced-in area where animals are kept
2. a tool used for writing

1. What part of speech is the word *pen*?
____
2. How many definitions of *pen* are listed in the dictionary entry?
____
3. What is the second definition of *pen*?
____

Tower Power

Have you ever visited an important monument?

1 When someone mentions Paris, France, you might think of the Eiffel Tower. Do you know why it was built?

2 In the 1880s, the people of Paris were getting ready to celebrate the centennial of the French Revolution. This anniversary was going to occur in 1889, and the French wanted to build a special monument for this important day. A contest was held for the best design. More than seven hundred entries were received. The tower designed by Alexandre–Gustave Eiffel was immediately chosen as the best, and in 1887 construction was begun.

3 It took two years to build the Eiffel Tower. On March 31, 1889, the tower was finished and a flag was flown from the flagpole at the top. At 1,052 feet, it was the tallest building in the world, and it held that record until 1930. During its first year, two million visitors came to see the tower. Some of them climbed the 1,665 steps to get to the highest platform. A person standing at the top can see 42 miles away on a clear day!

4 It might seem as though something as large as the Eiffel Tower would be very solid. In fact, the tower moves all the time. On windy days, it sways by almost five inches! The tower's height also changes by as much as six inches, depending on the weather.

5 Although the Eiffel Tower is very popular today, it was almost torn down in 1909 because there were not as many people coming to see it. Luckily, the invention of the radio saved the tower. Because the tower was so tall, it was the perfect place to put an antenna for sending and receiving radio waves. When television came along, the tower was also used to transmit television programs.

6 Over the years, people have done some strange things at the Eiffel Tower. In 1954, a mountaineer climbed the outside of the tower. In 1984, two people parachuted from the top deck. Someone even rode a bicycle down hundreds of stairs from the first platform to the ground.

7 Today, the Eiffel Tower is as popular as ever. With almost six million visitors a year, the Eiffel Tower has become the most well-known symbol of Paris.

NAME ______________________

Vocabulary Skills

Write the words from the article that have the meanings below.

1. marking the date of something that happened 100 years ago

   ______________________ Par. 2

2. the date every year that marks a special event

   ______________________ Par. 2

3. a statue or building that helps people remember something important

   ______________________ Par. 2

4. a raised surface, like a stage

   ______________________ Par. 3

5. moves back and forth

   ______________________ Par. 4

Circle the homophone that correctly completes each sentence below, and write it on the line.

6. The Eiffel Tower reaches so ____________ in the sky, it sways back and forth on windy days. (high, hi)
7. You can ______________ 42 miles away from the top of the tower on a clear day. (sea, see)
8. The Eiffel Tower ______________ as though it would be very solid. (seams, seems)
9. The Eiffel Tower has ______________ one of the most popular spots to visit in France for many years. (been, bin)

Fill in the blanks below with the possessive form of the word in parentheses.

10. ______________ most well-known monument is the Eiffel Tower. (France)
11. The ______________ construction took about two years. (tower)
12. Alexandre–Gustave ______________ design was chosen as the best. (Eiffel)
13. The ______________ invention saved the tower. (radio)

Reading Skills

1. Number the events below from **1** to **5** to show the order in which they happened.

   _____ A mountaineer climbed the side of the tower.

   _____ The Eiffel Tower was almost torn down.

   _____ Alexandre–Gustave Eiffel's design was chosen.

   _____ Two people parachuted from the top deck of the tower.

   _____ France celebrated its centennial.

2. Why was the Eiffel Tower built?

   ____

   ____

3. How long did it take to build the Eiffel Tower?

   ____

   ____

4. How far does the tower sway on windy days?

   ____

5. Do you think the French will want to tear down the Eiffel Tower in the future? Why or why not?

   ____

   ____

6. What saved the Eiffel Tower in 1909?

   ____

   ____

Impressive Paintings

Is there an art museum in your town?

1 The DiSalvos were spending the morning at the Louvre, the famous museum in Paris. "I think that we need to decide what we want to focus on today," said Dad. "The museum might be a little overwhelming otherwise."

2 Mom agreed. "When I studied art history in college," she said, "the Impressionists were always my favorite. That is where I'd like to begin. How does everyone else feel about it?"

3 "The brochure says that the Impressionist paintings are in the Musée d'Orsay," said Hannah.

4 "That is a part of the Louvre," said Mom. "It's on the left bank of the river. Let's start over there, and then maybe we'll come back here after lunch."

5 Hannah and Jack were surprised at how many of the Impressionist paintings they recognized. "Don't we have a calendar of this artist at home?" Jack asked Mom.

6 "Yes," said Mom. "His name is Claude Monet. He's one of my favorite artists. I'm impressed that you recognized his paintings, Jack."

7 Jack grinned. "I always thought they were kind of boring," he admitted. "They're definitely more interesting in real life." Mom laughed and patted Jack on the shoulder as they walked into the next room.

8 "Look at this!" said Dad. "This painting is magnificent!"

9 "Shhhh!" said Mom and Jack at the same time.

10 "Dad, you're supposed to talk quietly in museums," Jack said to his father with a stern look.

11 "Where's Hannah?" asked Mom suddenly.

12 Mom, Dad, and Jack looked all around, but they couldn't find Hannah anywhere. "Maybe she's still in the last room," suggested Jack. They checked the last room they had visited, but there was no Hannah.

13 Then, Jack spotted his sister through the doorway of a room they hadn't visited yet. A group of French students wearing uniforms were standing in front of a painting and listening to a man talk.

14 Jack walked over to the group and tugged on his sister's hand. "Come on," he whispered. "Mom and Dad think you're lost!"

15 "Hannah, what on earth were you doing?" asked Mom, as Hannah and Jack joined their parents.

16 "I'm sorry," said Hannah. "There is a girl in that class who speaks English. Her name is Adrienne. She was telling me what her teacher was saying. Did you know that people in France used to think that the Impressionists were just bad artists?"

17 Mom and Dad hugged Hannah. "We're glad you made a friend and that you're enjoying the paintings here, but you had us really worried. We need to stick together," said Mom.

18 "We should have a meeting place in case we get separated again," added Dad.

19 "How about the café?" asked Jack.

20 Mom and Dad laughed. "Someone's ready for lunch!" said Mom.

NAME ______________________

Vocabulary Skills

Write the words from the story that have the meanings below.

1. too much to handle at once

   ______________________ Par. 1

2. a pamphlet or booklet

   ______________________ Par. 3

3. had strong, positive feelings about

   ______________________ Par. 6

4. strict; serious

   ______________________ Par. 10

5. divided; set apart

   ______________________ Par. 18

Check the meaning of the underlined word in each sentence.

6. Jack <u>spotted</u> Hannah in another room.

   _____ noticed

   _____ covered with spots

7. Hannah's parents seem very <u>patient</u>.

   _____ a person who is receiving medical help

   _____ calm and understanding

8. The DiSalvos will probably want to <u>rest</u> after their long day.

   _____ the part that is leftover

   _____ relax; sleep

An **idiom** is a group of words that has a special meaning. For example, the idiom *hit the hay* means *to go to bed*. Write the idiom from paragraph 17 on the line next to its meaning.

9. stay in a group; not get separated

   ____

Reading Skills

1. Where are the Impressionist paintings located?

   ____

2. What is the name of one of Mom's favorite artists?

   ____

3. Why does Dad think the family should have a meeting place?

   ____

   ____

4. Do you think Hannah will want to come back to the Louvre on another day? Why or why not?

   ____

   ____

Write **H** on the line if the phrase describes Hannah. Write **J** if it describes Jack.

5. _____ recognizes Monet paintings from a calendar at home

6. _____ meets a French student named Adrienne

7. _____ tells Mom and Dad where the Impressionist paintings can be found

8. _____ suggests the café as a meeting place

Underline the word that best completes each sentence, and write it on the line.

9. Hannah and Jack ______________ many of the Impressionist paintings.

   recognize ignore dislike

10. For a few minutes, Hannah ______________ a group of French students.

    loses joins admires

A Museum Fit for a King

What museums have you visited?

1 Located on the Seine (SEN) River in the heart of Paris, the Louvre (LOOV) is the biggest art museum in the world. It has seven major areas, more than one hundred different rooms, and nearly 300,000 items in its collection. Even one whole day would not be enough to see the entire museum.

2 The Louvre is made up of several different buildings that were added over many centuries. The very first section, built more than eight hundred years ago, was originally used as a fortress to protect Paris from the Vikings. Within a hundred years, King Charles V had turned one of the towers into a library.

3 Even though it was used by French royalty to store their many possessions, it was not turned into a palace until the 1500s. During his reign, King Henry IV added a huge section called the Grande Galerie. This made the Louvre one of the biggest buildings in the world at that time. But the Louvre was not done growing yet! By 1624, King Louis XIII expanded it to almost four times the size it had been.

4 Meanwhile, the royal family continued to collect more and more art, which they kept at the Louvre. This art was only to be seen by the kings and queens and the people they might invite to view it. After the French Revolution, the art in the Louvre was available for everyone to enjoy. The museum opened to the public for the first time on November 8, 1793.

5 Today, the Louvre is owned and operated by the French government. French President François Mitterand understood how important the Louvre was to the world. In 1981, he announced a massive project that would not only remodel the old parts of the museum, but also make the museum nearly twice as big as it already was!

6 Mitterand also had the famous architect I. M. Pei (PAY) help solve a major problem. Because the museum was made up of so many buildings, visitors could not tell which door was the entrance. Pei's solution was to build a giant glass pyramid, which was based on the Louvre's Egyptian artifacts. The pyramid marks the entrance, and today everyone knows how to get inside.

7 Some of the most famous works of art ever created are on display at the Louvre. These include the *Mona Lisa*, painted by Leonardo da Vinci, as well as the sculptures *Winged Victory* and *Venus de Milo*. The museum also has important collections of artifacts from Islamic, Greek, and Roman history.

NAME ______________________

Vocabulary Skills

Write the words from the article that have the meanings below.

1. periods of one hundred years

   ______________________ Par. 2
2. things that someone owns

   ______________________ Par. 3
3. controlled or run by

   ______________________ Par. 5
4. to remake something, especially a structure or a building

   ______________________ Par. 5
5. someone who designs buildings

   ______________________ Par. 6
6. something created by humans during a certain period of history

   ______________________ Par. 6

Circle the homophone that correctly completes each sentence below, and write it on the line.

7. During the ______________ of King Henry IV, a large section was added to the Louvre. (reign, rain)
8. There were ______________ many buildings in the museum, people could not find the entrance. (sew, so)
9. The museum ______________ a clearly marked entrance. (kneaded, needed)
10. Before 1793, only royalty was ______________ to view the art. (allowed, aloud)

Reading Skills

1. What is the name of the river on which the Louvre is located?

   ____
2. Do you think the Louvre will grow even larger in the future? Why or why not?

   ____

   ____
3. Who owns and operates the Louvre today?

   ____
4. Name one famous piece of art on display at the Louvre.

   ____
5. After what major historical event could the public see the art at the Louvre?

   ____

Write **B** if the sentence describes something that happened before the Louvre opened to the public. Write **A** if the sentence describes something that happened after the Louvre opened to the public.

6. _____ Mitterand announced a project to expand the Louvre.
7. _____ The French Revolution began.
8. _____ One part of the Louvre protected Paris from the Vikings.
9. _____ I. M. Pei built a glass pyramid for the entrance.
10. _____ The Louvre was turned into a palace.

Seeing the World Through Different Eyes

What types of artwork do you like?

1 Today, artists can make whatever kind of art they want. A painting might be as realistic as a photograph, or it might look like smears and splashes across the canvas. Not very long ago, however, a powerful government organization in France decided what could and could not be be considered art. A brave group of painters, called the *Impressionists*, challenged these ideas and changed art forever.

2 In the middle of the 1800s, France was considered the most important place in the world for art. One reason for that was the Academy, a government organization with a strict set of rules about art. To be accepted by the Academy, an artist had to be very talented. Artists also had to paint exactly the way the Academy wanted them to. How could an artist be creative if he or she was told what to create?

3 Each year, the Academy had an exhibition of the art they had decided was the best. In 1864, a group of artists who did not get into the show became frustrated. They felt that their paintings were not bad; the paintings were just different. After complaining to the government, these artists were given their own show. It was called the *Salon des Refusés*, which means the *exhibition of rejects*.

4 The Academy thought all art should look realistic. The Impressionists wanted to explore other ideas. They were more interested in trying to show movement and the bright colors of daylight. For example, if you move your hand quickly in front of your face, it looks blurry. To the Impressionists, it was more real to show these blurry images than it was to paint a scene frozen like a photograph. It was also more interesting to show all of the different colors that occur when light hits an object like water.

5 By 1874, many different artists were painting in this new style, including Claude Monet. One of his paintings was titled *Impression: Sunrise*. A critic named Louis Leroy did not like these new artists. He thought their paintings looked unfinished. He used Monet's title to make fun of these painters by calling them "impressionists," meaning that they did not make real paintings, just sketches. The critics who liked these artists thought the word was just right. They began to use it in a positive way.

6 Some of the other Impressionists were Pierre-Auguste Renoir, Alfred Sisley, Edgar Degas, and Mary Cassatt. They thought it was more important to paint *how* they saw things, instead of just *what* they saw. Other artists around the world felt that they could have this freedom as well. Because of the Impressionists, the art world was never the same.

Regatta at Argenteuil by Claude Monet

Cliff Walk at Pourville by Claude Monet

NAME ______________________________

Vocabulary Skills

Write the words from the article that have the meanings below.

1. stood up against

   ______________________________ Par. 1

2. demanding and unchanging

   ______________________________ Par. 2

3. discouraged; puzzled and helpless

   ______________________________ Par. 3

4. resembling, or looking like, things that are real

   ______________________________ Par. 4

5. not being controlled by others

   ______________________________ Par. 6

Find an antonym in the article for each of the words below.

6. fearful ______________________________ Par. 1
7. rejected ______________________________ Par. 2
8. boring ______________________________ Par. 4
9. complete ______________________________ Par. 5
10. negative ______________________________ Par. 5

Reading Skills

1. What was the Academy?

   ____

   ____

2. Why didn't Louis Leroy like the paintings of the Impressionists?

   ____

   ____

3. Name two Impressionists other than Claude Monet.

   ____

   ____

4. Which came first—frustrated artists were given their own show by the Academy, or Louis Leroy came up with the name *Impressionists*?

   ____

   ____

Write **F** before the sentences that are facts. Write **O** before the sentences that are opinions.

5. _____ The Impressionists challenged ideas about art.
6. _____ It is not fair that artists couldn't create the art they wanted to create.
7. _____ The Impressionists wanted to show movement and light in their paintings.
8. _____ The paintings of the Impressionists look unfinished.
9. _____ Artists should be allowed to have the freedom they need to be creative.
10. Check the sentence that is the best summary for paragraph 4.

    _____ The Impressionists did not think that paintings that looked like photographs were very interesting.

    _____ Instead of painting realistically, the Impressionists wanted to explore light and movement.

    _____ According to the Academy, all art should look realistic.

An E-mail from Overseas

Have you ever written a letter or received one from abroad?

From: Hannah and Jack DiSalvo

Date: September 22, 2008

To: 4th and 5th graders at R.L.S. Elementary

Subject: Bonjour!

Bonjour! (That means *hello* in French.)

1 We hope you all had a great summer. Ours was a lot of fun. We have seen so many new things and met so many wonderful people. The French are very friendly. They have helped us adjust to living here and have made us feel welcome. There are so many things we want to share with all of you. We are going to have to send more than one e-mail, but here are our favorite highlights of our time in France so far. We are also including a few photos so you can see where we have been.

2 The best part of the summer was getting to see the Tour de France. It is the most famous bicycle race in the world. It is held every July. The riders travel more than two thousand miles over about a month! We got a quick glimpse of the riders as they sped past! After the race, our family rented bikes, and we rode along part of the route that the cyclists used. Here is a picture of us on our bikes in the heart of Paris.

3 A few of you asked whether the French really eat snails. The answer is yes. We went out to dinner a few weeks ago, and our parents ordered them. We each tried one, and it didn't taste too bad. The snails, called *escargots*, are served with lots of melted butter. They feel a little rubbery when you bite into them, but they don't actually have much taste. Jack's favorite food here is the French pastries. Hannah loves the fresh bread from the bakery down the street. Here is a picture of Jack eating a huge chocolate croissant.

4 We went to visit the Eiffel Tower a few weeks ago. We went all the way to the top. It was a sunny day, so we could see for miles and miles into the distance. Dad doesn't like heights, so he stayed at the bottom of the tower and took pictures from the ground.

5 We miss all of you a lot. Write back to us, and let us know what is new at home.

Au revoir! (Can you guess what that means in French?)

Hannah and Jack DiSalvo

NAME ______________________________

Vocabulary Skills

Write the words from the article that have the meanings below.

1. get used to

_______________________________ Par. 1

2. best parts

_______________________________ Par. 1

3. moved quickly

_______________________________ Par. 2

4. people who ride bicycles

_______________________________ Par. 2

5. sweet-tasting baked goods

_______________________________ Par. 3

Read each word below. Then, write the letter of its synonym on the line beside the word.

6. _____ wonderful	**a.**	section
7. _____ famous	**b.**	chewy
8. _____ part	**c.**	terrific
9. _____ answer	**d.**	well-known
10. _____ rubbery	**e.**	response

Write **S** if the possessive word is singular. Write **P** if it is plural.

11. _____ Hannah's

12. _____ classes'

13. _____ France's

14. _____ Jack's

15. _____ photograph's

16. _____ cyclists'

Reading Skills

1. What French word do Hannah and Jack use in the greeting of their e-mail?

____

2. What is the Tour de France?

____

____

3. Do you think Hannah and Jack will try more unfamiliar foods while they are in France? Why or why not?

____

____

4. Why didn't Mr. DiSalvo go to the top of the Eiffel Tower with his family?

____

5. Check the phrase that best describes the author's purpose.

_____ to persuade the reader to try *escargots*

_____ to tell a story about a family's experiences in France

_____ to convince the reader to take a trip to Paris

Circle the word that best completes each sentence, and write it on the line.

6. You can see far into the _______________ from the top of the Eiffel Tower.

height miles distance

7. Without the butter, the *escargots* would be mostly _______________.

tasteless rubbery cooked

8. The French have made the DiSalvos feel _______________.

ignored welcome friendly

Racing for the Yellow Jersey

What is the farthest you have ever ridden a bicycle?

1 Racing along country roads and through the cities of France each year, the best bicyclists in the world take part in the Tour de France. Not only is this contest one of the oldest and most popular sporting events on Earth, it is also one of the most difficult. Even though approximately 150 cyclists start each race, only about half reach the finish. That is not hard to believe when you learn that the Tour de France is nearly two thousand miles long and takes three weeks to complete!

2 In 1903, the race was held for the first time as a publicity event for the newspaper, *L'Auto*. It was an instant success. Every July since then, the race has taken place. Only war has been able to interrupt the annual Tour de France. The race was not held from 1915 until 1918 because of World War I and from 1940 to 1946 because of World War II.

3 The Tour de France is divided into different races for each day, called *stages*, so that the racers do not have to ride all night. These stages also allow the race to take place all over France and sometimes in other countries. In 1988, the race's first stage actually took place in Ireland. The competitors then traveled to France to continue the rest of the race.

4 Each stage is also a different style of bicycle racing. Sometimes the terrain is flat, so the race is a sprint. At other times, the race goes through the mountains, so the bicyclist needs to have better endurance. Judges give points to the winner of each stage. The racer who is winning the most sprints gets to wear a green jersey. The winner of the most mountain races wears a white jersey with red polka dots.

5 The most important jersey is for the bicyclist who is in the lead. The racer who is finishing the stages the fastest is considered the leader. This rider gets to wear a yellow jersey. At the end of the race, the yellow jersey is awarded to the winner as a trophy.

6 For the last stage of the race, the cyclists sprint to the finish line along the famous Champs-Élysées (shawns ell-ee-ZAY), a cobblestone street in downtown Paris.

7 Until a few years ago, all of the winners were from Europe. Most were from France. In 1986, American Greg LeMond became the first bicyclist who was not European to win the Tour de France. He won again in 1989 in the closest finish of all time—only eight seconds ahead of the next racer! Another American holds the record for the most Tour de France wins. Lance Armstrong has won the race seven times!

NAME ______________________________

Vocabulary Skills

Write the words from the article that have the meanings below.

1. information to let the public know about something

______________________________ Par. 2

2. something that happens once a year

______________________________ Par. 2

3. ground; land

______________________________ Par. 4

4. shirt without a collar

______________________________ Par. 4

5. a type of award

______________________________ Par. 5

Check the meaning of the underlined word in each sentence.

6. The racers must be careful not to <u>fall</u> when they are riding at such high speeds.

_____ autumn; the season that comes after summer

_____ to drop or tumble

7. Not every racer <u>can</u> complete the whole course.

_____ to be able to

_____ a metal container

8. Some cyclists like riding because it makes them feel like they can <u>fly</u>.

_____ an insect

_____ to move through the air with wings

Reading Skills

1. Check the phrase that best describes the author's purpose.

_____ to explain why the Tour de France is the most interesting race in Europe

_____ to share some facts about the Tour de France

_____ to entertain the reader with funny stories about cyclists

2. Check the sentence that best states the main idea of the selection.

_____ The Tour de France is the most difficult and popular bicycle race in the world.

_____ The Tour de France includes different stages so the riders do not have to bike all night.

_____ The racers may get to wear different colored jerseys throughout the race.

3. How many cyclists begin the race?

____

4. Why is the yellow jersey the most important?

____

5. Who was the first American cyclist to win the Tour de France?

____

6. What are two historical events that have interrupted the Tour de France?

____

Pedaling to Victory

How did Lance Armstrong become so strong? Where does he get his endurance?

1 Who is the greatest living athlete? Is it Michael Jordan? Mia Hamm? Maybe Tiger Woods? What about bicyclist Lance Armstrong? After his record-breaking seventh victory in the Tour de France, he is easily considered one of the best athletes in the world. He is also one of the most determined.

2 Lance Armstrong was born in Plano, Texas, in 1971. He says that his mother, Linda, is one of his greatest influences. As a teenager, he began competing in triathlons, which are extremely difficult competitions that involve swimming, biking, and running. It did not take Armstrong long to realize that biking was his strongest event. By 1991, Armstrong had proven himself to be the best young cyclist in America by winning the U. S. amateur championships.

3 His rise to the top of world cycling came quickly. Only two years later, in 1993, Armstrong became the youngest rider ever to win the World Cycling Championship. That same year he competed for the first time in the Tour de France, the longest and most famous bicycle race in the world. Armstrong did not yet have the strength and variety of biking skills needed for that race. He was not able to finish the two-thousand-mile course.

4 Back in America, though, Armstrong's victories continued. In both 1995 and 1996, he won the Tour DuPont, one of the most important races in the United States. He was now considered one of the top bicyclists in the world, but bad news was just around the corner.

5 In late 1996, doctors discovered that Armstrong had cancer. He would need to undergo surgery. He would also have to take very strong medicines that could affect his biking abilities. Armstrong's future as a professional cyclist was in doubt. His biking team even had to let him go. But the one thing Armstrong has shown throughout his career is an incredible amount of endurance. He never gives up.

6 By 1998, Armstrong was declared cancer-free, and he set his sights on the one major biking goal he had not yet accomplished, the Tour de France. This time, Armstrong was more than ready. His incredible endurance helped him to be the strongest cyclist on the difficult uphill climbs of the mountains. This skill allowed Armstrong to gain the lead and go on to win his first Tour de France in 1999. After that, he kept on winning! By 2005, Armstrong had won the race a record seven times, an incredible accomplishment for any athlete.

NAME ____________________

Vocabulary Skills

Write the words from the article that have the meanings below.

1. thought to be

_________________________ Par. 1

2. not professional; a beginner

_________________________ Par. 2

3. success in hard competitions

_________________________ Par. 4

4. the ability to do something for a long period of time

_________________________ Par. 5

Write the idiom from paragraph 4 on the line next to its meaning.

5. about to happen; coming up soon _______

____

Circle the homophone that correctly completes each sentence below, and write it on the line.

6. Lance Armstrong ______________ two thousand miles in the Tour de France. (rode, road)

7. Cyclists in the Tour de France ride ______________ several European countries. (threw, through)

8. Armstrong ______________ the race seven times! (one, won)

9 . Cyclists wear special ______________ when they are competing. (clothes, close)

Reading Skills

1. Number the events below from **1** to **5** to show the order in which they happened.

_____ Armstrong won the Tour de France for the seventh time.

_____ Armstrong became sick with cancer.

_____ Lance Armstrong was born in Plano, Texas.

_____ Armstrong began to compete in triathlons.

_____ Armstrong won the World Cycling Championship.

2. Check the words that best describe Lance Armstrong.

_____ determined

_____ lazy

_____ athletic

_____ scientific

_____ strong-willed

Circle the word that best completes each sentence, and write it on the line.

3. One of Armstrong's greatest ______________ is his mother.

influences regrets reasons

4. Armstrong did not ______________ cancer to stand in his way.

prove consider allow

5. Armstrong's biggest ______________ is winning the Tour de France seven times.

goal accomplishment future

6. What is the Tour DuPont?

____

The Peregrine Project

Have you ever gone to an Earth Day celebration? What was it like?

1 On April 22, Akiko and Ben's elementary school was going to have an Earth Day celebration. There would be a table that would teach students about recycling. There would be sign-up sheets for clubs that clean up litter around town. There would be games with Earth-friendly prizes. Of course, there would also be all sorts of healthful foods and snacks. Akiko and Ben wanted to contribute something really special.

2 "It just seems like all the good ideas are taken," complained Ben. "We have less than two weeks to put together something interesting."

3 "I know," agreed Akiko. "We just have to keep thinking. Let's sleep on it tonight, and then we'll share any new ideas at recess tomorrow."

4 "Okay," said Ben glumly.

5 The next day, Ben couldn't wait to talk to Akiko. "I have the perfect idea," he told her excitedly. "I was watching the evening news with my parents last night. There was a story about the peregrine falcons in New York City."

6 Akiko looked a little confused. "The falcons actually live in the city?" she asked. "I guess I thought that they would live in places out in the country. Actually, I think I heard that they make their nests on cliffs."

7 Ben nodded. "You're right. But they also live in cities. I guess that tall buildings and bridges seem sort of like mountaintops or cliffs to them. It's more dangerous for them to live in cities, though. That's why people have been helping to protect them. But I haven't even told you the best part yet," he added.

8 Akiko was starting to look excited, too. "What else did you find out?" she asked Ben.

9 "Well, there are about 15 nests in New York City right now. Some of them have 24-hour Web cams set up nearby."

10 Akiko nodded. "I see just where you are going with this idea. We can set up a computer that is hooked up to the Internet. Then, we can show what's happening in the nests right at that moment. This is so original. Mr. Rashad will love it!"

11 Ben looked pleased. "We're going to have the most popular table at the Earth Day celebration."

12 Akiko laughed. "Two weeks seems awfully far away, all of a sudden!"

NAME ______________________

Vocabulary Skills

Write the words from the story that have the meanings below.

1. a party for a special occasion

______________________ Par. 1

2. give or offer

______________________ Par. 1

3. sadly

______________________ Par. 4

4. mixed-up; puzzled

______________________ Par. 6

5. creative; first of its kind

______________________ Par. 10

Write the idiom from paragraph 3 on the line next to its meaning.

6. to think about something ______________

In each row, circle the word that does not belong.

7. bird falcon protect nests
8. recycle litter reuse environment
9. extinct cities skyscrapers bridges
10. original weird unique creative

Fill in the blanks below with the possessive form of the word in parentheses.

11. ______________ expression was confused. (Akiko)
12. Akiko liked ______________ idea. (Ben)
13. The ______________ nests were located in New York City. (falcons)
14. The ______________ tables would have many different themes. (students)

Reading Skills

1. On what day is Earth Day celebrated?

____

____

2. Why do you think it is more dangerous for peregrine falcons to live in cities?

____

____

3. What is Ben's perfect idea?

____

____

4. Why does Akiko say that Earth Day seems far away all of a sudden?

____

____

5. Check the words that describe Ben.

_____ lonely

_____ excited

_____ enthusiastic

_____ boring

_____ hilarious

_____ creative

6. On the lines below, write a summary for paragraph 1.

____

____

____

Keeping an Eye on Peregrine Falcons

Have you ever seen a peregrine falcon? If you have, was it in a zoo or in the wild?

1 Did you know that the peregrine falcon is one of the fastest animals in the world? It can fly at speeds of about 200 miles per hour. You might think a bird that could fly so fast would be safe from most types of danger. Unfortunately, that is not true. Once, there were about 350 breeding pairs of peregrine falcons in the United States. By the 1970s, they were considered an endangered species. What was causing the number of falcons to drop so quickly?

2 A pesticide, or chemical used to kill insects, called *DDT* was harming the peregrine falcon eggs. It made the shells too thin, and many of the babies could not survive. Luckily, DDT is no longer used as a pesticide. People also began breeding peregrine falcons in captivity. They were finally taken off the list of endangered species in 1999.

3 One thing that is unusual about peregrine falcons is that they like to make their nests in places that are very high in the air. In nature, they often nest on mountaintops and on the sides of cliffs. They have also adapted to life in cities. Peregrine falcons nest on tall buildings and bridges in cities. These nests can be as high as 50 to 200 feet in the air.

4 Pairs of peregrine falcons usually mate for life. They also like to return to the same nesting place every year. Both the mother and father falcons help to raise the babies. The mother spends more time in the nest. The father hunts and brings back food for her and the babies.

5 Many people all around the country work very hard to help peregrine falcons live to adulthood. There are even video cameras set up in places like New York and California to monitor the nests of peregrine falcons. This way, people can make sure that the birds and their eggs stay protected. Many of the cameras even broadcast live in nature centers and on the Internet. The peregrine falcons are lucky to have so many people who care about them.

NAME ______________________

Vocabulary Skills

Write the words from the article that have the meanings below.

1. having babies; reproducing

   ______________________ Par. 1

2. in danger of becoming extinct

   ______________________ Par. 1

3. not in the wild; under someone's control

   ______________________ Par. 2

4. become used to

   ______________________ Par. 3

5. watch closely

   ______________________ Par. 5

Write the words from the article that match the abbreviations below.

6. m.p.h. ______________________
7. NY ______________________
8. U.S. ______________________
9. CA ______________________
10. ft. ______________________

Reading Skills

1. What caused the falcons' eggshells to become too thin?

   ____

2. How high in the air do falcons make their nests?

   ____

3. How are the places that peregrine falcons nest in the wild similar to the places they nest in cities?

   ____

4. Do you think people will continue to help protect peregrine falcons in the future? Why or why not?

   ____

   ____

Write **T** before the sentences that are true. Write **F** before the sentences that are false.

5. _____ Only the mother raises the peregrine falcon babies.
6. _____ DDT is harmless to peregrine falcons.
7. _____ Peregrine falcons usually mate for life.
8. _____ Some peregrine falcons are bred in captivity.
9. _____ Peregrine falcons can fly almost 200 miles per hour.

Study Skills

The graph below shows the fastest speed at which each person or animal can move. Use the graph to answer the questions that follow.

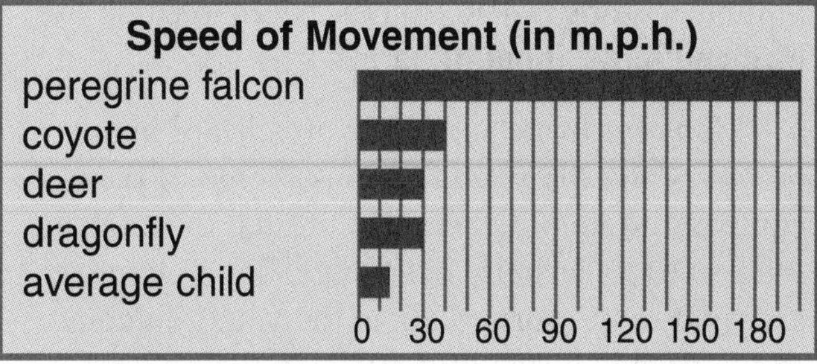

1. Which two animals travel at about the same speed?

   ______________ ______________

2. Which can move more quickly, a coyote or a deer?

   ____

Falcons in the City

What kinds of birds do you see in your neighborhood?

1 Salt Lake City, Utah, is famous for many things. It is named for the Great Salt Lake, which is the largest salt water lake in North America. The city hosted the 2002 Winter Olympic Games. Now, it is known for helping to protect a family of peregrine falcons at Temple Square, the headquarters of the Mormon Church.

2 Peregrine falcons usually lay about three or four eggs in a group called a *clutch*. When the babies are about five or six weeks old, they begin learning how to fly. It takes about a week for the parents to teach their fledglings. In natural areas, it is a bit safer for the young birds to take the risks that come with learning to fly. In urban areas, it can be more dangerous because the fledglings can crash into buildings or fly into traffic.

3 In Salt Lake City, volunteers wear bright orange vests to protect themselves as they keep an eye on the young birds. These volunteers actually put themselves in danger to save the birds. For example, if a peregrine falcon fledgling accidentally flies into traffic, one volunteer stops traffic. Another tries to catch the bird and move it out of harm's way.

4 Many birdwatchers in the area heard about the nests and the young falcons. Some of them came out to help. Others just wanted to watch as the babies took their first flights. The volunteers are right to be worried about the young falcons. In the decade of the mid-1980s to the mid-1990s, people counted 16 young peregrine falcons around downtown Salt Lake City. Only 11 of those birds survived. Of the 11 birds, six were helped by volunteers.

5 These numbers help the volunteers remember that the work they are doing really makes a difference. Some of them work 12-hour days to protect the peregrine falcons and their families. However, when the volunteers see a new generation of falcons that are ready to leave home, it makes all their work worthwhile.

NAME ______________________

Vocabulary Skills

Check the meaning of the underlined word in each sentence.

1. The volunteers stored their supplies in the trunk of the car.

   _____ the back of an automobile, often used for storage

   _____ the long nose of an elephant

2. Their goal was to save the young birds.

   _____ something a person works hard for

   _____ a score for driving a ball into a certain area

3. It does not take long for the fledglings to learn to fly.

   _____ to wish for something

   _____ having a great length

Reading Skills

Circle the word that best completes each sentence, and write it on the line.

1. It is not as _______________ to learn to fly in natural areas.

   fun dangerous interesting

2. Young falcons in _______________ areas can run into buildings or get hit by cars.

   urban country mountain

3. A _______________ is a bird that is learning how to fly.

   falcon fledgling volunteer

4. Name one thing for which Salt Lake City is famous.

   ____

5. How old are the peregrine falcon babies when they begin learning how to fly?

   ____

6. Why do the volunteers wear bright orange vests?

   ____

7. Why do the volunteers work such long hours to help save the young peregrine falcons?

   ____

   ____

8. Check the phrase that best describes the author's purpose.

   _____ to explain why peregrine falcons don't take good care of their babies

   _____ to entertain the reader with a funny story

   _____ to tell about a group of volunteers who saved some young peregrine falcons

Study Skills

Use the schedule of volunteer hours to answer the questions below.

Volunteer Schedule

Name	Mon.	Tues.	Wed.	Thurs.	Fri.
Margaret	8–12		8–12		
Omar	4–6	4–6	4–6	4–6	
Maria			1–5		1–5
Sam	12–4	12–4	12–4		12–4
Dennis		8–12		8–12	
Linh				12–6	12–6

1. Which day is Sam not scheduled to work?

   ____

2. How many days a week does Maria work?

   ____

The World of Tomorrow

What are some of the most recent inventions today?

1 "Grandpa, what is this?" Henry held a rolled-up poster in one hand. It was yellowed with age and seemed brittle.

2 Grandpa was putting price stickers on things that he wanted to sell in his yard sale. "I don't know, Henry. Let's unroll it and find out."

3 Grandpa and Henry slowly unrolled the old poster. They placed it on the folding table in the yard and set a book on each corner to anchor it. The poster revealed a faded picture of a large sphere and something that looked like an enormous spike. Below the picture were the words *New York World's Fair 1939–1940: Building the World of Tomorrow*. Grandpa smiled and gently smoothed the wrinkles in the poster.

4 "Did you go to this fair?" Henry asked Grandpa. "Were you even born yet?"

5 Grandpa laughed. "It does seem like a long time ago," he said. "I was just about your age when I went to the fair. It was one of the most memorable experiences of my life. My parents took me and my sister, Hillary," remembered Grandpa. "It was right after the Great Depression. There was no money for extras for several years. Everything we owned was used over and over again until it fell apart."

6 "What kind of a fair was it?" asked Henry. "The fairs I've gone to have rides and games and fair food, like elephants' ears and caramel apples."

7 "This fair had some of those things, too," nodded Grandpa. "But mostly the 1939 World's Fair was all about technology and things that were new. People in America wanted something to give them hope. They wanted to know that the world was changing for the better and that interesting things were coming their way."

8 "What kind of technology?" asked Henry. "I know that things like computers and cell phones weren't invented yet."

9 "Those types of technology were far off in the future," said Grandpa, "But I did get to see my first television there. It didn't look much like the televisions of today, but I remember how amazed we all were to see a picture moving inside that small box." Grandpa shook his head at the memory.

10 "What are those strange looking things?" asked Henry, gesturing to the poster.

11 "Those were the biggest attractions at the fair," answered Grandpa. "The Trylon was a 700-foot-tall structure that was shaped like a steeple or a large spike. The Perisphere was a 200-foot-tall building shaped like a ball. Inside the Trylon, people could ride up the world's largest escalator and make their way over to the Perisphere. Inside, I remember seeing a model of an incredible highway system where people could travel at speeds of 100 miles per hour."

12 "Wow!" exclaimed Henry. "That doesn't sound much like the fairs I've been to."

13 Grandpa nodded. "I know. It was a once-in-a-lifetime kind of experience."

NAME ______________________

Vocabulary Skills

Write the words from the story that have the meanings below.

1. easy to break

_______________________ Par. 1

2. to hold in place

_______________________ Par. 3

3. a solid geometric shape that looks like a globe

_______________________ Par. 3

4. the use of scientific knowledge to make new things

_______________________ Par. 7

5. pointing; motioning toward

_______________________ Par. 10

A **word family** is a group of words that have the same letter combinations. For example, the words *could*, *would*, and *should* are in the same word family because they all contain the *-ould* combination. Circle the words in each row that are part of the word family in parentheses.

6. (*-ight*) write delight tight tiger
7. (*-ought*) fought our brought broke
8. (*-ight*) night right rice sight

Fill in the blanks below with the possessive form of the word in parentheses.

9. _______________ memories of the fair make good stories. (Grandpa)
10. Grandpa went to the _______________ Fair in 1939. (World)
11. The _______________ purpose was to advertise the fair. (poster)
12. Henry remembers eating pastries called _______________ ears at a fair. (elephants)

Reading Skills

1. Number the events below from **1** to **5** to show the order in which they happened.

_____ Grandpa tells Henry that the fair was about technology and things that were new.

_____ Grandpa is pricing things to sell at a yard sale.

_____ Grandpa and Henry unroll the poster.

_____ Henry says the fair is not like the ones he has visited.

_____ Grandpa remembers seeing a television for the first time.

2. What major event in history did the 1939–40 World's Fair follow?

____

3. Why did Americans want something that could give them hope?

____

4. What were the biggest attractions at the fair?

____

5. Why do you think Grandpa says the fair was "a once-in-a-lifetime kind of experience"?

____

____

Circle the word that best completes each sentence, and write it on the line.

6. Grandpa _______________ the 1939 World's Fair in New York.

forgot attended disliked

7. People wanted to see the _______________ technology at the fair.

latest oldest strangest

A Fair to Remember

Have you ever been to a fair or a carnival?

1 Because people are always coming up with important, new inventions, the World's Fairs were started as a way to show all of the latest technology in one place. World's Fairs, also called *International Expositions*, are held every few years in different cities around the world.

2 The first big fair was the Great Exhibition, held in London, England, in 1851. A very large and unique glass building, the Crystal Palace, was built for the event. It still stands in London today. Although most of the pavilions for World's Fairs are not made to last, some still exist. For example, the Eiffel Tower was built to celebrate the centennial of the French Revolution at the Universal Exposition in Paris in 1889. The Biosphere, a giant metal ball, was created for the 1967 exposition in Montreal, Canada. It is still an attraction that people visit today.

3 Another important building is the Museum of Science and Industry in Chicago. It was built for the 1893 World Columbian Exposition. It was at this fair that many people saw electricity working for the first time. The fairgrounds were lit up by electric lights. Many of the exhibits showed different uses for electricity.

4 Chicago's fair was also the first World's Fair to have a section of amusement rides. The very first Ferris wheel was there, and it was huge. It stood 250 feet tall, and it could carry as many as 2,160 people! This fair also showed the world that Chicago had recovered from the Great Chicago Fire of 1871. Almost a third of the city had been destroyed at that time.

5 The biggest fair ever held was the 1904 St. Louis World's Fair in Missouri. There were 1,500 buildings. Sixty-two different countries took part. The 1904 Summer Olympics were even held at the fairgrounds! Many people have said that the St. Louis World's Fair is where hot dogs, hamburgers, and ice-cream cones were first eaten.

6 Although there have been many World's Fairs, a couple of others are notable. The 1939 New York World's Fair was planned as an event to cheer up people during the Great Depression. It had a time capsule that would not be opened until 6939. It also had one of the very first televisions. The 1939 World's Fair was an important influence on how Disneyland was built.

7 The most popular fair ever held was the 1967 exposition in Montreal. Fifty million people came to see the exhibitions at Expo '67. It was such a hit that the city named its baseball team after the event—the Montreal Expos!

NAME ______________________

Vocabulary Skills

Words that have two middle consonants are divided into syllables between the consonants, for example, *pic/ture* or *bas/ket*. Divide the words below into syllables using a slash (/).

1. p u r p o s e

2. b u r g e r

3. t a r g e t

4. c o m p a r e

Underline the compound word in each sentence. Then, write the two words that make up each compound.

5. The 1904 Olympics were held at the fairgrounds.

______________ ______________

6. The Montreal Expos are a baseball team.

______________ ______________

7. Ask your grandparents if they ever went to a World's Fair when they were young.

______________ ______________

8. Maria won a goldfish at her town's summer fair.

______________ ______________

Reading Skills

1. Why were World's Fairs first begun?

____

____

2. Why was it important for Chicago to host the World's Fair in 1893?

____

____

3. Name two structures that were built for a World's Fair but still exist today.

______________ ______________

4. How many countries were part of the largest fair in Missouri?

____

5. Why did people need to be cheered up during the Great Depression?

____

____

Write **F** before the sentences that are facts. Write **O** before the sentences that are opinions.

6. _____ The Museum of Science and Industry was built in Chicago.

7. _____ About 50 million people came to see Expo '67.

8. _____ The St. Louis World's Fair was the most exciting fair.

9. _____ The 1939 World's Fair had a time capsule.

10. _____ It is more fun to ride the Ferris wheel than any other amusement park ride.

11. Check the line beside the word that tells what type of selection this is.

_____ fiction

_____ fantasy

_____ nonfiction

What a Thrill!

Have you ever been to an amusement park? If you have, what was your favorite ride?

1 People have always liked to go on thrill rides. As early as the 1600s, Russians were building giant wooden slides during the winter and covering them in ice. Some were 80 feet tall. People would climb to the top of these slides and then ride down on sleds. Historians think of these rides as the earliest form of what we now call *roller coasters*.

2 The first rides to have cars that ran on tracks appeared in France during the early 1800s. At Frascati Gardens in 1846, the French built the first ride that looped upside down. These were not very fast or long rides, though, and they were not popular for long.

3 In 1872, in the mountains of Pennsylvania, an abandoned railroad track became the first roller coaster ride in the United States. When a coal-mining company built a tunnel through the mountain, a large section of track was no longer needed. It was turned into a thrill ride. The track ran straight down the mountain for 2,322 feet. The speeding train would reach 100 miles per hour. People loved it, and the Mauch Chunk Railway became a huge success. Every year, 35,000 passengers rode the train. It remained very popular until it closed during the Great Depression.

4 La Marcus Adna Thompson, a very successful inventor and businessman, designed and built the first real roller coaster set in an amusement park. Thompson's "Switchback Railway" opened in 1890 at Coney Island in Brooklyn, New York. Many more coasters were built after people saw how popular this ride could be.

5 In the 1920s, roller coasters were built all over the country. It was a time of great prosperity, called the "Roaring Twenties." People everywhere wanted to have fun and be playful. Then, the 1930s came and brought the Great Depression. Many of the amusement parks were closed because people did not have enough money to visit them. During World War II, lots of the old roller coasters were torn down. The wood and steel were reused in new ways to help fight the war.

6 Today, roller coasters are as popular as ever. You do not have to travel too far to get to an amusement park that has at least one. In fact, if you live in California or Ohio, you are in luck. Six Flags Magic Mountain in Valencia, California, and Cedar Point in Sandusky, Ohio, are tied for having the most roller coasters—16 each!

NAME ______________________

Vocabulary Skills

Write the words from the article that have the meanings below.

1. sudden and exciting

   ______________________ Par. 1

2. people who write or study about history.

   ______________________ Par. 1

3. well-liked

   ______________________ Par. 2

4. no longer used

   ______________________ Par. 3

5. success and wealth

   ______________________ Par. 5

Read each word below. Then, write the letter of its synonym on the line beside the word.

6.	_____ during	a.	demonstrate
7.	_____ show	b.	stay
8.	_____ constructed	c.	while
9.	_____ remain	d.	attempt
10.	_____ try	e.	built

Write **S** if the possessive word is singular. Write **P** if it is plural.

11.	_____ coaster's	12.	_____ park's
13.	_____ Russians'	14.	_____ rides'
15.	_____ mountain's	16.	_____ tracks'

Reading Skills

1. Which country had the first thrill ride that looped upside down?

   ____

2. How many people rode the Mauch Chunk Railway every year?

   ____

3. What was the name of the first roller coaster in an amusement park?

   ____

4. Why were old roller coasters torn down during World War II?

   ____

5. Many amusement parks closed during the Great Depression because ______________

   ______________________.

6. Number the events below from **1** to **5** to show the order in which they happened.

   _____ A coal-mining company built a tunnel through a mountain.

   _____ The Switchback Railway opened at Coney Island.

   _____ The Russians built wooden slides and covered them with ice.

   _____ Amusement parks in Ohio and California have the most roller coasters.

   _____ Many amusement parks closed during the Great Depression.

7. Check the sentence that best states the main idea of the selection.

   _____ Roller coasters are popular again, and you do not have to travel far to find one.

   _____ People around the world have loved thrill rides for many years and still do today.

   _____ People wanted to have fun and enjoy themselves during the "Roaring Twenties."

The Story of a Quilt

Do any objects in your home tell a story about you or your family?

1 Tess had been in bed with the flu for nearly a week. She was tired of feeling sick and achy. She missed going to school and seeing her friends. She missed playing in the park and going to the library.

2 On Friday, Tess's mom had to go back to work, so Tess's grandmother was coming to stay with her for the day. Tess loved spending time with Nonnie. She was hoping her grandmother would bring some homemade peach ice cream. Nonnie made the best ice cream in the world. Tess waited impatiently for her grandma to arrive. Finally, she heard voices downstairs. A couple of minutes later, Nonnie popped her head into Tess's bedroom.

3 "How's my girl?" she asked Tess. "I heard you were feeling under the weather." Nonnie was carrying a small blue bowl in one hand. A quilt was draped over her other arm.

4 "Hi, Nonnie!" said Tess cheerfully. "Is that peach ice cream for breakfast?" she asked.

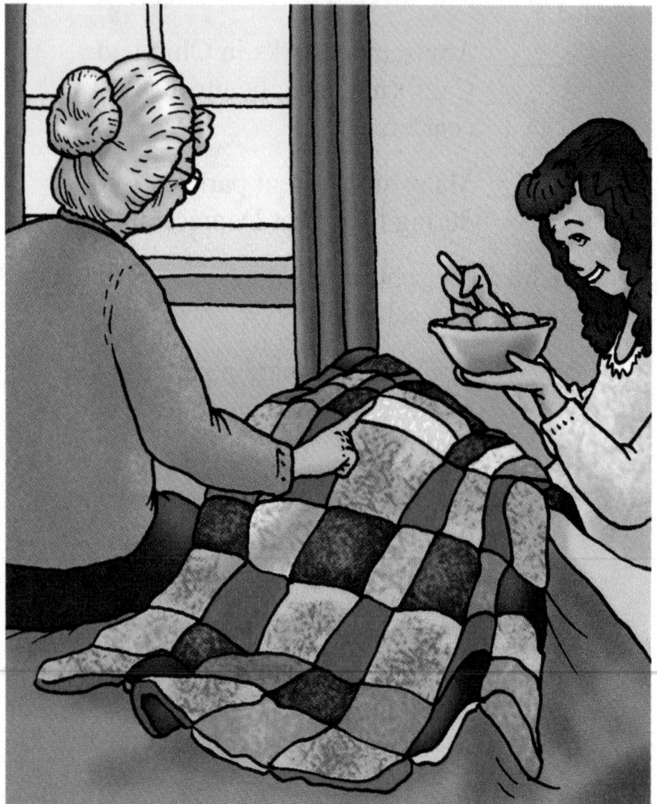

5 "How did you know?" said Nonnie. "I thought it might help you get your appetite back." She handed the bowl to her granddaughter.

6 "Why did you bring a quilt with you?" asked Tess.

7 "Well, I thought the quilt might make you feel better, too," said Nonnie. "It was your mother's favorite quilt when she was a little girl."

8 "Did you make it?" Tess asked her grandmother.

9 "No," answered Nonnie, "but my mother and my aunt made it when I was small. This quilt has seen a lot of things," she said softly.

10 Tess rubbed a corner of the quilt against her cheek. "I like this piece best, I think," she said, pointing to a large block of red flowered fabric.

11 "That was from the dress I wore for my sixth birthday," said Nonnie smiling. "It was my very favorite dress, but I outgrew it by my next birthday."

12 "What about this one?" Tess asked Nonnie.

13 "That piece was from my mother's favorite apron," said Nonnie, gently stroking a small piece of cotton. "She was wearing that apron the day my little brother fell in the creek. She ran out of the house when she heard us screaming for help," remembered Nonnie. "She tore the apron on a rock in the creek, but my brother was okay."

14 "Nonnie, do you have a story for every block in this quilt?" asked Tess.

15 "Almost every one," answered Nonnie. "Now that you know some of them, maybe you will remember and tell your own grandchildren these stories one day."

16 Tess thought for a moment. "Nonnie, you were right. This quilt *did* make me feel better. The peach ice cream didn't hurt, either!"

NAME ____________________

Vocabulary Skills

Write the words from the story that have the meanings below.

1. not bought at a store

____________________ Par. 2

2. not calmly

____________________ Par. 2

3. hung

____________________ Par. 3

4. desire for food

____________________ Par. 5

5. a piece of cloth that protects the clothes you wear beneath it

____________________ Par. 13

Write the idiom from paragraph 3 on the line next to its meaning.

6. not feeling well ____________________

7. Find a homophone in paragraph 13 for the word *peace*.

____

Write a compound word using two words from each sentence.

8. Tess was tired of being in the room where her bed was kept.

____

9. Tess had an ache in her head.

____

10. Because she was sick, Tess was wearing the gown that she usually wore at night.

____

Reading Skills

1. Do you think Tess will ask Nonnie to tell her more stories from the quilt? Why or why not?

____

____

2. Which piece of the quilt does Tess like best?

____

3. What does Nonnie mean when she says, "This quilt has seen a lot of things"?

____

____

4. How did Nonnie's mother tear her apron?

____

____

5. What problem does Tess have at the beginning of the story?

____

____

6. **Dialogue** is what a character says. The words in dialogue are always in quotation marks. On the line below, write the words that are dialogue in paragraph 12.

____

____

7. Check the phrase that best describes the author's purpose.

_____ to entertain the reader with a story about a girl who learns about her grandma's quilt

_____ to explain how to make a quilt at home

_____ to tell the reader facts about Nonnie's childhood

Patchwork History

Have you ever sewn anything? Does anyone in your family sew?

1 One of the earliest forms of quilting dates back to the Crusades in Europe in the 1400s. Turkish soldiers wore quilted material under their armor. It kept them warm, but it also added an extra layer of protection. This type of quilted material soon became used for bedding.

2 Quilts are made with two pieces of fabric that have a layer of batting, or padding, stuffed in between them. The layers are then sewn or tied together. Patchwork quilts are made of many tiny pieces of fabric sewn together, often in pretty or interesting patterns. For many years, quilts were made only by hand. Today, many quilts are still handmade, but some are made by machine.

3 Quilting became very popular in America in the mid-1800s. Colonial women did not have a lot of money or resources. Quilting became a way for women to make use of even the smallest scraps of material. They were able to make something practical and beautiful out of material that would have been wasted otherwise. Sometimes women would trade scraps of fabric with each other to add more variety to their quilts.

4 Quilting bees were popular gatherings. Women did not have many ways to express their creativity, but sewing beautiful quilts was one way they could. They got together in groups from time to time and helped each other with their quilts. Women worked very hard in the home. They often did not live close to other families, so they spent much time alone in the house. Quilting bees gave them a place to talk and socialize with other women while still completing useful projects. In fact, Susan B. Anthony first talked about women's suffrage, or the right to vote, at quilting bees.

5 The next time you see a quilt, think about all the work that went into it, especially if it was made by hand. Think about each scrap of material coming from a larger piece of cloth that was someone's dress, handkerchief, or shirt. Can you imagine all the stories each quilt has to tell?

NAME ___________________________

Vocabulary Skills

Write the words from the article that have the meanings below.

1. small pieces

_______________________ Par. 3

2. useful; having a purpose

_______________________ Par. 3

3. different types

_______________________ Par. 3

4. ability to make original or artistic things

_______________________ Par. 4

5. to talk and spend time with friends

_______________________ Par. 4

In each row, circle the word that does not belong.

6. colonial practical useful sensible
7. stitch sew express weave
8. pattern design decoration scrap

Divide the words below into syllables using a slash (/).

9. p r a c t i c e
10. f a b r i c
11. l a r g e r

Circle the homophone that correctly completes each sentence below, and write it on the line.

12. It takes many _______________ to sew a quilt by hand. (days, daze)
13. Today, some quilts are _______________ using a machine. (maid, made)
14. A decorative _______________ is often sewn around the edge of a quilt. (border, boarder)
15. It is not difficult for a quilter to fix a small _______________ in a quilt. (hole, whole)

Reading Skills

1. How did Turkish soldiers use quilted material?

____

____

2. What is a patchwork quilt?

____

____

3. What is a quilting bee?

____

____

4. Why were quilts practical?

____

____

5. What historical event was Susan B. Anthony a part of?

____

____

6. How can a quilt tell a story?

____

____

7. Check the sentence that best states the main idea of the selection.

_____ A quilt is made of two pieces of fabric with a layer of batting sewn in between.

_____ Quilting bees were a good place for women to socialize while they were still doing useful work.

_____ Quilts, which are both beautiful and practical, were a way for women throughout history to reuse scraps of material to make something useful.

The Mystery of the Quilt Codes

What are some ways to communicate without talking?

1 Quilts can be used to keep warm on a cool night. They can be decorative objects. They can be passed along from one generation to the next. But did you ever think that quilts could be used to communicate, or send messages?

2 Some people believe that quilts made by slaves were used to give information to other slaves who were planning to escape on the Underground Railroad. The Underground Railroad was not actually a railroad. It was the name used for the system that helped slaves travel north, where they could live freely. This trip was very dangerous for slaves. If they were caught, their lives were in danger.

3 Ozella McDaniel said that she had learned the secret codes of the quilts from her relatives. Her ancestors had been slaves. The codes were passed down to her through the generations. The patterns in the quilts contained messages about the journey north. The escaping slaves would memorize the messages so they could take the information with them without being caught.

4 Some of the symbols McDaniel said the slaves used in the quilts were the log cabin, the wagon wheel, the bear's paw, and the star. The log cabin told slaves to look for safe houses. The wagon wheel let them know that they were about to go on a long trip. The bear's paw told the slaves to walk north over the Appalachian Mountains. Also, bears know where to find water and berries. If the slaves ran out of food on their journey, following bear prints could help them survive. The star pattern let the slaves know they should follow the North Star toward freedom.

5 Not everyone believes that slaves used quilts this way. Unfortunately, none of the quilts have survived long enough to prove the stories. Also, the stories were not written down by the slaves. Instead, they were passed down through oral tradition, or storytelling.

6 The historians who study this time in history do not all agree about the meanings of slave quilts. They have different opinions about the purpose of the quilts. We may never know the truth behind the quilts that were made so long ago. However, the work of historians and the legends of storytellers may bring us a bit closer to figuring out the mysteries of the quilts.

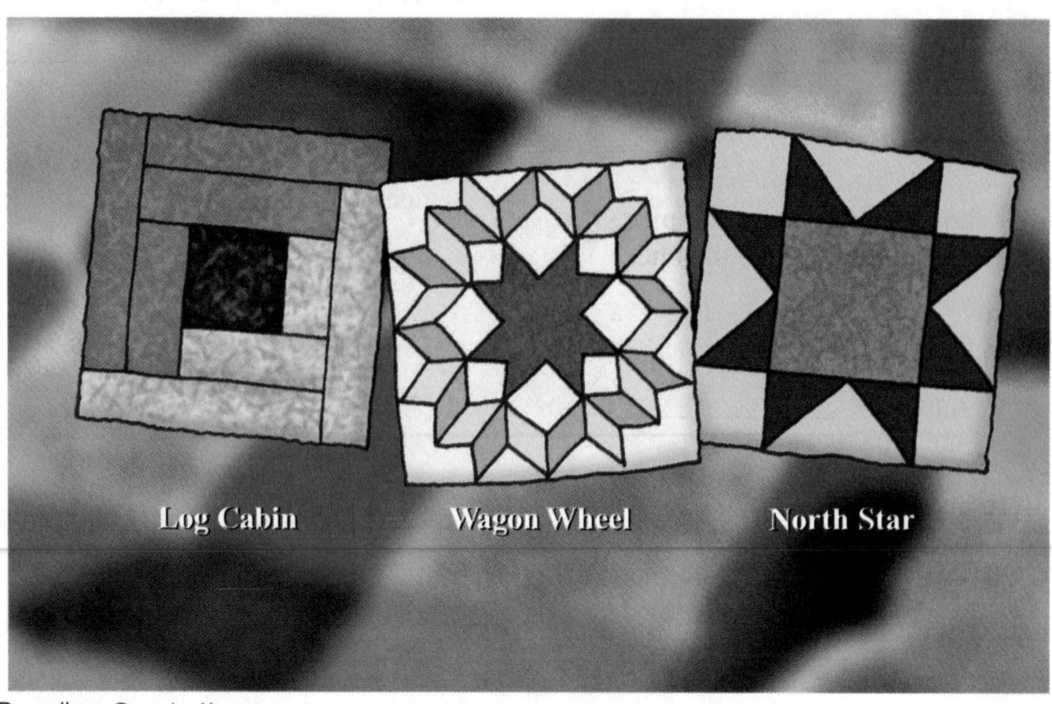

NAME ______________________

Vocabulary Skills

Find a synonym in the article for each of the words below.

1. colorful ______________________ Par. 1
2. journey ______________________ Par. 2
3. captured ______________________ Par. 2
4. relatives ______________________ Par. 3

Circle the words in each row that are part of the same word family.

5. (*-ight*) moonlight fright excite frost
6. (*-ought*) fought bought fox boot
7. (*-ould*) should cold could wood

Reading Skills

1. Check the sentence below that is the best summary for paragraph 4.

   _____ Some people think that patterns like the log cabin, the wagon wheel, the bear's paw, and the star were used to tell secret codes.

   _____ The bear's paw told the slaves to walk north over the mountains.

2. What was the Underground Railroad?

   ____

   ____

3. What did a star pattern on a quilt mean?

   ____

4. Why did the slaves want to travel north?

   ____

5. Why don't historians know for certain whether the quilts were used by slaves to communicate information about escaping?

   ____

6. Do you think the mystery of the slave quilts will be solved in the future? Why or why not?

   ____

   ____

Circle the word that best completes each sentence, and write it on the line.

7. Quilts may have been used to pass ____________ to other slaves.

   information generations patterns

8. None of the quilts ____________ long enough for historians to study.

   agreed survived proved

9. Some historians have ____________ ideas about the purpose of the quilts.

   few studied different

Study Skills

Guide words are printed at the top of each page in a dictionary. The guide word at the left is the first word on the page. The guide word at the right is the last word on the page. Check each word that could be found on a page having the guide words shown in dark print.

1. **answer—appear**

   _____ anteater _____ apple _____ annex

2. **wheel—wing**

   _____ wind _____ wax _____ where

3. **ridge—roar**

   _____ rind _____ reality _____ route

Make Your Own Quilt

What story do you want your quilt to tell about you?

Things you will need:

- 25 four-inch squares of paper (colored or patterned papers will work best)
- crayons and markers
- glue stick, rubber cement, or two-sided tape

1. First decide what type of quilt you want to make. You can make two different patterns of squares and alternate them, or you can create your own design. For example, you may want to have alternating squares all around your quilt and a different pattern in the center.
2. Once you have decided what your quilt will look like, you can begin coloring or decorating your squares. Remember that some of your squares can have pictures or symbols on them that are meaningful to you. Your quilt will tell a story about you.

   Here are some ideas of pictures you can include on your quilt squares:

   - your family
   - your pets
   - your friends
   - your house, neighborhood, or school
   - things you like to do
   - places you have visited
   - memories of things that are special to you

   Not every square needs to have a picture on it. You can make a pattern (like polka dots, checks, or swirls) on some pieces, or you can use colored or patterned paper to add variety to your quilt.
3. When you have finished making the quilt squares, spread them out on the top of a large table. Arrange them in an order that you think looks nice. You should have a total of five rows made up of five squares each.
4. Now you can begin attaching the squares to each other, one row at a time. Use a small amount of glue or tape on the edge of each square. When you have five rows completed, you can begin attaching the rows together.
5. If you used glue, allow your quilt time to dry before you hang it up on the wall. See if your friends can determine what story your quilt tells about you.

NAME ______________________

Vocabulary Skills

Write the words from the article that have the meanings below.

1. to happen in turns; every other one

_______________________ Step 1

2. full of importance

_______________________ Step 2

3. place in a particular order

_______________________ Step 3

4. figure out; decide

_______________________ Step 5

Check the meaning of the underlined word in each sentence.

5. Sewing with a machine can make quite a racket.

_____ a loud noise

_____ a paddle used to hit a ball

6. Even a scrap of material can be used in a quilt.

_____ an argument

_____ a small piece

Reading Skills

1. Check the phrase that best describes the author's purpose.

_____ to persuade the reader that quilts are difficult to make

_____ to explain how to make a paper quilt

_____ to tell about the history of quilts

2. Name two ideas of pictures you could include in your quilt.

_______________ _______________

3. How big should the squares of paper be?

____

4. What information should people be able to get by looking at your quilt?

____

5. Number the steps below from **1** to **5** to show the order in which they appear in the selection.

_____ Decorate your squares of paper.

_____ Decide what type of quilt to make.

_____ Attach the rows of squares using tape or glue.

_____ Arrange the squares on a table.

_____ Gather the materials you will need.

6. Check the line beside the word or words that tell what type of nonfiction selection this is.

_____ biography

_____ how-to text

_____ history

Study Skills

Use the index below to answer the questions that follow.

Index

1. On what pages can you find information about patterns?

____

2. Which topic is covered on the greatest number of pages?

____

A Musical Discovery

What kinds of music do you enjoy?

1 "*Ahhhhchoo!*" Devon sneezed. He was helping his great-uncle Frank clean out the attic on a cool fall morning.

2 "It looks like we had better open a window," said Uncle Frank. "I think several years' worth of dust have accumulated up here." The floorboards squeaked as Uncle Frank stepped carefully over a few boxes and opened a small window. He took a deep breath of the crisp fall air and made his way back over to Devon.

3 "Uncle Frank, what are these records from?" asked Devon, holding up a stack of records in white paper sleeves.

4 "Hmm," said Uncle Frank. He picked up the records and looked at the faded dates that were written on the sleeves. "I haven't heard these in ages!" he exclaimed. "I thought they had disappeared years ago."

5 "They look pretty old," commented Devon.

6 "They are very old," agreed Uncle Frank. "Let's go downstairs and see if we can find somewhere to play them. I have a feeling they might surprise you."

7 A few minutes later, Devon and his great-uncle sat on the comfortable old sofa and began listening to the records. The music was strong and clear, and it made Devon want to tap his toes and drum his fingers on the coffee table.

8 "This is great!" he said. "Did you know the people in this band or something?"

9 "Yes, I did," said Uncle Frank with a smile. "I knew them very well. In fact, I married the singer."

10 "Aunt Clara was the singer on these records?" asked Devon with a surprised expression on his face. "I never knew she could sing."

11 "She had a beautiful voice," remembered Uncle Frank. "It was as smooth as honey. I was playing the trumpet in the last song we heard. Those were some good times."

12 "I never even knew that you and Aunt Clara were in a band," said Devon shaking his head. "Do you still play? What was the name of your band? Were you famous?"

13 "I haven't picked up a trumpet in years," answered Uncle Frank. "Our group was called the *Frank Mack Quartet*. We weren't famous, but in the late 1940s and the early 1950s we were pretty popular at some Missouri jazz clubs. I think I even signed a few autographs when I was young and handsome." Uncle Frank chuckled at the memory.

14 "The best parts of being in that group were meeting your great-aunt and being around people who loved jazz music just as much as we did," said Uncle Frank. "Being famous would have just been icing on the cake."

15 "Uncle Frank," said Devon, "if we find your trumpet in the attic, will you teach me how to play?"

16 Uncle Frank nodded. "Once the jazz bug bites you, there's no going back!"

NAME ____________________

Vocabulary Skills

Write the words from the story that have the meanings below.

1. built up over time

_______________ Par. 2

2. lost color or brightness

_______________ Par. 4

3. a look that shows a mood

_______________ Par. 10

4. a group of four people

_______________ Par. 13

5. signatures of a famous person

_______________ Par. 13

6. Find the simile in paragraph 11, and write it on the lines below.

____

____

7. Write the idiom from paragraph 14 on the line next to its meaning.

something extra; a bonus _______________

Divide the words below into syllables using a slash (/).

8. i t e m

9. r e c o r d

10. r e l a x

Reading Skills

Write **F** before the sentences that are facts. Write **O** before the sentences that are opinions.

1. _____ Uncle Frank's band was the best jazz band of the last 50 years.

2. _____ Devon is helping Uncle Frank clean the attic.

3. _____ Devon should learn how to play the trumpet.

4. _____ Uncle Frank's band played at Missouri jazz clubs.

5. _____ Aunt Clara was in the same band as Uncle Frank.

Write **D** before the phrases that describe Devon and **F** before the phrases that describe Uncle Frank.

6. _____ sneezes because of the dust in the attic

7. _____ has never played the trumpet before

8. _____ thinks Aunt Clara had a beautiful voice

9. _____ has not played the trumpet in many years

10. _____ holds up a stack of records

11. What do you think Uncle Frank means when he says, "Once the jazz bug bites you, there's no going back"?

____

12. What does Devon want to do when he hears the music on the records?

____

13. Do you think Devon will learn to play the trumpet in the future? Why or why not?

____

____

Trumpet Talk

Have you ever seen someone play the trumpet?

1 Musical horns were given their name for a very good reason: they were made from the hollowed out horns of animals. People found that making a noise at the small end of a tube produced a louder sound at the large end. These horns, as well as some large shells, were the earliest versions of what we now know as the *trumpet*.

2 As far back as the ancient Egyptians, human beings were making trumpets out of silver and bronze. The first horns did not look like the trumpets you might see today. Instead, the tubes were long and straight, not coiled around in a loop. These horns were used for ceremonies, but more importantly, they were used to communicate.

3 The horn was also used for communication in medieval times. Different sections of the army would use the trumpet to tell each other important information, similar to the way more modern armies used the bugle.

4 During the 1800s, the trumpet was finally recognized as an important instrument for musicians. This happened partly because of the introduction of valves to the trumpet. Because the first horns had just a straight tube, the trumpeter could only play certain notes. Coiling the tube into a loop and adding extra tubes to the sides meant that the horn could now make a large variety of sounds.

5 How does a trumpet work? There are three main sections: the mouthpiece, the tubes and valves, and the bell. The mouthpiece is where the trumpeter blows into the horn. This sounds simple, but it is not as easy as blowing up a balloon. The player has to vibrate his or her lips to create the right sound. The mouthpiece is shaped like a cup, so there is room for the lips to *buzz* into the trumpet.

6 This vibration is then carried through the coiled tubes. Pushing down the valves will open the side tubes so that the vibration has to go farther. In a horn, the longer the sound has to go, the lower the note will be. If the trumpeter does not push down any valves, the sound will go straight through the trumpet and produce the highest note. Different valves open tubes of different lengths, so the player can create all of the notes needed for a song.

7 The last part of the trumpet is the bell. This section is where the sound leaves the horn and blasts into the room. The size of the bell also affects the sound. Wider bells produce a softer sound. Narrower bells give off a sharper sound. Some trumpeters even plug the bell with a mute so that the sound is muffled. Miles Davis, one of the greatest trumpeters ever, often used a mute when he played.

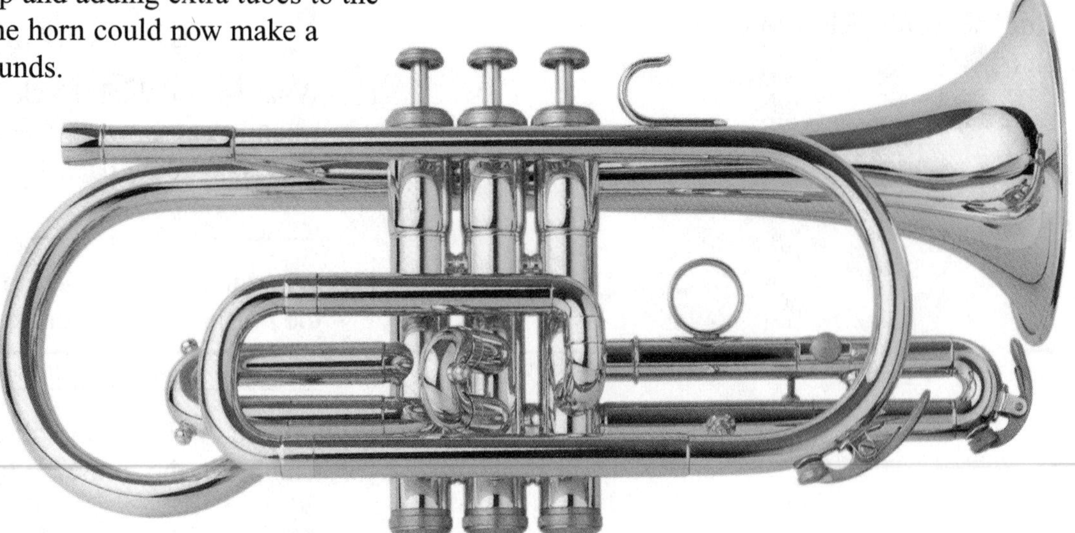

NAME ______________________

Vocabulary Skills

Write the words from the article that have the meanings below.

1. different forms of something

   ______________________ Par. 1

2. twisted into a spiral

   ______________________ Par. 2

3. the Middle Ages in Europe, around A.D. 500 to 1450

   ______________________ Par. 3

4. something that blocks an opening but can be opened or closed

   ______________________ Par. 5

Find an antonym in the article for each of the words below.

5. latest ______________________ Par. 1
6. modern ______________________ Par. 2
7. lowest ______________________ Par. 6
8. wider ______________________ Par. 7

Write a compound word using two words in each sentence.

9. The trumpeter puts his or her mouth on the piece shaped like a cup.

   ____

10. A shell that was found near the sea was one early version of a trumpet.

    ____

11. The members of the band boarded a plane that would fly through the air.

    ____

12. The band had to be in St. Louis by the end of the week.

    ____

Reading Skills

Circle the word that best completes each sentence below, and write it on the line.

1. In a horn, the longer the sound has to go, the ______________ the note will be.

   higher louder lower

2. ______________ bells produce a softer sound.

   Wider Narrower Older

3. The trumpeter has to ______________ his or her lips in the mouthpiece.

   place vibrate stop

4. In what way did people in medieval times use the trumpet to communicate?

   ____

   ____

5. Why do some trumpeters use a mute?

   ____

   ____

6. What kind of sound will a trumpet make if the trumpeter does not push down any valves?

   ____

   ____

7. What was one reason the trumpet became recognized as an important musical instrument?

   ____

   ____

8. On the lines below, write a summary for paragraphs 2 and 3.

   ____

   ____

   ____

King of the Trumpet

Have you ever played a musical instrument?

1 John Birks Gillespie was born in 1917 in Cheraw, South Carolina. He was the youngest of nine children. John taught himself to play the trombone when he was young and switched to the trumpet when he was 12 years old. After his father died, 18-year-old John and his widowed mother moved to Philadelphia. This was an important move for the young trumpet player. There was a busy musical scene in Philadelphia, and John got a lot of experience performing in public. He also earned the nickname "Dizzy," a name that he would be known by for the rest of his life.

2 Dizzy became well known for the unusual way he played music. He put notes together in a way that no one else ever had. The notes did not seem like they should go together, but somehow the music always worked as a whole.

3 Dizzy also had the opportunity to play with saxophonist Charlie Parker. Charlie was doing new and interesting things on the saxophone the same way Dizzy was doing them on the trumpet. Together, Dizzy and Charlie started a new type of jazz music called *bebop*. Bebop was different than the type of jazz most people were familiar with. It moved more quickly, and the notes were played in an irregular pattern. In the 1940s, the two musicians made several records together. Today, these records are still thought of as some of the greatest in jazz history.

4 There were two things that were especially memorable about watching Dizzy perform. One is that his trumpet looked strange because it was bent. Someone had once accidentally fallen on Dizzy's trumpet. It turned out that he actually liked it better that way and never had it fixed. Dizzy's cheeks also puffed out to look like two small balloons when he played the trumpet. He was a great comedian, so it was always entertaining to watch him perform.

5 Dizzy Gillespie was not just a talented jazz musician. He also cared about social causes. He did some work for the United Nations and eventually even formed a band called the *United Nations Orchestra*. He was also a civil rights activist. He worked to make sure that all Americans would have the same rights, regardless of their race, religion, gender, or social class. Dizzy Gillespie may be best remembered for the ways he changed jazz music. But during his lifetime, Dizzy made a difference in many people's lives.

NAME ____________________

Vocabulary Skills

Write the words from the article that have the meanings below.

1. doing something in front of an audience

   ______________________ Par. 1

2. a name that is used instead of a given name

   ______________________ Par. 1

3. not following a usual pattern

   ______________________ Par. 3

4. easy to remember

   ______________________ Par. 4

5. fun and interesting; amusing

   ______________________ Par. 4

Read each word below. Then, write the letter of its antonym on the line beside the word.

6. _____ unusual		**a.**	regular
7. _____ purposely		**b.**	accidentally
8. _____ united		**c.**	stingy
9. _____ generous		**d.**	divided

Divide the words below into syllables using a slash (/).

10. n i c k n a m e

11. l i f e t i m e

12. k e y b o a r d

Write **S** if the possessive word is singular. Write **P** if it is plural.

13. _____ Dizzy's **14.** _____ band's

15. _____ musicians' **16.** _____ records'

Reading Skills

1. How many children were there in Dizzy Gillespie's family?

   ____

2. What instrument did Charlie Parker play?

   ____

3. Name one thing that was different about bebop.

   ____

4. Why was Dizzy's trumpet bent?

   ____

5. How do we know that Dizzy cared about social causes?

   ____

   ____

Read the phrases below. Write **D** next to the phrase if it describes Dizzy, write **C** if it describes Charlie, and write **B** if it describes them both.

6. _____ born in South Carolina
7. _____ played the saxophone
8. _____ made bebop popular
9. _____ played a bent trumpet
10. Check the sentence that best states the main idea of the selection.

    _____ Dizzy Gillespie was a talented musician and a caring person.

    _____ Dizzy Gillespie was the youngest of nine children.

    _____ Dizzy Gillespie played with saxophonist Charlie Parker.

For the Love of Jazz

Where did jazz music begin?

1 Many people call the United States of America a "great melting pot" where all of the different cultures of its citizens combine to make one diverse culture. A perfect example of this idea is jazz. Jazz began when African American musicians, who listened to a lot of different kinds of music, started to play in a way that combined them all.

2 In the late 1800s, many African Americans who had been slaves were still alive. The songs they had sung while working were based on folk music from Africa. A popular form of this music was hopeful and sad at the same time. It was known as the *blues*. These songs were not written down with notes and lyrics. Instead, the singer or musician would learn the basic melody and then perform it with his or her own personal interpretation. This way of performing is called *improvising*. It is the most important element of jazz music.

3 Originally, jazz was played mostly in New Orleans, Louisiana. Railroads and phonographs helped it become known around the country. Many African American men worked for the Pullman Company, which operated sleeper cars for railroad travel. The men who worked for Pullman told people all around the country about this new, exciting music called *jazz*. They also brought along records, a new invention, so that people could actually hear jazz as well.

4 The trumpeter Louis Armstrong is considered by many historians to be the most important musician of early jazz. In addition to being a fantastic trumpeter, he also invented "scat" singing. Scatting is when a singer does not sing actual words but uses his or her voice to make nonsense sounds that are more like the music an instrument would make. Ella Fitzgerald was another famous scat singer.

5 During the 1920s, jazz finally became popular with Americans of all races. In fact, it was so popular that the 1920s are still known as the "Jazz Age." Jazz also helped lead to the end of segregation. In the 1930s, the white bandleader Benny Goodman hired an African American pianist and guitarist. At that time, bands were supposed to be all white or all black. Most musicians understood how ridiculous this idea was. No matter how different they might look, deep down they all loved jazz!

NAME ____________________

Vocabulary Skills

In each row, circle the words that belong together.

1. music jazz railroad blues
2. different similar variety diverse
3. popular words lyrics singing
4. records train railroad sleeper car

Underline the compound word in each sentence. Then, write the two words that make up each compound.

5. The railroad tracks run near my apartment building.

   ________ ________

6. The afternoon train will arrive at 3:00.

   ________ ________

7. Louis Armstrong was an outstanding musician.

   ________ ________

8. Without jazz, the world of music would be very different.

   ________ ________

Reading Skills

1. Why is America called "a great melting pot"?

   ____

2. What are two adjectives the author uses to describe the blues?

   ________ ________

3. What two things helped jazz become known around the country?

   ________ ________

4. What sorts of sounds does a singer who is scatting make?

   ____

5. How did jazz help end segregation?

   ____

   ____

Write **T** before the sentences that are true. Write **F** before the sentences that are false.

6. _____ The blues are a type of railroad car.
7. _____ The 1940s were known as the Jazz Age.
8. _____ Many African American men worked for the Pullman Company.
9. _____ At first, jazz was mostly played in Georgia.
10. _____ Ella Fitzgerald was a famous scat singer.

Study Skills

You can use a computer's reference system to help you find a book you want in a library. Use the information below to answer the questions that follow.

Call No:	667.42 HO
Author:	Hoffman, William C.
Title:	Jazz Through the Years
Publisher:	Avondale Press

1. What is the title of the book?

   ____

2. What is the author's last name?

   ____

3. What is the book's call number?

   ____

A Bebop Afternoon

Have you ever listened to music at an outdoor festival?

1 Devon, his mom, and his friend Will shook out the checkered picnic blanket. They placed it on the grass under the shade of a large maple tree. Families were setting up all around the park where the jazz festival was taking place. Devon's mom had brought a picnic basket with her, and the boys helped her unload the lunch she had packed. They laid out two kinds of sandwiches, pretzels, apples, lemonade, and fresh brownies.

2 "When do you think the music is going to start, Mom?" asked Devon, helping himself to a turkey and cheese sandwich. He'd been looking forward to the festival for months, ever since Uncle Frank told him that he'd be performing.

3 "It looks like they are almost done setting up," responded Mom. "They'll probably start playing in about 15 minutes."

4 "How long has it been since your uncle played in front of a crowd?" asked Will, biting into a crisp apple.

5 "About 30 years," replied Devon. "We found his trumpet and some old records when we were cleaning out his attic last fall. Uncle Frank started giving me lessons on the trumpet, and he started playing it again himself. He joined the band a couple of months ago."

6 "Is he nervous?" asked Will.

7 "Nope," said Devon. "I think he is just excited. Last week he told me that he hadn't realized how much he missed playing music and being surrounded by people who love it the way he does."

8 "What are they doing now, Mom?" Devon asked. He could hear music coming from the small stage, but it didn't sound like a song.

9 "I think they are just warming up and preparing to begin," said Mom. "You know, your father and I saw Uncle Frank and Aunt Clara perform years and years ago in a club in Missouri. Dad and I weren't married yet. I think it was one of our first dates. That was one of the last times your aunt and uncle performed together."

10 Suddenly, the bandleader tested the microphone. He introduced the members of the band. He even added how happy they were to have Uncle Frank come out of retirement to play again.

11 Devon leaned back and grinned at his mom and Will. The sounds of his uncle's trumpet filled the summer air. He tapped his fingers in time to the rhythm of the music. Devon couldn't wait to learn to play the way his uncle did.

NAME ______________________

Vocabulary Skills

Write the words from the story that have the meanings below.

1. an event that celebrates something

   ______________________ Par. 2

2. became aware of; figured out

   ______________________ Par. 7

3. having all around

   ______________________ Par. 7

4. getting ready

   ______________________ Par. 9

5. a time in an older person's life when he or she stops working

   ______________________ Par. 10

6. a regular beat or sound

   ______________________ Par. 11

Circle the homophone that correctly completes each sentence below, and write it on the line.

7. Devon's mom ______________ a lunch to eat at the festival. (packed, pact)

8. Uncle Frank ______________ into the mouthpiece of the trumpet. (blue, blew)

9. Uncle Frank and Aunt Clara made a wonderful ______________. (pear, pair)

10. Mom ______________ Uncle Frank's band play in Missouri. (heard, herd)

Underline the prefix in each word. Then, write the meaning of the word.

11. impolite ______________________

12. nonidentical ______________________

13. redeliver ______________________

Reading Skills

1. Check the phrase that best describes the author's purpose.

   _____ to persuade the reader to learn how to play a musical instrument

   _____ to entertain the reader with a story about a boy watching his uncle perform

   _____ to explain how to play the trumpet

2. Name two things that were in the picnic lunch Mom packed.

   ______________ ______________

3. Why does Will think Uncle Frank might be nervous?

   ____

   ____

4. Why has Uncle Frank started playing the trumpet again?

   ____

   ____

5. Why do you think Devon grins at his mom and Will at the end of the story?

   ____

   ____

6. Check the words that you think describe Devon.

   _____ curious

   _____ excited

   _____ stingy

   _____ supportive

   _____ angry

   _____ impatient

Plants on the Move

What kinds of plants do you think Beatriz and Abby will discover at the conservatory?

1 On Tuesday afternoon, Mrs. Singh's class walked through the large glass doors of the conservatory. Everyone in the class was supposed to choose one plant that was his or her favorite. When they returned to school, they would write about that plant and share the information they found with the rest of the class.

2 The first room they visited was the rain forest room. The air inside was warm and slightly damp. Beatriz took a deep breath. The air smelled earthy, the way it did in the spring when it had been raining for days.

3 "Is that a palm tree?" Beatriz asked the guide, Mr. Cooney. She pointed to an enormous plant that towered over the room. It had large spiky green leaves that looked a little like the palm trees Beatriz had seen when her family went on vacation in Florida. This tree seemed much larger though.

4 "You're right," said Mr. Cooney. "It is a type of palm tree. It is called an *Alexandria palm*."

5 "I like palm trees," Abby told Beatriz, "but I don't think they are my favorite type of plant."

6 In the next room they visited, Mr. Cooney showed the class a *mimosa*, or sensitive plant. "Does anyone know why it is called a sensitive plant?" he asked.

7 Terrell raised his hand. "Because its feelings get hurt easily?" he joked. The class laughed.

8 "Actually, that's not a bad guess," said Mr. Cooney. "Watch what happens when I touch the leaves of the plant." He ran one finger gently down the long spine, and the tiny leaves on either side folded up. "This plant reacts to touch, as you can see, but it also reacts to wind or heat the same way."

9 "Wow," said Beatriz. "I never knew plants could move like that."

10 "What about the Venus flytrap?" asked Abby. "My brother used to have one, and it could move, too."

11 "That's right," said Mr. Cooney. "The Venus flytrap is native to North and South Carolina. The plant gives off a sweet liquid that attracts insects. There are trigger hairs on the inside of the leaves. When an insect touches the trigger hairs, the plant snaps shut and traps the insect inside. Even small animals like frogs can become trapped."

12 "I think the Venus flytrap might be my favorite because it is so unusual," Beatriz said to Abby.

13 "I like the sensitive plant the best," said Abby.

14 "You might not want to make up your minds too soon," said Mrs. Singh, smiling at the girls. "We've only seen a small portion of the plants that are displayed here."

15 Beatriz laughed. "I think I'm going to end up with a whole list of favorites!"

NAME ______________________________

Vocabulary Skills

Write the words from the story that have the meanings below.

1. a greenhouse where plants are grown and displayed

   ______________________________ Par. 1

2. rose very high in the air

   ______________________________ Par. 3

3. easily affected by something

   ______________________________ Par. 6

4. responds

   ______________________________ Par. 8

5. from a particular place

   ______________________________ Par. 11

Read each pair of words listed below. If the words are synonyms, write **S** on the line. If the words are antonyms, write **A** on the line.

6. _____ enormous huge
7. _____ gently harshly
8. _____ unusual common
9. _____ traps captures
10. _____ smiling grinning

Write the possessive form of the word in parentheses on the line below.

11. Mrs. _______________ class visited a conservatory. (Singh)
12. The palm _______________ leaves were green and spiky. (tree)
13. The class laughed at _______________ joke. (Terrell)
14. The _______________ assignment was to choose a favorite plant. (students)

Reading Skills

1. What happens if a person touches the leaves of the sensitive plant?

   ____

2. What is another name for the sensitive plant?

   ____

3. Where does the Venus flytrap grow in the wild?

   ____

4. How does the Venus flytrap know that an insect has landed on it?

   ____

5. Do you think Beatriz and Abby will visit the conservatory again? Why or why not?

   ____

   ____

6. Check the sentence below that is the best summary for paragraph 11.

   _____ The Venus flytrap lives in the Carolinas.

   _____ The Venus flytrap attracts and captures insects and small animals.

   _____ The Venus flytrap has sensitive trigger hairs.

Read the sentences below. Write **A** next to the sentence if it describes Abby. Write **B** if it describes Beatriz.

7. _____ Her brother had a Venus flytrap.
8. _____ She didn't know that plants could move.
9. _____ The Venus flytrap is her favorite.
10. _____ The sensitive plant is her favorite.

Make Your Own Terrarium

What kinds of plants grow well in a terrarium?

Materials you will need:

- a large glass or plastic jar with a lid; a fish bowl covered with plastic wrap will also work
- potting soil
- gravel or small rocks
- small plants that like shade and moisture

1 A terrarium is a great way to have your own miniature garden. It is easy to put one together, and it does not require a lot of care. The lid on the terrarium keeps moisture from escaping. This means that you rarely have to water the plants in your terrarium. After you water the plants the first time, the moisture will evaporate and then condense on the sides of the container. The water keeps getting recycled.

2 Terrariums also do not need a lot of light. When you choose plants for your terrarium, make sure to look for ones that like shade and warm, moist conditions. Here are some examples of plants that do well in terrariums: small ferns, moss, violets, baby tears, and begonias.

A. Place a small layer of gravel at the bottom of the jar or bowl. Then, add a layer of soil to the jar.

B. Now, add the plants to your terrarium. First, decide how you would like to arrange them. Then, make a small hole in the soil and place a plant in it. Pat the soil around the plant to make sure it stays in place. Continue with the next plant.

C. When you have finished planting, you can add a bit of moss or some decorative rocks to your terrarium.

D. Now, place your terrarium in a place where it will receive a bit of sunlight every day. It should not get too much direct light, but it also should not be in complete shade.

E. If you accidentally put too much water in your terrarium, just take off the lid or the plastic wrap for a couple of days. This will allow the extra water to evaporate into the air so that the plants do not rot.

F. If the soil begins to look too dry, you may have to water it a bit. If the plants start getting too large, you can trim them, or you can place them in an even larger terrarium.

G. Now, sit back and enjoy the miniature world you created!

NAME ______________________

Vocabulary Skills

In each row, circle the word that does not belong.

1. light moss fern violet
2. pebbles gravel jar stones
3. moist damp dry wet
4. total part complete entire

Check the meaning of the underlined word in each sentence.

5. A fern has many small <u>leaves</u>.

   _____ to go away

   _____ the flat green part of a plant

6. A terrarium does not need much <u>light</u>.

   _____ a form of energy from the sun

   _____ not heavy

7. If there is not room in the <u>yard</u> for a garden, make a terrarium.

   _____ the area around a house

   _____ 36 inches

Reading Skills

1. Check the phrase that best describes the author's purpose.

   _____ to show that terrariums are the best type of gardens to have

   _____ to tell the history of terrariums

   _____ to explain how to assemble and care for a terrarium

2. What kind of a container can you use to make a terrarium?

   ____

   ____

3. Why don't you have to water the plants in a terrarium very often?

   ____

   ____

4. Name two types of plants that do well in terrariums.

   ______________ ______________

5. What kind of light will your terrarium need?

   ____

   ____

6. What can happen if you put too much water in a terrarium, and you do not take off the lid to let some of the water evaporate?

   ____

   ____

Study Skills

A table of contents is one of the first pages in a book. It shows the chapters that are in a book. It also shows the page on which each chapter begins. Use the table of contents below to answer the questions.

Table of Contents

1. What is the title of Chapter 3?

   ____

2. On what page does Chapter 5 begin?

   ____

3. What chapter would you use if you wanted some information about terrarium animals?

   ____

A Special Garden

Why do people need to make sure that endangered plants survive?

1 What would you see if you were to go on a tour of the United States Botanic Garden in Washington, D.C.? You would have a chance to see some of the 26,000 plants they care for!

2 Plants are important for many reasons. They provide the oxygen we breathe. They also provide materials for many types of food, shelter, medicine, and fuels that human beings use. One out of every eight species of plants in the world is endangered. The people at the U.S. Botanic Garden know how important plants are, so they do their best to raise, conserve, and study plants from all around the world.

3 In 1842, the United States sent an expedition to the South Seas. It was led by Admiral Wilkes. The expedition brought back all sorts of living plants. The U.S. Botanic Garden was founded so there would be a place where the plants could be cared for and studied. The Garden moved to its current location in the Nation's Mall at the foot of the United States Capitol in 1933. In addition to the conservatory, you can visit Bartholdi Park, an outdoor garden that contains about four thousand plants.

4 There are many different areas you can visit at the U.S. Botanic Garden. Each area focuses on a different category of plant. For instance, you might not realize how many plants can grow in the desert. If you visited the Desert House, you could see all kinds of cacti and succulents. These are plants that store water in their leaves so that they can live in very dry places.

5 In the Rare and Endangered House, you would see plants that conservationists worked very hard to find. For example, there is a rare plant called the *Brighamia insignis* that grows on the sea cliffs of a Hawaiian island. Scientists had to climb steep cliffs to gather seeds from these plants to bring back to the U.S. Botanic Garden.

6 In the Medicinal Plant House, you could see plants that are used in making many different medicines. Some of these plants have saved lives. But as more and more of Earth's forests are cut down, there are fewer opportunities for discovering new medicinal plants. There may be plants we have not even discovered yet that hold the key to curing some of the worst illnesses. This is why the Botanic Garden has such an important role in preserving plants.

NAME ______________________

Vocabulary Skills

Write the words from the article that have the meanings below.

1. to be careful not to use up

   ______________________ Par. 2

2. a journey that is made for a specific purpose

   ______________________ Par. 3

3. created or established

   ______________________ Par. 3

4. threatened; exposed to danger

   ______________________ Par. 5

5. people who work to preserve and protect something

   ______________________ Par. 5

Write the idiom from paragraph 6 on the line next to its meaning, and write it on the line.

6. have the solution ______________________

Circle the homophone that correctly completes each sentence below.

7. The bloom of the plant beside you is a beautiful ______________ yellow. (pail, pale)

8. I ______________ the Orchid House without going inside. (past, passed)

9. There is a large ______________ of stained glass in the window of the conservatory. (pane, pain)

Reading Skills

1. Where is the United States Botanic Garden located?

   ____

2. Name two things plants provide for people.

   ______________ ______________

3. Who was Admiral Wilkes?

   ____

   ____

4. Why do you think that different categories of plants are located in different areas at the U.S. Botanic Garden?

   ____

   ____

5. How can plants help save people's lives?

   ____

   ____

6. Do you think the U.S. Botanic Garden will continue to grow and preserve new kinds of plants? Why or why not?

   ____

   ____

Write **F** before the sentences that are facts. Write **O** before the sentences that are opinions.

7. _____ Plants provide the oxygen we breathe.

8. _____ The most interesting plants are the ones in the Desert House.

9. _____ Admiral Wilkes led the expedition to the South Seas.

10. _____ The *Brighamia insignis* grows in Hawaii.

11. _____ The orchid is the most beautiful type of plant at the U.S. Botanic Garden.

Something in the Air

Why are people so excited to visit the titan arum?

1 When you think about flowers, what sorts of smells do you think of? Most people think of flowers as having a pleasant or even beautiful scent. That is probably because they have never encountered the titan arum, the world's smelliest flower.

2 Not only does it have a strong odor, the titan arum is also the largest flower in the world. In the wild, it can grow to be 20 feet tall with a bloom that is about 6 feet tall and 3 feet wide!

3 Where can you find this unusual specimen? It grows in the rain forests of Sumatra, Indonesia. In the United States, fewer than 20 have been successfully raised in greenhouses and conservatories.

4 It is best known for the awful odor that it produces once the flower has opened. People think the smell is terrible, but insects disagree. In the wild, the smell attracts insects that pollinate the flowers. The bright colors attract birds that eat the seeds. This allows the plant to eventually grow in new places.

5 One reason that this plant is so rare is that both male and female flowers are needed for pollination. Both flowers exist in the large spike in the center of the petals. However, the male and female flowers do not usually bloom at the same time. If another plant is nearby, the flowers can still be pollinated. Because these plants are so rare in the United States, people usually have to help with the pollination process.

6 Another interesting thing about the titan arum is how quickly the bloom dies. People wait years and years to see this amazing plant bloom. Even if a titan arum plant lives to be 40 years old, it may bloom only two or three times. There are usually video cameras that capture every second of the bloom. Television and radio stations have frequent updates. But after only one or two days, the bloom dies.

7 This does not stop people from streaming in for an opportunity to see the plant. During the 18 days before, during, and after the blooming of the titan arum at Huntington Botanical Gardens in California, 76,000 people came to visit this stinky plant!

NAME ____________________

Vocabulary Skills

Write the words from the article that have the meanings below.

1. come in contact with

_______________________________ Par. 1

2. a smell

_______________________________ Par. 2

3. a sample that is used for scientific study

_______________________________ Par. 3

4. sometime in the future

_______________________________ Par. 4

5. can be found

_______________________________ Par. 5

Find a synonym in the story for each of the words below.

6. unusual _______________________ Par. 5
7. moment _______________________ Par. 6
8. often _______________________ Par. 6
9. chance _______________________ Par. 7

Underline the compound word in each sentence. Then, write the two words that make up each compound.

10. Some plants are raised in greenhouses.

_____________ _____________

11. People like to have frequent updates when the titan arum is blooming.

_____________ _____________

12. Everyone seems to be interested in this enormous, stinky plant!

_____________ _____________

13. Television stations videotape the plant while it is in bloom.

_____________ _____________

Reading Skills

1. For what is the titan arum best known?

____

2. Where does the titan arum grow in the wild?

____

3. Why do you think people are so eager to see the titan arum?

____

4. The next time a titan arum blooms in the United States, do you think people will line up to see it? Why or why not?

____

____

5. Why does the titan arum smell so awful?

____

6. Check the sentence that best states the main idea of the selection.

_____ The bloom of the titan arum lasts only one or two days.

_____ The titan arum grows in the rain forests of Sumatra, Indonesia.

_____ The titan arum is fascinating because it is rare, and it is the largest and smelliest flower in the world.

Write **T** before the sentences that are true. Write **F** before the sentences that are false.

7. _____ The titan arum can be found growing in the wild all around the United States.
8. _____ Both male and female flowers exist in the center spike of the titan arum.
9. _____ The titan arum has an awful odor.
10. _____ The bloom of the titan arum can last for two to three weeks.

A Family Decision

If you could choose a place for your family to go on vacation, where would you choose to go?

1 "We're having a family meeting," Dad told Juan and Maria. "We have to decide where we'll go on vacation this summer. Start brainstorming places you'd like to visit."

2 A few minutes later, Maria and Juan sat down at the dining room table with their parents. Dad wore a sun visor, sunglasses, flip-flops, and a Hawaiian shirt. Maria and Juan burst into laughter as soon as they saw their father.

3 "Dad, we're not on vacation yet!" exclaimed Juan.

4 "I know, I know," said Dad. "Can you guess where I'd like to go?"

5 Maria nodded. "I'm guessing that you want to go to the beach."

6 Dad grinned. "I thought we could go to Florida. We could swim in the ocean, eat fresh seafood, and collect shells."

7 Mom had a pad of paper in front of her. She wrote down *Dad: Florida (ocean, seafood, shells)*. "Okay, who else has a suggestion?" she asked.

8 "I'd like to go camping," said Juan. "My friend Sophie went camping last year with her aunt, uncle, and cousins. She said they had a great time. They went hiking, cooked-out, and swam in a lake. They had campfires every night and took turns telling scary stories. That's what I'd like to do," said Juan.

9 Mom wrote down *Juan: camping (hiking, cook-outs, swimming, campfires, scary stories)*. "Maria, you're next," said Mom. "Where would you like to go?"

10 Maria thought for a moment. "At the end of the year, my class did a unit about National Parks. Going to Yellowstone National Park in Wyoming would be really interesting. We learned about all kinds of amazing wildlife that you can see there. I'd also love to see the geysers."

11 Mom wrote down *Maria: Yellowstone (Wyoming, wildlife, geysers)*. Then, she put down her pen and looked at the pad of paper. "All of those ideas sound good to me," she said. "I think that camping at Yellowstone might be a good compromise. I know that there isn't an ocean or seafood or shells there," she said, smiling at Dad, "but that way we could do the things that both Juan and Maria want to do on vacation. Also, we went to Florida last year."

12 "You're right," said Dad. "None of us has ever been to Wyoming or seen a geyser. I haven't been camping in years. I think it will be fun to try something new."

13 "Shall we have an official vote?" asked Mom. "Are we agreed that we'll camp at Yellowstone?" Before the words were even out of her mouth, Dad, Juan, and Maria had raised their hands.

14 "Looks like it is unanimous!" laughed Mom. "The Garzas are going to Yellowstone!"

NAME ______________________________

Vocabulary Skills

Write the words from the story that have the meanings below.

1. thinking of ideas

______________________________ Par. 1

2. an idea

______________________________ Par. 7

3. hot springs that spray steam and water into the air

______________________________ Par. 10

4. to make a decision that pleases everyone

______________________________ Par. 11

5. complete agreement

______________________________ Par. 14

Circle the homophone that correctly completes each sentence below, and write it on the line.

6. Maria hopes to see a ______________ and other animals at Yellowstone National Park. (bare, bear)

7. Mom ______________ that the family could reach a compromise. (knew, new)

8. The Garzas will ______________ many friendly people on their trip. (meat, meet)

Underline the suffix in each word. Then, write the meaning of the word.

9. thoughtless ______________________

10. government ______________________

11. fearless ______________________

12. comfortable ______________________

Reading Skills

Circle the word that best completes each sentence below, and write it on the line.

1. Dad ______________ the family for a meeting.

   gathers commands requests

2. Mom ______________ everyone's vacation ideas.

   changes records ignores

3. Dad thinks that going someplace new would be a(n) ______________.

   journey adventure mistake

4. Name two things Dad says the family could do in Florida.

   ______________ ______________

5. Do you think the Garzas will be happy with their decision to camp at Yellowstone? Why or why not?

   ____

   ____

6. How can you tell that Dad wants to go to the beach?

   ____

   ____

7. What problem are the Garzas trying to solve in the story?

   ____

Read the phrases below. Write **M** if it describes Maria. Write **J** if it describes Juan.

8. _____ has a friend named Sophie who went camping

9. _____ guesses that Dad wants to go to the beach

A Library Expedition

What kind of information do you think the Garzas will find at the library?

1 Juan, Maria, and Mr. and Mrs. Garza were on their way to the library to research what kinds of things they would need for their camping trip to Yellowstone National Park. They were borrowing a tent from Sophie's family, but they weren't sure what other equipment they would need for their trip.

2 When they got to the library, they decided to split up. Juan and Mom were going to look for books about camping. Dad and Maria were going to look for books about Yellowstone.

3 "Let's meet by the reference desk in half an hour," suggested Dad. Then, he and Maria headed over to the travel books, while Mom and Juan sat down at the computers. In just a few minutes, Dad and Maria had pulled out a stack of books about national parks, Wyoming, and Yellowstone.

4 "Can I look through the books about Yellowstone?" asked Maria.

5 "Sounds good to me," replied Dad. "I'll start scanning the ones on national parks and Wyoming."

6 Meanwhile, Mom and Juan made a list of call numbers for books about camping. It didn't take them long to select several books that looked interesting. They spread the books out on a table and began looking through them.

7 A few minutes later, Dad and Maria wandered by with their pile of books.

8 "Wow!" said Mom, looking at all the books on the table. "It certainly looks like we'll have plenty of information to work with here."

9 "Look at this list," said Juan, pointing to a page in the thick green book he was holding. "It's a checklist of the things we'll need for camping. It divides the materials into categories. For example, they have lists of things we'll use for cooking and eating, hiking, and setting up our campsite."

10 "That book seems very practical," said Mom. "I like the way it's organized."

11 "Dad and I found some really great books about Yellowstone Park," said Maria. "This one is by Camilla Jackson. She is a park ranger at Yellowstone. It explains what kinds of clothes we'll need. It can become pretty cold at night. She recommends that we bring lots of layers to wear. There is also a whole chapter in this book about wildlife. I know just what to do if we see a bear. Dad and I can also identify several types of snakes."

12 As the Garzas left the library later that afternoon, Mom said, "We still have a lot of work to do to prepare for our trip, but we got a good start today. We'll just keep on checking things off our lists until we have everything we need. Then, we'll be on the road to Wyoming!"

NAME ______________________

Vocabulary Skills

Find a synonym in the story for each of the words below.

1. responded ______________________ Par. 5
2. choose ______________________ Par. 6
3. separates ______________________ Par. 9

Fill in the blanks below with the possessive form of the word in parentheses.

4. The ______________ vacation was going to be in Wyoming. (Garzas)
5. The ______________ selection of books was very helpful. (library)
6. It was ______________ idea to go to Yellowstone. (Maria)
7. ______________ family was going to lend the Garzas a tent. (Sophie)
8. Mom thought the ______________ list would be useful. (book)

Reading Skills

Write **B** next to the sentence if it happened before the Garzas had chosen their books and met at the table. Write **A** if it happened afterward.

1. _____ The Garzas left the library.
2. _____ Mom and Juan made a list of call numbers.
3. _____ Dad scanned books about Wyoming and national parks.
4. _____ Mom and Juan spread out books on a table.
5. _____ Maria said that they should bring layers of clothes to wear.

Circle the word that best completes each sentence below, and write it on the line.

6. Sophie's family would ______________ the Garzas a tent.

   loan borrow sell

7. The materials were ______________ into categories.

   removed explained divided

8. Check the sentence that best states the main idea of the selection.

   _____ The Garzas go to the library to find out how to prepare for their trip to Yellowstone.

   _____ The Garzas agree to meet by the reference desk.

   _____ Juan finds a helpful book that includes different types of checklists.

Study Skills

Use the information below to answer the questions that follow.

Call No:	462.65 KE
Author:	Kean, Maggie
Title:	Visiting the National Parks
Publisher:	Merli & Ball Publishing

1. Circle the call number of the book that would be closest on the shelf to the book listed above.

   462.65 PO 464.45 KA 460.65 MI

2. What is the book's title?

   ____

The Wolves Are Back!

Why do you think the wolves disappeared from Yellowstone National Park?

1 If you were to take a trip to Yellowstone National Park, there is a good chance that you would be able to catch a glimpse of a wolf during your visit. More than 250 wolves live in Yellowstone National Park today. But if you had visited just a few years ago, you would not have had a chance to see one of these beautiful, independent creatures.

2 Between 1926 and 1995, there were no wolves living in Yellowstone. Because wolves did live there in the past, scientists decided to try to bring them back to the park. In 1995, the United States Fish and Wildlife Service captured 14 wolves in Canada and released them in the park. A year later, they caught and released 17 more wolves. By the third year of the program, 64 wolf pups had been born. The wolves were breeding and raising their young even more quickly than the scientists had hoped!

3 Today, scientists say that Yellowstone National Park has the major predators that it once had before humans interfered. You might wonder why animals that hunt and kill other animals are so important, but everything in nature has a role to play. Think of nature as a see-saw that always wants to be balanced. A big change in nature will cause the "see-saw" to become unbalanced. Human beings, who believed wolves were a dangerous annoyance, caused things to go out of balance at Yellowstone.

4 Scientists call wolves one of the keystone species. This means that many other plants and animals depend on them. Some scientists believe that wolves affect as many as 25 other species at Yellowstone. For example, wolves mostly hunt elk and deer. Other animals that live in the area eat the leftover meat wolves leave behind. This means that those animals may eat fewer plants. More plants grow, and they may be larger than before. This provides shelter for some animals and insects.

5 At Yellowstone, the environment began to change not long after the wolves were brought back. It is quickly becoming more like it was hundreds of years ago. Many people have heard about the program and are interested to hear how the wolves are doing. Scientists are glad that more people are learning about endangered species and how important even a single type of animal can be to the environment.

NAME ______________________

Vocabulary Skills

Write the words from the article that have the meanings below.

1. not controlled by anyone else

______________________ Par. 1

2. let go

______________________ Par. 2

3. animals that hunt and kill other animals

______________________ Par. 3

4. got in the way

______________________ Par. 3

5. all sides are equal

______________________ Par. 3

Check the meaning of the underlined word in each sentence.

6. If you camp at Yellowstone, you might hear a wolf <u>bay</u> at night.

_____ part of a sea

_____ howl

7. Wolves usually travel in a <u>pack</u>.

_____ to fill with things

_____ a group

Write a compound word using two words in each sentence.

8. Antoine will carry a pack on his back when he hikes at the park.

____

9. The family will bring some trail mix they made at home.

____

Reading Skills

Write **F** before the sentences that are facts. Write **O** before the sentences that are opinions.

1. _____ Wolves are beautiful creatures.
2. _____ Yellowstone currently has the major predators it had throughout history.
3. _____ Wolves are an annoyance.
4. _____ Wolves mostly hunt elk and deer.
5. _____ More than 250 wolves live in Yellowstone today.
6. What caused the "see-saw" to become unbalanced at Yellowstone?

____

____

7. If another species disappears at Yellowstone in the future, what do you think scientists might do?

____

____

8. What is a keystone species?

____

____

9. Did the environment at Yellowstone begin to change right before or right after the wolves were brought back?

____

____

10. What problem did some people have with wolves in Yellowstone?

____

____

____

Geyser Capital of the World

What do you think creates a geyser?

1 What would you think if you saw water shooting straight up out of the ground? Unless you were near a fountain or a sprinkler, you would probably be quite surprised. When a geyser erupts, however, that is exactly what happens. You would not want to play in its spray, though. The water and steam shooting out of a geyser are more than 212 degrees Fahrenheit!

2 Unless you have taken a trip to Yellowstone National Park, you have probably never seen a geyser. Although single geysers are located in a few places, there are only six spots on Earth where large groups of geysers exist. Geyser fields can be found in New Zealand, Japan, and Iceland, but the largest field by far is in the United States. Yellowstone contains nearly 400 geysers—as many as the rest of the world combined. The geysers at Yellowstone are also among the most active.

3 The word *geyser* comes from an Icelandic word that means *to gush*. Geysers are formed when heated water is trapped deep underground. This water becomes hot when it comes into contact with magma. Magma is a type of rock that is so hot it has turned into liquid. When a volcano erupts, magma comes out in the form of lava.

4 The boiling water and steam in the geyser get trapped because the way to the surface is blocked by cooler water on top. Normally, steam can float away into the air like it does when a pot boils on the stove. The steam in a geyser has nowhere to go. Pressure keeps building until small amounts of cold water are pushed out of the top. Eventually, the pressure from the hot water underground becomes stronger than the weight of cold water on top, and the geyser explodes into the air.

5 Once all of the pressure is released, the eruption ends, and the whole process begins again. Although every geyser is different, the time each geyser takes to erupt can be predicted. For instance, Old Faithful in Yellowstone erupts every 30 to 90 minutes. Each geyser also shoots to a different height. Old Faithful sprays as high as 170 feet in the air. The tallest geyser in the world is Steamboat Geyser, also located at Yellowstone. It can shoot water 350 feet into the air.

6 Today, you do not have to go all the way to Wyoming to see Old Faithful erupt. You can see it from home or school on the Internet. The National Park Service has set up a Web cam that shows Old Faithful in action. Just visit www.nps.gov/yell/oldfaithfulcam.htm to see Old Faithful live.

NAME ______________________

Vocabulary Skills

Write the words from the article that have the meanings below.

1. suddenly bursts out

   ______________________ Par. 1

2. water in the form of a gas

   ______________________ Par. 1

3. all together

   ______________________ Par. 2

4. a strong force

   ______________________ Par. 4

5. said that something would happen in the future

   ______________________ Par. 5

Check the correct meaning of the underlined word in each sentence.

6. Old Faithful is the most <u>famous</u> geyser.

   _____ capable of fame

   _____ has much fame

   _____ to be without fame

7. Kyra was <u>speechless</u> the first time she saw a geyser.

   _____ without speech

   _____ capable of speech

   _____ the act of speech

8. I just read an excellent <u>nonfiction</u> book about Yellowstone.

   _____ the act of fiction

   _____ before fiction

   _____ not fiction

Reading Skills

1. Why do geysers erupt?

   ____

   ____

2. About how often does Old Faithful erupt?

   ____

3. Name two places other than Yellowstone where geysers can be found.

   __________ __________

4. How far into the air can Steamboat Geyser shoot water?

   ____

5. What happens when the pressure of the hot water underground is greater than the cold water on top?

   ____

   ____

6. Check the sentence below that is the best summary for paragraph 4.

   _____ The steam in a geyser has nowhere to go.

   _____ Boiling water and steam build up below the cold water until the pressure is too great and the geyser erupts.

   _____ When a pot boils on a stove, the steam can evaporate.

Write **T** before the sentences that are true. Write **F** before the sentences that are false.

7. _____ There are almost 400 geysers at Yellowstone.

8. _____ After all the pressure is released, the eruption ends.

9. _____ All geysers shoot water into the air at the same height.

A Natural Beauty

Have you ever visited a national park? Which one would you most like to visit?

1 Who first thought of creating national parks, a place where we could preserve some of the most important parts of our natural and cultural history? Artist George Catlin was one of the first people to have such an idea. He was concerned about the effect of Americans moving westward in the 1830s. He worried about wildlife, wilderness, and Native American cultures in the West being changed as more people moved and the area became more crowded.

2 In 1864, Congress donated Yosemite Valley to California. It would become the first state park. Yellowstone National Park in Wyoming was created in 1872, and many others followed during the next 50 years. The government wanted to preserve these beautiful natural areas. However, the railroad companies were interested in the creation of these parks for different reasons. They wanted more people to travel greater distances. They liked the idea of new tourist attractions all around the country. They also built new hotels near the parks so people would want to visit.

3 Over the years, the types of areas that were preserved expanded. Congress wanted to protect places where there were ancient Native American ruins and artifacts. In 1889, Arizona's Casa Grande Ruin was the first to be preserved. In 1906, Congress passed the Antiquities Act. It allowed presidents to set aside areas that were historically important to our country as national monuments. Theodore Roosevelt created 18 national monuments while he was president. Some of these, like Arizona's Petrified Forest and the Grand Canyon, later became national parks.

4 The national parks were not done growing yet. In the 1930s, the National Park Service was given the monuments of the War Department. This meant that they were in charge of all kinds of historic sites and battlefields. Several years later, they even added some seashores and lakeshores to the system.

5 Today, there is an enormous variety of things to do and see in the national parks. If you visit Alaska, you can see nearly 50 million acres of national park wilderness. At the Assateague Island National Seashore in Maryland and Virginia, there are bands of wild horses that run freely. In California's Redwood National Park, you can visit some of the tallest and oldest trees in the world. The redwoods there can grow to be more than 300 feet tall and live to be about 2,000 years old.

6 What would have happened to all these places of natural beauty if they had not been preserved as national parks? No one really knows. The important thing is that we remember how lucky we are to have them and do our best to save them for future generations to enjoy.

NAME ______________________________

Vocabulary Skills

Write the words from the article that have the meanings below.

1. protect; make something last a long time

______________________________ Par. 1

2. worried

______________________________ Par. 1

3. someone who travels to different places for fun

______________________________ Par. 2

4. became bigger

______________________________ Par. 3

5. buildings or statues that help remind people of something

______________________________ Par. 3

Read each sentence below. Then, write a word from the **-ought** word family that best completes the sentence.

6. Who ______________ of creating national parks?

7. Throughout history, many people have ______________ to preserve natural areas.

8. Some wealthy Americans have ______________ land and donated it to the national parks.

Reading Skills

1. Why were the railroad companies happy about the creation of the national parks?

____

____

2. How tall can redwoods grow to be?

____

3. Name one of the national monuments that was created while Theodore Roosevelt was president.

____

4. Do you think more national parks will be founded in the future? Why or why not?

____

____

5. Number the events below from **1** to **4** to show the order in which they happened.

_____ George Catlin was concerned about people moving westward.

_____ The National Park Service was given the War Department's monuments.

_____ Yellowstone National Park was created.

_____ Congress passed the Antiquities Act.

Study Skills

A **time line** shows the order in which things happened. Use the time line below to answer the questions that follow.

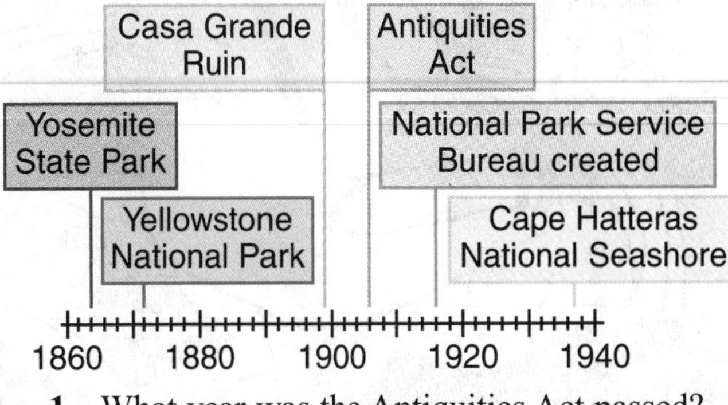

1. What year was the Antiquities Act passed?

____

2. Which park was created in 1872?

____

3. Was Yosemite or Yellowstone created first?

____

Mars Mission

Will Max make it to Mars someday?

1 *Max had an itch on his knee. It was hard to reach through the bulky astronaut suit he wore. Max unsnapped portions of the suit until he could finally reach the annoying spot.*

2 *"I sure hope that wasn't a bite from the first flea to travel into space, Winnie," said Max, patting his dog on her head. Winnie wagged her tail and looked up at Max. Max was glad that his dog had been able to come with him on the first manned flight to Mars. He thought about how lonely he would be without Winnie for company.*

3 *Max checked a number on the brightly lit panel in front of him. "We're almost there, Winnie," said Max excitedly. "If my calculations are correct, we should be arriving on Mars in less than an hour!" Winnie wagged her tail and gave a sharp bark.*

4 *"You're not getting cold feet, are you girl?" Max asked his dog. "I don't want you to be nervous. We've been preparing for this journey for so long, I know that we'll do fine. Just think, your picture will be in all the history books as the first dog to visit Mars." Winnie just looked at Max. Then, she settled down and rested her chin on her paws.*

5 *Max turned his attention to the small window. He could see that his ship was rapidly approaching the giant red planet. Max performed one last check of his equipment. "Prepare for landing!" he shouted. Winnie lifted her head for a moment and then rested it on her paws again. There was a loud* whooooshing *sound, and then an enormous thud as the spacecraft landed on Mars.*

6 *"We did it, Winnie!" shouted Max, hugging his dog. "We made it to Mars!" Max took his digital camera out of its case and began snapping photos through the porthole. The surface of Mars looked like a rocky, rust-colored desert. In the distance, Max could see something that looked like a massive crater. He tried to position the camera so he could take a photo of it to send back to the scientists at NASA. He was bobbing up and down in the ship when. . .*

7 Max opened his eyes. He looked around him. He was bouncing up and down, but he wasn't in a spaceship. He definitely wasn't on Mars. Max was in his own bedroom. Winnie was prancing around on Max's waterbed, which made him feel like he was bobbing up and down. Winnie barked.

8 Max sighed. "It's time for your breakfast, isn't it, girl?" he asked. Winnie barked again. Max started to get out of bed. "It could happen," he said to himself, remembering the rocky red planet and his bulky spacesuit. Max bent down to scratch an itch on his knee. "It could happen."

NAME ______________________________

Vocabulary Skills

Write the words from the story that have the meanings below.

1. large and oddly shaped

______________________________ Par. 1

2. the use of math to figure out or estimate something

______________________________ Par. 3

3. getting closer to

______________________________ Par. 5

4. a small round window, usually on the side of a ship

______________________________ Par. 6

5. enormous; very large

______________________________ Par. 6

Write the idiom from paragraph 4 on the line next to its meaning.

6. getting nervous ______________________

Read each pair of words listed below. If the words are synonyms, write **S** on the line. If the words are antonyms, write **A** on the line.

7.	_____	correct	wrong
8.	_____	massive	enormous
9.	_____	nervous	worried
10.	_____	calm	excited
11.	_____	rapidly	quickly
12.	_____	remember	forget

Reading Skills

1. Check the words that describe Max.

_____ competitive

_____ adventurous

_____ curious

_____ imaginative

_____ shy

2. Why was Max glad to have Winnie with him on the spacecraft?

____

3. What was Max trying to take a picture of when he woke up?

____

4. In his dream, Max thinks he is bobbing up and down in the air as he is trying to snap a photo. What is happening in real life that makes him think this?

____

5. On the line below, write the words that are dialogue in paragraph 5.

____

If the event described takes place in reality, write **R** on the line. If it takes place in Max's fantasy, write **F** on the line.

6. _____ Winnie was trying to let Max know it was time for her breakfast.

7. _____ Max took a picture from the porthole of the spaceship.

8. _____ Max unsnapped parts of his spacesuit.

9. _____ Max got out of bed.

10. _____ Max told Winnie her picture would be in a history book.

The Mysteries of Mars

Do we have neighbors in the solar system?

1 You might not know what a Venusian or a Uranian is, but you have probably heard of a Martian. If there are seven planets besides Earth, why do people commonly think only of Mars when talking about life on other planets?

2 Part of the reason is the Italian astronomer Giovanni Schiaparelli (shee AW pah REL lee). While observing Mars through his telescope in the 1800s, Schiaparelli noticed lines that ran across the surface of the planet. He called these lines *canali*, an Italian word that means *channels*. Schiaparelli used that word because he thought the lines might carry water the way channels, like the English Channel, do on Earth. An amateur American astronomer named Percival Lowell misunderstood what Schiaparelli meant.

3 Lowell read the paper about Mars and saw the word *canali*. He thought that the Italian astronomer meant that he saw canals on the surface of Mars. Canals are human-made structures that carry water from one place to another. Lowell began the theory that an advanced civilization on Mars had built canals all over the planet. He published his articles in newspapers across America. The idea that human beings have neighbors on Mars became very popular.

4 Beginning in 1960, different countries, including the United States, started trying to send spacecraft to Mars. In early 1965, the National Aeronautics and Space Administration, or NASA, launched the *Mariner 4* spacecraft. By July, it was circling Mars and sending back photos and scientific measurements that put a serious dent into any theories about life on Mars. The photos showed a dry planet covered with craters, similar to Earth's moon.

5 *Mariner 9* was launched in 1971. It showed a different part of the planet. This area of Mars had volcanoes, canyons, and mysterious channels that once might have carried water. Scientists knew that if the planet had once had flowing water, there was at least a chance that it also might have had life. The scientists now needed to prove that Mars once had water.

6 In January of 2004, NASA landed two spacecrafts on Mars, *Spirit* and *Opportunity*. Called *rovers*, they were equipped with very advanced tools. They could drive around on the planet but be controlled by scientists on Earth. They made an amazing discovery. The rocks that the rovers picked up and examined showed the scientists that Mars did have flowing water in the past. The news excited scientists worldwide, and the search for life on Mars continues.

NAME ______________________________

Vocabulary Skills

Write the words from the article that have the meanings below.

1. an expert in the study of the universe

   ______________________________ Par. 2

2. watching closely

   ______________________________ Par. 2

3. ahead of its time

   ______________________________ Par. 3

4. to send upward with great force

   ______________________________ Par. 4

5. prepared with things that are necessary

   ______________________________ Par. 6

Circle the homophone that correctly completes each sentence below, and write it on the line.

6. ______________ planet may not be the only one that has ever supported life. (Hour, Our)

7. They ______________ an amazing discovery. (made, maid)

8. Sending spacecrafts to Mars was quite a ______________. (feet, feat)

9. NASA's space program has ______________ over the years. (grown, groan)

Write **S** if the possessive word is singular. Write **P** if it is plural.

10. _____ astronomers' **11.** _____ Mars's

12. _____ spacecraft's **13.** _____ NASA's

14. _____ newspapers' **15.** _____ scientists'

Reading Skills

1. What did Percival Lowell think Schiaparelli saw on the surface of Mars?

   ____

2. What was the name of the American spacecraft that was sent to Mars in 1965?

   ____

3. Do you think that scientists will continue to look for life on Mars? Why or why not?

   ____

   ____

4. In the passage, what problem did Percival Lowell have?

   ____

5. Does this selection take place in reality, or is it a fantasy? How can you tell?

   ____

6. Check the phrase that best describes the author's purpose.

   _____ to explain why there is no life on Mars

   _____ to tell about the search for life on Mars

   _____ to persuade the reader to visit Mars someday

Read each sentence below. If the event took place before 1965, write **B** on the line. If it took place after 1965, write **A** on the line.

7. _____ *Spirit* and *Opportunity* landed on Mars.

8. _____ Schiaparelli noticed lines that ran across the surface of the planet.

9. _____ Lowell created the theory about canals and civilization on Mars.

Space Travelers

Do you have what it takes to be an astronaut?

1 Although it is still rare, space travel is becoming more and more common. There have now been 440 people from more than 30 countries who have flown in space. In English-speaking countries, they are known as *astronauts*. This word comes from the Latin words *astrum*, which means *star*, and *nauta*, which means *mariner*, or the person who plots the course of a ship. You have to fly more than 62 miles above Earth to officially be in space!

2 The first human to fly in space was a *cosmonaut*, the Russian word for *astronaut*. In April 1961, cosmonaut Yuri Gagarin orbited Earth in the spacecraft *Vostok 1*. Only one month later, Alan Shepard became the first American astronaut, although he did not fly completely around the planet. John Glenn was the first American to do that. He orbited Earth three times in 1962. He also became the oldest astronaut when he returned to space in 1998 at the age of 77. The first woman to fly in space was also a Russian cosmonaut. Valentina Tereshkova went into space on *Vostok 6* in June of 1963.

3 At first, almost all astronauts were pilots. The earliest space flights were made just to see if humans could make the journey into space. For this reason, the main job for the astronaut was flying the spacecraft. Today, astronauts need to be able to perform many more tasks. They do not just fly space shuttles. They also take part in planning the flights and the experiments. Astronauts are now scientists, engineers, medical doctors, and sometimes pilots as well.

4 To be an astronaut, the first thing you need is a college education. Your degree should be in math, science, or engineering so that you are able to plan experiments or operate the computer controls on the shuttle. You should also be in great physical condition because space flight is hard on the human body. If you want to be a shuttle pilot, you also need incredible eyesight and at least one thousand hours of flying experience. All astronauts need to be trustworthy, reliable, and excellent communicators.

5 If you have met all of those requirements, you are ready to start astronaut training. For at least a year, astronaut candidates learn how the shuttle works, how to survive crashes, and how it feels to be in outer space. They train inside a simulator, which is like a very realistic computer game that looks and feels like the inside of the shuttle. Pilots also practice landing the shuttle by flying an STA, or Shuttle Training Aircraft.

6 Even after astronauts have finished their training, they still do not fly right away. New astronauts will first take part in planning experiments, testing computer software, and helping to prepare the launch site. Eventually, the day arrives when they are selected to go on a flight!

NAME ______________________

Vocabulary Skills

Check the word that is a synonym for each word listed below.

1. brave

_____ courageous _____ afraid
_____ thoughtful

2. goal

_____ effort _____ purpose _____ idea

3. strength

____ attitude ____ weakness _____ power

Underline the word with a prefix in each sentence. Then, write the meaning of the word on the line.

4. The astronaut's children love it when she retells the story of her flight into space.

____

5 Astronauts do things people once thought would be impossible.

____

6. An astronaut should not be a dishonest person.

____

7. It is important that an astronaut does not misunderstand directions he or she is given.

____

Reading Skills

1. What is the first thing you need to do if you want to become an astronaut?

____

2. What was the profession of most of the first astronauts?

____

3. Why do you need to be in good shape to be an astronaut?

____

4. Why do you think astronauts need to be good communicators?

____

5. What is a simulator?

____

6. On the lines below, write a summary for paragraph 4.

____

____

____

7. Write **T** before the sentences that are true. Write **F** before the sentences that are false.

_____ New astronauts can fly as soon as they have finished their training.

_____ Today, astronauts need to be able to perform many tasks.

_____ Alan Shepard was the oldest astronaut to go into space.

_____ If you fly 40 miles above Earth, you are officially in space.

_____ You need to have good eyesight to be a shuttle pilot.

Study Skills

Use a dictionary to help you divide these words into syllables.

1. astronaut ______________________
2. orbit ______________________
3. scientist ______________________
4. engineer ______________________

A Friendly Lesson

Have you ever been afraid of something but tried to do it anyway?

1 Maggie sat dangling her feet into the sparkly blue water of her family's swimming pool. She had been anticipating the new pool for months. Now that it was there, though, she didn't feel as happy as she thought she would.

2 "What's wrong?" asked her mom.

3 Maggie sighed. "Amelia is scared of the water. She doesn't know how to swim. I thought that she would be playing with me in the pool all summer. I miss Amelia. Nothing is as much fun without her," said Maggie, lightly splashing water over her knees.

4 "Hmmm," said Mom. "Why don't you go call Amelia and see if she can come over? Maybe if you and I both get in the pool with her, we can help her feel safe in the water. Remember how we taught your little brother to swim? Now, he swims like a dolphin!"

5 Maggie looked a little more cheerful. "You're right, we did teach Tyler to swim. He was pretty scared the first time we took him to the pool, wasn't he?" asked Maggie. "I think I'll go call Amelia right now and see if her dad can bring her over."

6 Later that afternoon, Amelia came over with her dad. "Are you sure you don't want me to stay?" he asked.

7 Amelia nodded. "I think I'm ready to do this," she said. "I'm tired of being scared of the water. I don't want to miss a whole summer of swimming with Maggie."

8 "I'm proud of you," said her dad. "I'll be back in a couple of hours, okay?" Amelia nodded again and sat on the side at the shallow end of the pool.

9 All afternoon, Maggie and her mom worked with Amelia in the water. They taught her how to blow bubbles so she wouldn't get water in her nose. They taught her to kick across the width of the pool holding a kickboard. When Amelia's dad came to pick her up, everyone was surprised the time had gone so quickly.

10 "Watch this, Dad!" shouted Amelia. "I can float on my back. Maggie's mom can even let go for a few seconds, and I can do it on my own!" She proudly demonstrated her new skills for her father.

11 "This is amazing!" said Amelia's dad. "You two must be incredible teachers."

12 Maggie and her mom smiled at each other. "I think Amelia was just ready to learn," said Maggie's mom. "She set her mind to it and did all the work herself."

13 "Can we come back tomorrow, Dad?" asked Amelia. Everyone laughed.

14 "I have a feeling that I'm going to have a prune for a daughter all summer!" said Amelia's dad.

NAME ______________________

Vocabulary Skills

Write the words from the story that have the meanings below.

1. hanging down

______________________ Par. 1

2. looking forward to something

______________________ Par. 1

3. feeling pleased about something that you or someone else has done

______________________ Par. 8

4. a measurement from side to side

______________________ Par. 9

5. showed

______________________ Par. 10

Find the simile in paragraph 4, and write it on the line below.

6. ______________________

Find an antonym in the story for each of the words below.

7. everything ______________ Par. 3
8. depressed ______________ Par. 5
9. disappointed ______________ Par. 8

Divide the words below into syllables using a slash (/).

10. k i c k b o a r d
11. b a r e f o o t
12. l i f e g u a r d

Circle the word in each row that does not belong.

13. happy glum excited cheerful
14. brave teach instruct show
15. swim kick sit paddle

Reading Skills

1. Check the words that describe Amelia.

_____ funny

_____ brave

_____ determined

_____ suspicious

_____ proud

Circle the word that best completes each sentence, and write it on the line.

2. Mom and Maggie helped Amelia ______________ her fear of the water.

ignore overcome explain

3. Maggie ______________ Amelia's company.

enjoys dislikes forgets

4. Amelia's dad had not ______________ her to learn so much in one afternoon.

wanted expected selected

5. Why does Maggie feel sad at the beginning of the story?

____

6. What does Dad mean when he says, "I'm going to have a prune for a daughter all summer"?

____

7. Why does Amelia want to learn how to swim?

____

____

8. Why does Amelia say that she wants to come back tomorrow?

____

____

Sink or Swim

Why do things float?

Materials:

- a large bowl of water
- an apple
- a carrot

1 What do you think will happen when you place the apple and the carrot in the water? Will they sink or float?

2 Put the carrot and the apple in the bowl one at a time. The carrot will sink, but the apple will float. This is because apples and carrots contain different amounts of air. Air is lighter, or less dense than water. Something that contains more air will float better than something that is denser.

3 The cells of a carrot are packed together tightly. There is more air in the cells of the apple. This allows the apple to float and causes the carrot to sink.

Materials:

- two clear glasses
- warm water
- two grapes
- 3 teaspoons salt
- a spoon

4 Now, think about salt water. Do you think that things are more or less buoyant in salt water than in fresh water?

5 Fill both glasses with warm water. Then, add the salt to one glass. Stir the water until the salt dissolves. Now, place one grape in each glass of water. The grape in the glass of fresh water will sink. The grape in the glass of salt water will float. How is this possible?

6 The weight of the grapes is not different. If something is heavier than the same volume of water, it will sink. If something is lighter, it will float. Salt water is heavier, or denser, than fresh water. This means that it can support heavier things than fresh water can.

7 If you ever visit the Dead Sea near Israel, you can try this experiment with your own body. The human body is made mostly of water. The Dead Sea is much saltier than other oceans. In fact, it contains more than 30 percent salt and minerals. In comparison, the Pacific Ocean only has about 3 percent salt and minerals. Because the Dead Sea is so salty, your body is much less dense than the water. This means you could float without even trying!

NAME ___________________________

Vocabulary Skills

Write the words from the article that have the meanings below.

1. packed tightly together; heavy

_____________________ Par. 2

2. able to float

_____________________ Par. 4

3. melts; turns from a solid into a liquid

_____________________ Par. 5

4. the amount of space something takes up

_____________________ Par. 6

Check the meaning of the underlined word in each sentence.

5. The carrot should <u>sink</u> in the first experiment.

_____ go below the surface

_____ a container with faucets and a drain

6. Please turn down the <u>volume</u> on your stereo.

_____ the degree of loudness

_____ the amount of space something takes up

7. The grape will <u>float</u> in fresh water but not in salt water.

_____ a large exhibit in a parade

_____ to stay above the surface

Fill in the blanks below with the possessive form of the word in parentheses.

8. A _______________ cells are packed together more tightly. (carrot)

9. The Dead _______________ water is much saltier than the water of other oceans or seas. (Sea)

Reading Skills

Circle the word that best completes each sentence, and write it on the line.

1. Salt water is _______________ than freshwater.

denser colder deeper

2. Something that is _______________ than the same volume of water will sink.

older heavier stronger

3. The Dead Sea is _______________ than the oceans of the world.

lighter fresher saltier

4. Check the phrase that best describes the author's purpose.

_____ to explain how to conduct two experiments about floating

_____ to persuade the reader to become a scientist

_____ to show why the water in the Dead Sea is so salty

5. Why do you think you need to use warm water in the second experiment?

____

____

6. Why does the apple float while the carrot sinks?

____

____

7. What do you think would happen if you used an egg instead of a grape in the second experiment?

____

8. Where is the Dead Sea located?

____

Flood Watch!

How will the Lopez family keep their basement from flooding?

1 Teresa and Manuel sat on the couch in the living room. They could not think of a single thing to do. It had been raining steadily for four days. Teresa and Manuel had done all the rainy day activities they could think of.

2 They played games. They set up easels and painted. They made cookies. They watched all their favorite movies. They even helped their mom clean out all the closets in the house. They were out of ideas.

3 Mr. Lopez walked by carrying a basket of laundry. He stared at Manuel and Teresa slouched on the couch. "What are you kids doing?" he asked.

4 "There is absolutely nothing left to do in this house!" said Teresa dramatically. "It may never stop raining!"

5 "All we want to do is go outside," agreed Manuel. "It feels like we haven't left the house in a month."

6 "I'm sure I can think of something..." began Mr. Lopez. Just then, Mrs. Lopez came running into the room.

7 "I was just listening to the local news on the radio," she said. "Sawmill Creek is rising very quickly. It's already overflowed its banks in some places. The rain isn't supposed to let up anytime soon, so it's probably going to flood in our neighborhood, too. I think it's time for us to sandbag the house." Teresa and Manuel sat up. They were excited to have something finally happen!

8 "Kids, if you want to help, you need to put on your rain jackets and boots," said their dad. "If we hurry, we may be able to keep the basement from flooding too badly."

9 The Lopez family quickly put on their rain gear and headed outside. The small creek that normally trickled quietly behind their house was rushing loudly now. The grass squished under their feet as they walked across the lawn toward the garage. Mr. Lopez grabbed several large bags that were on a shelf in the garage.

10 "Okay, Teresa and Manuel, you can start filling the bags with sand from these containers," said Mr. Lopez. Mom and I will carry the bags outside and start piling them around the base of the house."

11 "Won't the water leak around the bags?" asked Teresa.

12 "Maybe a little," said Mom. "But we're going to overlap the bags so that there aren't any gaps between them. Then, we're going to cover the bags with sheets of plastic. That will help make them even more watertight."

13 After a few trips, Dad paused and grinned at Manuel and Teresa. "You said you wanted to get out of the house. This isn't what you had in mind, is it?"

14 Manuel and Teresa laughed. "No, but at least it's more exciting!" said Manuel.

NAME ______________________________

Vocabulary Skills

Write the words from the story that have the meanings below.

1. without stopping

   ______________________________ Par. 1

2. flowed over the top of

   ______________________________ Par. 7

3. equipment for a particular activity

   ______________________________ Par. 9

4. flowed in a thin stream

   ______________________________ Par. 9

5. to cover one thing with part of another thing

   ______________________________ Par. 12

Underline the word with a suffix in each sentence. Then, write the meaning of the word on the line below it.

6. This was the closest the Lopez family had been to having their house flooded.

   ____

7. The members of the family gave each other a lot of encouragement as they worked.

   ____

8. Mom and Dad carried the heaviest bags.

   ____

Reading Skills

1. Name two rainy day activities Teresa and Manuel did.

   ______________ ______________

2. Why did the grass squish beneath their feet as they walked across it?

   ____

3. Where did Mrs. Lopez hear the news that Sawmill Creek was flooding?

   ____

4. If the story continued, what do you think would happen next?

   ____

   ____

5. Name one way that Teresa and Manuel are similar.

   ____

   ____

   ____

Write **F** before the sentences that are facts. Write **O** before the sentences that are opinions.

6. _____ At the beginning of the story, Teresa and Manuel are bored.
7. _____ Keeping the basement from flooding is exciting.
8. _____ Sawmill Creek is rising quickly.
9. _____ Mom and Dad overlap the sandbags so there are not gaps between them.
10. _____ Rainy days are boring.

Study Skills

Check each word that could be found on a page having the guide words shown in dark print.

1. **bread—broccoli**

   _____ brick _____ brush _____ brittle

2. **wallow—water ski**

   _____ walrus _____ wasp _____ web

3. **hoax—hooked**

   _____ hoarse _____ homestead
   _____ honk

The Flood of the Century

What contributed to the disaster of the Johnstown Flood?

1 The city of Johnstown is located in southwestern Pennsylvania. In the late 1800s, it was a nice, quiet place to live, with a steel company that employed many of its citizens. The town was built on a floodplain, but most people did not pay too much attention to that fact. As the town grew, it moved closer and closer to the banks of Stony Creek and the Little Conemaugh River.

2 South Fork Dam lay 14 miles upstream from the city of Johnstown. It held Lake Conemaugh on the side of a mountain, 450 feet above the city of Johnstown. The South Fork Fishing and Hunting Club owned the dam. They had turned the lake into a resort area. The dam was not in good repair, but the club did not have it fixed. Some people worried that one day, the dam would no longer be able to hold back the water, but nothing was done in time to save the town.

3 On May 31, 1889, after heavy rains, the dam burst. It sent 20 million tons of water rushing down the Little Conemaugh River at speeds of about 40 miles per hour. As it approached Johnstown, the wall of water was nearly 60 feet tall in some places.

4 The people of the town were caught by surprise. Many tried to escape, but the water moved too quickly. Some people managed to climb onto pieces of debris and use them as rafts. Some were able to survive by hiding in their attics until help could reach them. Others were not so lucky. The Johnstown Flood ended up taking the lives of 2,209 people.

5 It took years for the city of Johnstown to clean up the mess created by the disaster. It took even longer for the people to recover from the loss of so many lives. Some people blamed South Fork Fishing and Hunting Club for not keeping the dam in good repair. They believed that if the dam had been maintained, it might have saved the lives of many people who drowned during the Johnstown Flood.

6 Today, you can visit the Johnstown Flood National Memorial in southwestern Pennsylvania. There is a 165-acre national park there, as well as the remains of the South Fork Dam. You can see photos of Johnstown before and after the flood. It is sad to see the wreckage the flood created, but the fact that Johnstown exists today shows the strength and determination of people who faced one of the worst disasters in American history.

NAME ____________________

Vocabulary Skills

Read each word below. Then, write the letter of its antonym on the line beside the word.

1. _____ closer **a.** destroyed

2. _____ mountain **b.** farther

3. _____ created **c.** wonderful

4. _____ terrible **d.** valley

Circle the words in each row that are part of the same word family.

5. (*-ought*) thought thank sought thump

6. (*-ight*) sunlight sundae fling flight

7. (*-ould*) wonder would could wound

Underline the compound word in each sentence. Then, write the two words that make up each compound.

8. The city was built on a floodplain in Pennsylvania.

____________ ____________

9. South Fork Dam was 14 miles upstream.

____________ ____________

10. People received help from places that were far from southwestern Pennsylvania.

____________ ____________

Reading Skills

1. Who owned South Fork Dam at the time of the flood?

____

2. Why does the author say that the fact that Johnstown exists today shows the strength of people in that town?

____

____

3. What problem did the people of Johnstown have in the selection?

____

____

4. Number the events below from **1** to **5** in the order in which they happened.

_____ Some people were worried that the dam might not hold.

_____ The dam sent 20 million tons of water rushing down the Little Conemaugh River.

_____ The Johnstown Flood National Memorial was founded.

_____ The South Fork Fishing and Hunting Club bought the South Fork Dam.

_____ The people of the town were caught by surprise.

5. Check the sentence that best states the main idea of the selection.

_____ The water flooded Johnstown at speeds of about 40 miles per hour.

_____ The city of Johnstown is located in southwestern Pennsylvania.

_____ The Johnstown Flood in 1889 was one of the worst disasters in American history.

6. Check the line beside the word or words that tell what type of nonfiction selection this is.

_____ biography

_____ history

_____ how-to text

7. Does this story take place in reality, or is it a fantasy? How can you tell?

____

____

Career Day

Have you ever thought about what kind of career you might like to have as an adult?

1 Hiroshi sat at the kitchen table. He stared at the blank sheet of paper in front of him. Then, he stared out the window. For a homework assignment, Hiroshi was trying to decide what kind of career he wanted to have. Once he chose a career, he was supposed to research it so he could share the information with the rest of the class.

2 Hiroshi wasn't sure what he wanted to be. When he was younger, he thought that he might like to be a firefighter. Hiroshi liked the idea of helping people. He also liked the trucks firefighters drove and thought that it would be an exciting job. After Hiroshi went to his first professional baseball game the summer before, he thought he might like to play baseball professionally. He knew that becoming a professional ballplayer was a long shot, so he wanted to think of some other ideas that were more realistic.

3 When Hiroshi's sister Saki came into the kitchen for a snack a few minutes later, Hiroshi was still sitting there with the blank piece of paper in front of him.

4 "What are you doing?" she asked, grabbing a green apple and a handful of cheese crackers.

5 "I need help," said Hiroshi. "I'm trying to think of things that I might like to do for a career. I don't know where to start."

6 Saki shrugged. "That doesn't sound too hard," she said, taking a bite of her apple. "I thought your class went on a field trip to a Frank Lloyd Wright building a few months ago and you decided you wanted to be an architect."

7 "I forgot all about that trip!" exclaimed Hiroshi. "I thought that Fallingwater was amazing. I've never seen another building like that. It felt like the house was part of the forest and the waterfall was part of the house." He grinned at his sister. "I would love to design buildings like that." Hiroshi wrote down *architect* at the top of his paper.

8 "And didn't you tell Mom and Dad that you wanted to be an oceanographer after you saw that biography of Jacques Cousteau on television?" asked Saki.

9 Hiroshi nodded. "I can't believe you remembered that," he said. "That would be an amazing job, too. There are so many things that humans don't know about the ocean yet. I like the mystery of it." He added *oceanographer* to his list.

10 "I also seem to remember that someone wanted to be a clown when he was little," teased Saki.

11 Hiroshi laughed. "Sometimes, I wish you didn't have such a good memory. Thanks, but I think I'll stick with the first two careers on my list."

NAME ______________________

Vocabulary Skills

Write the words from the story that have the meanings below.

1. a job or profession

_________________________ Par. 1

2. practical; similar to the way things are in real life

_________________________ Par. 2

3. someone who designs buildings

_________________________ Par. 6

4. someone who studies oceans and ocean life

_________________________ Par. 8

5. the story of someone's life

_________________________ Par. 8

Write the idiom from paragraph 2 on the line next to its meaning.

6. something that is not likely ____________

In each row, circle the words that belong together.

7. ocean underwater career amazing
8. biography career job profession
9. structure information building forest

Write **S** if the possessive word is singular. Write **P** if it is plural.

10. _____ Saki's
11. _____ ballplayers'
12. _____ Hiroshi's
13. _____ firefighters'
14. _____ house's
15. _____ apple's

Reading Skills

1. What is Hiroshi's homework assignment?

____

____

2. What did Hiroshi like about Fallingwater?

____

____

3. How does Saki tease her brother at the end of the story?

____

4. What made Hiroshi want to be an oceanographer?

____

5. On the line below, write the words that are dialogue in paragraph 4.

____

Read the sentences below. Write **H** next to the sentence if it describes Hiroshi. Write **S** if it describes Saki.

6. _____ eats a green apple
7. _____ wanted to be a firefighter
8. _____ has a good memory
9. _____ likes the mystery of the ocean
10. _____ makes a list of career ideas

Study Skills

Use a dictionary to help you divide these words into syllables.

1. information ____________________
2. professional ____________________
3. oceanographer ____________________
4. assignment ____________________

The Wright Stuff

What is the most unusual building you've ever seen?

1 Many people think that Frank Lloyd Wright was the most important architect of the twentieth century. He introduced new ways of thinking about architecture. Wright believed that buildings should not just be big boxes with doors and windows. He thought that a building's shape should fit in with its natural environment.

2 Wright also wanted to make sure that people would always be able to experience the natural world, even when inside a building. For these reasons, Wright's building style was called "organic architecture."

3 Frank Lloyd Wright was born in 1867 and grew up in Wisconsin. In 1887, when he was twenty, he moved to Chicago, Illinois, to work and learn at an architecture firm. After only five years, Wright was ready to go out on his own as a designer. Many of his buildings can be found in Illinois, although he built all over the world.

4 One of his early and very popular designs was called the prairie house. This style of house is a great example of organic architecture. Wright wanted to design a house that imitated the landscape of Illinois and the rest of the Midwest. Because the middle section of the United States is mostly flat farmland that was originally prairie, the prairie houses were very flat and spread out. People loved the way they looked!

5 Wright's most famous house might be Fallingwater in Pennsylvania. This house was built right on top of a stream and waterfall! A stairway leads from the living room right down to the water. Wright also wanted to make sure that the surrounding woods would be a major part of the house. By putting lots of windows in every room, the outdoors would always be visible.

6 Homes were not the only things Wright designed. The headquarters for the Johnson Wax Company is another famous building. This time, Wright used a forest as inspiration for the main work area inside. The large room has many towering columns that become thinner as they reach the ceiling, imitating the way tree trunks grow smaller toward their tops.

7 The last building Wright completed during his lifetime was the Guggenheim Museum in New York City. Many people think it is his masterpiece. Wright's design for the museum is based on the spiral shape of a shell. Both the inside and the outside of the building loop around like a spring. Wright's interesting and unusual museum is far from looking like a box, which is just the way he wanted it.

Frank Lloyd Wright found inspiration for his buildings in the natural world.

NAME ______________________________

Vocabulary Skills

Write the words from the article that have the meanings below.

1. natural; made of living things

   ______________________________ Par. 2

2. copied

   ______________________________ Par. 4

3. able to be seen

   ______________________________ Par. 5

4. something that creates new ideas

   ______________________________ Par. 6

5. an artist's greatest work

   ______________________________ Par. 7

Write the words from the article that match the abbreviations below.

6. WI ______________________________
7. IL ______________________________
8. PA ______________________________

Reading Skills

1. How were the prairie houses similar to the landscape of the Midwest?

   ____

   ____

2. How do you think Fallingwater got its name?

   ____

   ____

3. What is the shape of the Guggenheim Museum in New York City?

   ____

4. What do you think Wright's feelings about the natural world were?

   ____

5. Check the sentence below that is the best summary for paragraph 4.

   _____ One of Wright's most popular designs was the prairie house, which imitated the Midwest landscape.

   _____ The Midwest contains many areas of flat farmland.

6. Check the words that describe Wright.

   _____ imaginative _____ unique

   _____ talkative _____ rude

   _____ creative

7. Check the line beside the word or words that tell what type of selection this is.

   _____ biography _____ myth

   _____ how-to

Study Skills

Use the table below to answer the questions that follow.

Frank Lloyd Wright Buildings		
1909	Robie House	Chicago, IL
1911	Taliesin	Spring Green, WI
1915	Imperial Hotel	Tokyo, Japan
1936	Johnson Wax Headquarters	Racine, WI

1. Which building was built in 1915?

   ____

2. In what year was the Robie House built?

   ____

3. Which building is located in Spring Green, Wisconsin?

   ____

The World Underwater

How do you think the wreckage of the Titanic *was discovered?*

1 People are fascinated by the exploration of space. They like the idea that so many things about our solar system are a mystery. But there are still some very mysterious places on Earth that have not been explored yet. The ocean is one of those places, and Robert Ballard is one of its lucky explorers.

2 Robert Ballard was born in 1942 in Kansas. He grew up in San Diego, California, where he first developed an interest in the ocean and ocean life. One of his favorite books as a child was Jules Verne's *20,000 Leagues Under the Sea*. That novel, and the influence of his parents, are two of the most important reasons Ballard wanted to become an undersea explorer.

3 As a young man, Ballard earned degrees in chemistry and biology. He also spent some time in the Navy, working as a marine biologist. After he left the Navy, Ballard returned to school, where he studied geology and geophysics. Then, Ballard spent several years mapping underwater mountain ranges on the ocean floor.

4 One of the most interesting discoveries Ballard made was of giant worms on the ocean floor. The tubeworms, called *Riftia*, were an important discovery because scientists did not think that any organisms could survive so deep underwater. Nearly all forms of life need the energy of the sun. The sun's rays do not reach all the way to the dark ocean floor, so scientists thought that no plants or animals could live there.

5 While on a trip to the Galápagos Islands in 1977, Ballard discovered worms that were more than 10 feet long. They lived near underwater hot springs and received energy from the springs rather than from the sun. This discovery changed scientists' ideas about life on this planet, as well as on other planets.

6 In 1985, Ballard finished work on his first remote-controlled robot, *Argo*. *Argo* changed the way the underwater world was explored. Now, remote-controlled underwater cameras could take photographs and send the pictures to computers on the surface. *Argo* helped Ballard with the discovery of the luxury ocean liner the *Titanic* in 1985, his most well-known accomplishment.

7 The *Titanic* struck an iceberg on her maiden voyage in 1912. More than 1,500 people lost their lives when the enormous ship sank. Ballard was part of the crew that used sonar to discover the wreckage of the *Titanic* more than 12,000 feet underwater. Ballard then had to wait an entire year before weather conditions were good enough for exploring one of the most famous shipwrecks of all time.

8 Robert Ballard's childhood dreams of being an undersea explorer came true. His talent, hard work, and imagination have allowed him to see some amazing parts of the Earth that few people ever experience.

NAME ______________________

Vocabulary Skills

Write the words from the article that have the meanings below.

1. very interested in

______________________ Par. 1

2. making a map of

______________________ Par. 3

3. any living creatures

______________________ Par. 4

4. something expensive and pleasurable that isn't really necessary

______________________ Par. 6

5. first or earliest

______________________ Par. 7

6. a device that uses sound waves to find underwater objects

______________________ Par. 7

Check the correct meaning of the underlined word.

7. The ocean is a mysterious place.

_____ capable of mystery

_____ without mystery

_____ full of mystery

8. Ballard's enjoyment of the ocean makes his hard work worthwhile.

_____ full of enjoying

_____ the act of enjoying

_____ without enjoying

Reading Skills

Write **F** before the sentences that are facts.
Write **O** before the sentences that are opinions.

1. _____ Robert Ballard is the greatest living scientist today.
2. _____ Ballard grew up in San Diego.
3. _____ More money should be spent on space exploration than on ocean exploration.
4. _____ The *Titanic* sank on her maiden voyage in 1912.
5. _____ Ballard discovered tubeworms near the Galápagos Islands.
6. What is one way in which outer space and the oceans are similar?

____

7. Why was Ballard's discovery of deepwater tubeworms so important?

____

____

8. What did *Argo* send back to the surface from deep underwater?

____

9. Why did Ballard have to wait a year before exploring the *Titanic*?

____

10. Who is the author of the novel *20,000 Leagues Under the Sea*?

____

E-mail Advice

What is it like to be an architect?

From: Hiroshi Ishikawa
Date: November 13, 2008
To: Mr. Daley
Subject: Architect career

Dear Mr. Daley,

1 My aunt said that you would be expecting to hear from me. My name is Hiroshi, and I am interested in becoming an architect. I would like to learn more about what it is like to be an architect. Can you tell me a little more about your career? What do you like best about it? I would be happy to receive any advice you have.

2 Thank you for your time. I look forward to hearing from you.

Sincerely,

Hiroshi Ishikawa

From: Andrew Daley
Date: November 15, 2008
To: Hiroshi Ishikawa
Subject: RE: Architect career

Dear Hiroshi,

3 I am happy to hear that you would like to become an architect! Your aunt tells me that you are a good student and a hard worker, so I already know that you'll be able to accomplish whatever you put your mind to.

4 You have chosen a difficult but rewarding career. Architecture is unusual because it is a blend of both art and science. You need to be creative to think of new and interesting designs. You also need to be good at math and science so that you can translate your creative ideas into structures that are safe and useful. Even English is important to an architect. You need to be able to express your ideas clearly so that other people can understand them.

5 Think about all the different kinds of buildings people need: houses, apartments, schools, office buildings, grocery stores, churches, malls, hotels, factories, gymnasiums, airports, hospitals. Architects figure out the best way to build each building so that it is interesting to look at, safe, and easy to use.

6 First, the architect usually creates a proposal that shows the customer his or her idea for the building. If the customer likes it, then the architect keeps working. He or she comes up with a plan that shows all the details of how the building will be constructed. The architect does not actually build the structure. But questions often come up during the construction, so the architect always needs to be available.

7 My favorite part of being an architect is seeing the idea that I had in my mind become an actual building. That never stops being exciting for me!

8 Please let me know if you have any other questions. You are also welcome to schedule a day to shadow me at work.

Good luck, Hiroshi!

Andrew Daley

NAME ______________________

Vocabulary Skills

Write the words from the story that have the meanings below.

1. satisfying

_______________________ Par. 4

2. to express in a different language or a different way

_______________________ Par. 4

3. built or put together

_______________________ Par. 6

4. to follow

_______________________ Par. 8

Circle the homophone that correctly completes each sentence below, and write it on the line.

5. Hiroshi's ______________ told Mr. Daley to expect an e-mail from her nephew. (aunt, ant)

6. The greeting Hiroshi uses in his e-mail is "______________." (dear, deer)

7. The architect does not actually ______________ the structure. (billed, build)

8. A person who plans to ______________ a house might meet with an architect. (bye, buy)

Fill in the blanks below with the possessive form of the word in parentheses.

9. ______________ aunt is Mr. Daley's friend. (Hiroshi)

10. An ______________ job is to make a building interesting, safe, and easy to use. (architect)

11. ______________ designs are created by architects. (Schools)

Reading Skills

1. How do you think Hiroshi was introduced to Mr. Daley?

____

2. Why does Mr. Daley say that architecture is unusual?

____

3. What is Mr. Daley's favorite part of being an architect?

____

4. Name four types of buildings an architect might design.

____

____

5. Do you think that Hiroshi and Mr. Daley will ever meet in person? Why or why not?

____

____

6. Check the phrase that best describes the author's purpose.

_____ to entertain the reader with a story about how a boy learns what an architect does

_____ to persuade the reader to become an architect

_____ to describe the schooling an architect needs

7. Check the words that describe Mr. Daley.

_____ helpful

_____ kind

_____ unpredictable

_____ intelligent

_____ stingy

On the Mail Trail

What was the Pony Express, and how did it work?

1 Think about the last time you mailed a letter. Maybe you were writing to a grandparent who lives in another state or a friend who moved away. What did you do with your letter? You probably placed it in a mailbox, where a postal carrier picked it up. Eventually, your letter would have traveled by truck or by airplane to its destination.

2 In the 1800s, things were not so simple. The country was expanding westward. After the California Gold Rush, more and more people were moving west. Telegraph lines reached from the East Coast to Missouri, but there was no quick way to get information to California.

3 Then, in 1860, the Pony Express began to transport mail from St. Joseph, Missouri, to Sacramento, California. The Pony Express riders were able to carry mail almost two thousand miles in just 10 days! Then, a boat picked up the mail and carried it to San Francisco.

4 Stations were set up about 25 miles apart between Missouri and California. Each rider would cover about 75 miles a day. The horses could travel about 10 miles per hour, and riders received a fresh horse every 10 or 15 miles. When they changed horses, they would quickly transfer their saddlebags, called *mochilas*, to the new horse.

5 The Pony Express riders were usually young men around 20 years old. They had to be thin and small, because that allowed the horses to travel farther and faster. The riders also had to be willing to risk their lives because the route was so dangerous.

6 Although the Pony Express existed for less than two years, it carried some very important news. When Abraham Lincoln was elected president of the United States in 1860, the Pony Express riders carried the news west to California. They even alerted the people of California when the Civil War began.

7 By October 1861, the Pony Express was no longer needed. The Pacific Telegraph Company completed its line to San Francisco. The Pony Express was not a success as far as its owners were concerned. It actually lost money in the short time it operated. But the Pony Express remains an interesting piece of American history and an exciting story of the American West.

PONY EXPRESS

ST. JOSEPH, MISSOURI to CALIFORNIA
in 10 days or less.

WANTED

YOUNG, SKINNY, WIRY FELLOWS

Must be expert riders,
willing to risk death daily.
Wages $25 per week.

APPLY, **PONY EXPRESS STABLES**
St. Joseph, MISSOURI

NAME ____________________

Vocabulary Skills

Write the words from the article that have the meanings below.

1. the place someone or something is going

   ____________________ Par. 1

2. a way of sending messages by wire to a receiving station

   ____________________ Par. 2

3. to move from one place to another

   ____________________ Par. 4

4. occurred; was real

   ____________________ Par. 6

5. warned; let someone know

   ____________________ Par. 6

Circle the homophone that correctly completes each sentence below and write it on the line.

6. The Pony Express riders ____________ many miles to deliver the mail. (road, rode)
7. A rider's ____________ was important because it could affect how fast a horse could travel. (wait, weight)
8. The Pony Express route was ____________ dangerous that the owners suggested the riders be orphans. (so, sew)
9. A rider got a new ____________ every 10 to 15 miles. (horse, hoarse)

Find the compound words from the selection that contain the words below.

10. parent ____________________
11. mail ____________________
12. air ____________________

Reading Skills

1. What is a *mochila*?

   ____

2. Why was the Pony Express originally needed?

   ____

3. Name one important message that was carried to California by the Pony Express.

   ____

   ____

4. Why did Pony Express riders have to be small and light?

   ____

   ____

5. About how long was the route between St. Joseph, Missouri, and San Francisco, California?

   ____

6. Check the line beside the word or words that tell what type of selection this is.

   _____ fiction

   _____ historical nonfiction

   _____ fantasy

7. Number the events below in the order in which they happened in the selection.

   _____ The Pony Express was founded.

   _____ The first rider left St. Joseph on horseback.

   _____ The Pacific Telegraph Company completed its line to San Francisco.

   _____ People began moving to the American West.

   _____ Abraham Lincoln was elected president.

The Trail West

What will Kenji and Alexi find out about the trail of the Pony Express?

1 Kenji and Alexi sat at a table at the library after school on Thursday afternoon. The previous day, their class had taken a field trip to visit the Pony Express National Museum in St. Joseph, Missouri. Their homework assignment was to choose something about the museum and the Pony Express that interested them. Then, they were supposed to do some research to find out more about the topic they selected. Kenji and Alexi were best friends, and they had decided to work on the project together.

2 "It's hard to pick just one part of our trip that was the most interesting," said Kenji.

3 "I know," agreed Alexi. "I think I'd like to learn more about the trail and the route the riders took. We know that they started out right here in St. Joseph. I wonder if it is still possible to follow the trail today."

4 Kenji and Alexi used the library's computer catalog to find several books about the Pony Express. One of the books included a map of the route. "This is just what we were looking for!" exclaimed Kenji.

5 Alexi looked over Kenji's shoulder and pointed to a spot on the map. "After the riders left Missouri, it looks like they traveled through a small part of northern Kansas before they continued into Nebraska. Then, they headed into Wyoming."

6 "Wait," said Kenji, pointing to the map. "This part of the route crosses a tiny bit of Colorado first."

7 "You're right," said Alexi.

8 "Look how big Wyoming is," commented Kenji. "That must have been one of the longest parts of the trip. I remember our tour guide yesterday saying that some of the roughest terrain and harshest weather was in Wyoming."

9 "Next, the trail passed through Utah and Nevada," continued Alexi. "Finally, the riders made it to Sacramento!"

10 "Look at this, Alexi," said Kenji, opening another book. "It says that there is a group of people who belong to the National Pony Express Association. They live in the seven states that the trail passed through."

11 "Some of them probably live right here in St. Joseph," commented Alexi.

12 "They actually reenact the ride every June," Kenji continued. "They dress in authentic clothes, and they try to keep the same schedule that the riders did. One difference, though, is that they use their own horses."

13 "Does each rider travel as far as the original riders of the Pony Express did?" asked Alexi.

14 "No," said Kenji. "They only ride about five miles. When they reach the next person, they transfer the mochila. About six hundred people participate!"

15 "The next reenactment is only a month away," said Alexi excitedly. "We'll have to see if our parents will take us there to cheer the riders on."

NAME ______________________

Vocabulary Skills

Find an antonym in the story for each of the words below.

1. less ______________________ Par. 1
2. shortest ______________________ Par. 8
3. closing ______________________ Par. 10
4. different ______________________ Par. 12

Write **S** if the possessive word is singular. Write **P** if it is plural.

5.	_____ riders'	**6.**	_____ Kenji's
7.	_____ schedule's	**8.**	_____ friends'
9.	_____Alexi's	**10.**	_____ books'

Reading Skills

1. Where did Kenji and Alexi's class go on their field trip?

____

____

2. Which state does Kenji say has rough terrain?

____

3. How often do the members of the National Pony Express Association do a reenactment?

____

____

4. What is one difference between the reenactors and the original Pony Express riders?

____

____

5. Check the line beside the word or words that tell what type of selection this is.

_____ biography

_____ fiction

_____ historical nonfiction

Read the phrases below. Write **K** next to the phrase if it describes Kenji. Write **A** if it describes Alexi. Write **B** if it describes both Kenji and Alexi.

6. _____ says that the trip through Wyoming must have been difficult
7. _____ lives in St. Joseph, Missouri
8. _____ visited the Pony Express Museum the day before
9. _____ wants to cheer on the reenactors as they ride through St. Joseph

Study Skills

Use the information below to answer the questions that follow.

Pony Express Museum Information

Tickets:

Adults	$4.00	Students (7–18)	$2.00
Seniors	$3.00	Kids 6 and under	Free

Hours:
Mon.–Sat.: 9–5
Sun.: 1–5

1. How much is admission for a student?

____

2. What are the museum's hours on Sunday?

____

3. Who can get into the museum for free?

____

4. Which type of ticket is most expensive?

____

The Riders of the Pony Express

What was it like to ride the Pony Express?

1 Who were the riders of the Pony Express? They were young men who were adventurous and courageous. They were willing to risk their lives to be a part of the bold new plan to carry mail on horseback from Missouri to California. The trail could be unpredictable. Riders never knew what kinds of problems they might encounter. In the winter, they faced blizzards and blinding snow. Heavy rains could cause some roads to become impassable. There was also the threat of conflict with bandits and Native Americans.

2 There were about 80 Pony Express riders at any one time. They were paid about one hundred dollars a month for their work, which was a large sum, especially for riders who were so young. The youngest rider was said to be only 11 years old, and the oldest was in his 40s. Because the riders had to be lightweight, most of them were very young.

3 Johnny Fry is usually recognized as being the first westbound Pony Express rider. Fry was only 20 years old when he signed up to ride. He weighed less than 120 pounds and was an experienced rider. Fry rode the 80 miles from St. Joseph, Missouri, to Seneca, Kansas. He was able to cover about 12 miles an hour and made it to Seneca without any problems. When the Civil War began, Fry enlisted and fought on the side of the Union. He died in combat in Kansas in 1863. Johnny Fry, pioneer of the Pony Express, was only 23 years old.

4 Buffalo Bill Cody is probably the most well-known rider of the Pony Express. Cody was only 15 years old when he began riding for the Pony Express. Although he was young, he quickly proved himself to be fearless. He was given one of the most dangerous sections of the route through the state of Wyoming.

5 By some accounts, Cody was the rider who completed the longest nonstop ride. The story has it that Cody reached the station where he was supposed to be relieved by another rider. He found that the other rider had been killed, so Cody continued on the route. He rode a total of 322 miles in a little more than 20 hours.

6 Other accounts say that "Pony" Bob Haslam held the record for the longest continuous ride at 370 miles. However, there were few records kept of such information. Much of it was passed along by word-of-mouth, so it is not always easy for historians to know which pieces of information are facts and which have been exaggerated.

7 The one thing that we know for sure is that the young riders of the Pony Express will always be remembered for their unique role in American history.

NAME ____________________

Vocabulary Skills

Write the words from the article that have the meanings below.

1. hard to tell what is coming

   ____________________ Par. 1

2. impossible to be crossed or traveled past

   ____________________ Par. 1

3. versions of a story

   ____________________ Par. 5

4. something that people tell each other instead of writing down

   ____________________ Par. 6

5. said to be bigger or more interesting than it actually is

   ____________________ Par. 6

Check the correct meaning of the underlined word.

6. Riders on the Pony Express were <u>courageous</u> young men.

   _____ capable of courage

   _____ full of courage

   _____ without courage

7. The stories about Buffalo Bill Cody say that he was <u>fearless</u>.

   _____ without fear

   _____ full of fear

   _____ fear again

Reading Skills

1. Who was Johnny Fry?

   ____

2. What sorts of difficulties did riders face on the trail?

   ____

   ____

3. About how much were the Pony Express riders paid?

   ____

4. Who did Johnny Fry fight for during the Civil War?

   ____

5. Why aren't historians sure who made the longest ride on the Pony Express?

   ____

Write **T** before the sentences that are true. Write **F** before the sentences that are false.

6. _____ Buffalo Bill Cody started riding for the Pony Express when he was 11 years old.
7. _____ Johnny Fry rode from St. Joseph, Missouri, to Seneca, Kansas.
8. _____ There was the frequent threat of bad weather on the route.
9. _____ Johnny Fry was killed during the Civil War.
10. _____ Most of the Pony Express riders weighed more than 150 pounds.

Study Skills

Use a dictionary to help you divide these words into syllables.

1. courageous ____________________
2. Americans ____________________
3. experienced ____________________
4. dangerous ____________________
5. information ____________________

Lone Star Camels

Have you ever heard of the U.S. Camel Corps? Keep reading to learn more about it!

1 When you think of camels, where do you imagine they live? You probably picture them in the deserts of the Middle East, in countries like Egypt or Saudi Arabia. But those are not the only places camels have ever lived. In the second half of the 1800s, a group of camels lived in Texas!

2 How did camels end up so far from their homeland in the Middle East? In 1852, Jefferson Davis, U.S. Secretary of War, recommended that the army try using camels for carrying military provisions in the American Southwest. In 1855, Congress approved the use of $30,000 dollars for the first and only U.S. Camel Corps.

3 Later that year, several U.S. military personnel set sail for North Africa. They had a hard time finding available camels there, so they tried again in Malta, Greece, and Turkey. Finally, after learning much about camels, they landed in Egypt. When their ship sailed for home, it had a number of new passengers, 33 camels and 5 people to care for the animals and show American soldiers how to work with them.

4 The camels were taken to Camp Verde, near San Antonio, Texas. A year later, 41 more camels arrived. Although there were now more than 70 camels in the United States, they were not used often until the Camel Corps was assigned to explore some unfamiliar territory between El Paso and the Colorado River.

5 The camels proved themselves on this trip. They were tougher than the horses and the mules. When the expedition became lost, the soldiers' camels led the people to water. The soldiers were overjoyed. The camels, however, could have continued on for several more days without any water.

6 Even though the camels had proved that they were useful to the military, there were still several problems. Some soldiers did not like the camels at all. They thought the animals were bad tempered. When the camels were irritated or annoyed by something, they reacted by kicking or spitting. They also had a very strong odor that the soldiers did not like. The odor caused other animals that were not used to being around camels to become skittish and upset.

7 Another problem was that the Camel Corps still was not used very often. It was seen as an unnecessary expense for the military. When the Civil War began, the camels were mostly forgotten. Some were sold to places like zoos or circuses. Others were eventually released into the desert.

8 By the mid-1860s, the U.S. Camel Corps no longer existed. Even so, camels still roamed through areas of Nevada, Idaho, Texas, California, and Arizona. The last confirmed sightings were during the early 1900s. Some people claim that camels still live in remote areas of the Southwest desert today, but no one has been able to prove it.

NAME ______________________

Vocabulary Skills

Write the words from the article that have the meanings below.

1. stored food and supplies

______________________ Par. 2

2. extremely happy

______________________ Par. 5

3. nervous; easily frightened

______________________ Par. 6

4. able to be proven true

______________________ Par. 8

5. faraway; hard to reach

______________________ Par. 8

Write the words from the story that match the abbreviations below.

6. TX ______________________
7. CO ______________________
8. NV ______________________
9. ID ______________________

Divide the words below into syllables using a slash (/).

10. t h e m s e l v e s
11. o v e r j o y e d
12. s o u t h w e s t

Write **S** if the possessive word is singular. Write **P** if it is plural.

13. _____ military's
14. _____ camels'
15. _____ Congress's
16. _____ animals'

Reading Skills

1. What kinds of problems was the U.S. military having with the camels?

____

2. Do you think there are any camels still living in the U.S. deserts today? Explain your answer.

____

____

3. Check the line beside the word or words that tell what type of selection this is.

_____ fairy tale

_____ nonfiction

_____ biography

4. How did the camels help the people when the expedition became lost?

____

5. Why did some soldiers dislike the camels?

____

6. Number the events below in the order in which they happened in the selection.

_____ The U.S. Camel Corps no longer existed.

_____ Jefferson Davis recommended that the army try using camels for transporting things in the desert.

_____ The last confirmed camel sighting happened in the American desert.

_____ Members of the U.S. military went to North Africa to look for camels to purchase.

_____ Another 41 camels arrived in the United States.

One Hump or Two?

Read the following selection to learn more interesting facts about camels.

1 The camel is one of the strangest and oldest creatures living today. Scientists believe that millions of years ago, ancestors of camels lived in North America. There was a bridge of land over the Bering Strait that led to Asia. One group of animals migrated to Asia. These animals developed into the camels of today. Another group migrated to South America. This group developed into the llama, an animal in the same family as the camel.

2 There are two types of camels, the *dromedary* and *Bactrian*. The dromedary has one hump and is found mostly in Arabian countries. The Bactrian camel has two humps and is found in Asian countries. All dromedary camels today are domesticated. Bactrian camels can still be found in the wild in areas of Mongolia and China. The Bactrian camel is shorter and heavier than the dromedary. Also, the pads on its feet are thicker so that it can walk in colder, rockier places than the dromedary.

3 The camel has many interesting characteristics. For example, unlike most animals, it lifts both feet on one side at the same time when it runs. This causes it to rock from side to side when it runs. Another unusual characteristic is the camel's ability to eat almost anything if it becomes hungry enough. It might even eat its own leather harness, part of a tent, or a straw basket if it cannot find the grass it prefers.

4 Camels are the best pack animal in the world. They can carry loads as heavy as 600 pounds 25 miles a day. They can also go without water for as long as two weeks in the winter. They do not like to work though, so areas where camels are being loaded and unloaded are often very noisy.

5 You might think that a camel stores extra food and water in its hump or humps. This is what human beings thought for many years, but it is not true. A camel's hump is made of fat and muscle. If a camel has to go without food for several days, it can use the fat in its hump for energy. The camel conserves water in its tissues and cells. Its body does not use the water to cool off the way the human body does. That is why a camel's body temperature can vary, or change, by as much as 11 degrees.

NAME ______________________

Vocabulary Skills

Write the words from the article that have the meanings below.

1. moved from one country or area to another

_____________________________ Par. 1

2. turned into; became

_____________________________ Par. 1

3. trained; used by human beings

_____________________________ Par. 2

4. features or qualities

_____________________________ Par. 3

Circle the words in each row that are part of the same word family.

5. (*-ought*) bought sigh sing brought
6. (*-ight*) fight right ton tonight
7. (*-ought*) trout fought thought thimble

Underline the word with a suffix or a prefix in each sentence. Then, write the meaning of the word on the line.

8. The camel is one of the strangest animals alive today. ______________
9. It is incorrect to believe that camels store extra water in their humps. ______________

____

10. Camels do not show a great enjoyment of the work they do. ______________
11. Sarah felt like the luckiest girl in the world when she got to ride a camel on her trip to Egypt. ______________

Reading Skills

Write **F** before the sentences that are facts. Write **O** before the sentences that are opinions.

1. _____ There are two types of camels.
2. _____ Camels can go without water for long periods of time.
3. _____ Camels are more interesting than horses or mules.
4. _____ A camel's body temperature can vary by 11 degrees.
5. _____ Camels are very strange-looking animals.
6. How did camels travel from North America to Asia millions of years ago?

____

____

7. Name one way the dromedary and the Bactrian camel are alike.

____

____

8. Name one way the dromedary and the Bactrian camel are different.

____

____

9. What is a camel's hump made of?

____

____

10. Why does a camel rock from side to side when it runs?

____

____

Survivors in the Desert

How do plants and animals survive in the desert?

1 "I'd like you to think of one thing you could not live without," Mr. Patel told his class. The class was quiet for a moment, and then students began raising their hands. Mr. Patel wrote their answers on the board as the students spoke: *CD players, chocolate ice cream, my bike, computers, pizza, music, my skateboard, movies, weekends, the beach, soccer*.

2 "These are all good answers," said Mr. Patel, turning around to face the class. "Unfortunately, none of them are correct. You all answered my question differently, but the answer I was looking for applies to all of you. Does anybody have any ideas?"

3 Dajuan raised his hand. "Is it water?" he asked.

4 "Excellent!" said Mr. Patel. "Who can tell me why we could not live without water?"

5 "Well," said Gabrielle, "every living creature needs water to survive. I think that more than half of the human body is made of water."

6 "You are right," nodded Mr. Patel. "We are starting our unit about the desert today, and water is scarce in the desert. Plants and animals that live there have had to adapt to those conditions.

7 "Plants have adapted to life in the desert in three different ways," said Mr. Patel. "Some of them have changed their structures. The cactus is one example of this type of plant. It stores water so that it can go for long periods of time without rain. The stem is thick and has a waxy skin, which holds the moisture inside the plant instead of letting it evaporate. The cactus also has spines that give it some shade from the hot desert sun.

8 "Another type of desert plant has adapted by growing very long roots," Mr. Patel continued. This allows it to reach water that is far below the surface of the desert. The third major type of desert plant is dormant during the dryer seasons. This is a sort of sleeping time for plants when they do not continue to grow. It is similar to the way some animals hibernate in the winter. When there is rain and the desert is not so hot, this type of plant comes to life."

9 "What about animals that live in the desert?" asked Carson. "They don't have stems that conserve water or long roots like plants do."

10 "That's true," said Mr. Patel. "But they have found other ways to adapt. Some desert animals are nocturnal. This means that they are only active at night when the desert becomes cooler. During the day, they burrow underground or sleep in caves that are protected from the sun. Some desert animals get moisture from plants. Animals that eat other animals, like vultures, get enough liquid from their food.

11 "After lunch, we'll talk more about life in the desert. You might want to have a big glass of cold water with your lunch. We have a long, dry afternoon ahead of us!" laughed Mr. Patel.

NAME ______________________

Vocabulary Skills

Write the words from the story that have the meanings below.

1. not enough of something that is needed

    ______________________ Par. 6

2. change in order to survive in different conditions

    ______________________ Par. 6

3. not active for a period of time

    ______________________ Par. 8

4. active only at night

    ______________________ Par. 10

5. to dig a hole in the ground

    ______________________ Par. 10

Check the meaning of the underlined word in each sentence.

6. Mr. Patel turned around to <u>face</u> the class.

    _____ to look at

    _____ the front part of the head

7. Mr. Patel discussed three <u>major</u> types of desert plants.

    _____ an officer in the military

    _____ important; basic

8. The cactus is one <u>type</u> of desert plant.

    _____ a group that has common characteristics

    _____ to write using a computer

Find the compound words from the selection that contain the words below.

9. ground ______________________
10. skate ______________________
11. after ______________________

Reading Skills

1. What is one way the cactus has adapted to life in the desert?

    ____

    ____

2. How are a dormant plant and a hibernating animal similar?

    ____

    ____

3. What do nocturnal desert animals do during the day?

    ____

    ____

4. How do the long roots of some desert plants help them survive?

    ____

    ____

5. About how much of the human body is made of water?

    ____

    ____

6. On the line below, write the words that are dialogue in paragraph 3.

    ____

7. Check the sentence that best states the main idea of the selection.

    _____ Some desert animals are nocturnal and avoid the most extreme heat of the day.

    _____ Mr. Patel's class learns about how plants and animals survive in the desert.

    _____ Water is necessary to all forms of life.

Answer Key

3

Vocabulary Skills

Write the words from the story that have the meanings below.

1. changed someone's mind — convinced (Par. 4)
2. talked about — discussed (Par. 6)
3. very small — miniature (Par. 10)
4. ocean water that moves in and out several times a day — tide (Par. 12)
5. not deep — shallow (Par. 12)

A **synonym** is a word with the same or nearly the same meaning as another word. Find a synonym in the story for each of the words below.

6. laughed — chuckled (Par. 5)
7. swallow — gulp (Par. 6)
8. several — few (Par. 10)
9. yelled — shouted (Par. 10)

A **prefix** is a group of letters added to the beginning of a word to change its meaning. The prefix **pre-** means *before.* For example, *preheat* means *to heat before.* Add **pre** to each word below. Then, use each new word in a sentence.

10. pre view Answers will vary.
11. pre pay Answers will vary.
12. pre wash Answers will vary.

Reading Skills

Write **T** before the sentences that are true. Write **F** before the sentences that are false.

1. F Cameron is visiting his grandpa in Massachusetts.
2. F Cameron wakes up before Grandpa does.
3. T Grandpa makes blueberry pancakes for breakfast.
4. T Cameron and Grandpa plan to go fishing in the afternoon.
5. F Cameron and Grandpa have to drive to get to the beach.
6. F Grandpa finds the tide pool before Cameron does.
7. Name one thing Cameron wants to do when he goes exploring.
   follow the path to the beach, go to the little island, catch some fish

Study Skills

Guide words are printed at the top of each page in a dictionary. The guide word at the left is the first word on the page. The guide word at the right is the last word on the page. Check each word that could be found on a page having the guide words shown in dark print.

1. **crate—crib**
   ✓ crayon ___ cringe ✓ create
2. **mile—mix**
   ✓ minus ✓ minute
   ___ microphone
3. **paint—park**
   ___ paste ___ packet ✓ pants

5

Vocabulary Skills

Write the words from the article that have the meanings below.

1. to stay alive — survive (Par. 2)
2. area around you; surroundings — environment (Par. 2)
3. to catch or capture — trap (Par. 4)
4. gives or offers — provides (Par. 7)
5. to look — peek (Par. 8)

Read each word below. Then, write the letter of its synonym on the line beside the word.

6. c difficult		a.	totally
7. a completely		b.	walk
8. d usually		c.	hard
9. b stroll		d.	often

A word that means the opposite of another word is an **antonym**. Find an antonym in the story for each of the words below.

10. huge — miniature (Par. 1)
11. slowly — quickly (Par. 6)
12. few — many (Par. 7)

The prefix **non-** means *not.* For example, *nontoxic* means *not toxic.* Add **non** to each word below. Then, use each new word in a sentence.

13. non sense Answers will vary.
14. non stop Answers will vary.
15. non swimmer Answers will vary.

Reading Skills

Circle the word that best completes each sentence and write it on the line.

1. Plants and animals must be strong to survive in a tide pool.
   weak large (strong)
2. When water dries up, it evaporates.
   (evaporates) dies melts
3. Starfish and sea urchins have sticky feet.
   backs eyes (feet)
4. Which type of tide pool is most difficult for animals to live in?
   high-level
5. What is one way humans use kelp?
   as an ingredient in ice cream
6. Check the reason the author probably wrote this story.
   ___ to entertain the reader
   ✓ to give some facts about tide pools
   ___ to teach people about ocean tides

7

Vocabulary Skills

Write the words from the story that have the meanings below.

1. getting ready — preparing (Par. 1)
2. very tired — exhausted (Par. 2)
3. take it easy; unwind — relax (Par. 2)
4. tried; tasted — sampled (Par. 4)
5. most of the time — usually (Par. 9)

Check the meaning of the underlined word in each sentence.

6. Cameron and Grandpa picked two buckets of blueberries.
   ___ chose
   ✓ gathered
7. Cameron thought the northern lights looked like a spaceship in the sky.
   ✓ appeared
   ___ stared
8. You can see the northern lights in parts of the world that are closer to the poles.
   ___ long, thin sticks
   ✓ the most northern and southern ends of Earth

The prefix **mis-** means *badly.* For example, *misspell* means *to spell badly.* Add **mis** to each word below. Then, write the meaning of the new word.

9. mis behave Answers will vary.
10. mis match Answers will vary.
11. mis count Answers will vary.
12. mis understand Answers will vary.
13. mis use Answers will vary.

Reading Skills

Write **C** before the groups of words that describe Cameron and **G** before the groups of words that describe Grandpa.

1. G said that spring and fall are better times for seeing the northern lights
2. C thought the northern lights were a spaceship
3. G started a fire in the fire pit on the beach
4. C wants to move to Maine
5. G said blueberries would turn their fingers blue

Write **T** before the sentences that are true. Write **F** before the sentences that are false.

6. F Cameron and Grandpa bought some blueberries at the store.
7. F Grandpa picked up Cameron's parents at the airport.
8. T Dinner reminds Mom of summers in Maine when she was little.
9. F Grandpa has never seen the northern lights before.
10. T The northern lights are usually seen only in places with high latitudes.
11. Name one thing Cameron and Grandpa do to prepare for Cameron's parents.
    Possible answer: opened windows, did laundry, picked blueberries

9

Vocabulary Skills

Read each word below. Then, write the letter of its antonym on the line beside the word.

1. c dangerous		a.	creates
2. a destroys		b.	closer
3. e apart		c.	harmless
4. b farther		d.	separate
5. d collide		e.	together

Think of the meaning of the prefix in each word. Then, write the meaning of the word.

6. precook to cook before
7. nonfiction not fiction
8. misspell spell badly
9. nonsense not sense
10. preschool before school

Reading Skills

Circle the word that best completes each sentence and write it on the line.

1. Some people made up legends to explain the lights they saw in the sky.
   paintings (legends) experiments
2. Solar particles and gases collide in Earth's atmosphere to create the northern lights.
   (gases) light ice
3. Scientists do not think the northern lights make any sounds.
   explosions steam (sounds)
4. In Roman myths, who was Aurora?
   goddess of dawn
5. Toward which two areas of Earth does solar wind move?
   the poles
6. About how far away from Earth is the lowest section of the northern lights?
   40 miles
7. Check the sentence that best states the main idea of the selection.
   ___ The northern lights are amazing the first time you see them.
   ✓ Collisions of solar particles create lights in the night sky.
   ___ The northern lights are also called *aurora borealis.*

Study Skills

An **outline** is used to put ideas in order. It shows the important facts in a story. Use the facts from paragraph 1 to complete Part I. Use the facts from paragraph 3 to complete Part II.

I. Northern lights in history
   A. People saw moving colors in sky and were frightened
   B. Made up legends to explain what they saw
   C. Aurora was Roman goddess of dawn

II. How northern lights are created
   A. Solar particles get trapped in Earth's atmosphere
   B. Collide with gases
   C. Energy from collision creates light
   D. When lots of collisions happen at once, northern lights can be seen

Answer Key

Vocabulary Skills

Write the words from the story that have the meanings below.

1. small town
   village Par. 1
2. not known
   unfamiliar Par. 2
3. not bright
   dim Par. 3
4. threw
   tossed Par. 6
5. jumped
   leaped Par. 8
6. twinkling
   shimmering Par. 9

In each row, circle the three words that belong together.

7. (years) (days) path (minutes)
8. (leaped) (jumped) (hopped) quickly
9. (hand) shoe (shoulder) (arm)

The prefixes **im-** and **in-** mean *not*. For example, *impossible* means *not possible*. *Inexact* means *not exact*. The prefix **im-** is usually used before words that begin with *b*, *m*, or *p*. The prefix **in-** is usually used before words that begin with other letters. Add **im** or **in** to each word below. Then, write the meaning of the new word.

10. in expensive Answers will vary.
11. im perfect Answers will vary.
12. in correct Answers will vary.

Reading Skills

1. Number the events below from **1** to **5** to show the order in which they happened in the story.
   5 Whenever the chief and his son saw the northern lights, they thought of the children playing ball.
   3 The chief and the old man watched the braves play ball.
   1 The boy's parents were worried about him.
   4 The boy asked the chief if he was angry.
   2 The boy followed the trail of the Milky Way.
2. The boy's parents were worried about him because he did not run and play with other children in the village.
3. How did the boy and the chief get to the Land of the Northern Lights?
   They followed the trail of the Milky Way.
4. What were the belts the braves wore made of?
   rainbows
5. What do you think the boy taught the children in the Wabanaki village when he got home?
   He taught them to play ball.

11

Vocabulary Skills

Write the words from the story that have the meanings below.

1. closed loudly
   slammed Par. 4
2. lots; many
   plenty Par. 8
3. busy
   occupied Par. 8
4. collected or brought together
   gathered Par. 13

A word that means the opposite of another word is an **antonym**. Write the pair of antonyms from each sentence.

5. Madison worried it would get cold soon, and she wouldn't be able to ride her bike until warm weather came again.
   cold warm
6. Malaika and her siblings never had bikes, but they always found fun things to do.
   never always
7. One team will use the right side of the egg carton, and the other team will use the left.
   right left

When you add an apostrophe (') and the letter **s** to a singular noun, it shows that a person or thing owns something. Write the possessive form of each word in parentheses.

8. Madison's family is hosting an exchange student. (Madison)
9. There were spots of rain on Malaika's glasses. (Malaika)
10. The sky's color grew darker and darker. (sky)
11. The team's goal is to win the game. (team)
12. The game's rules are easy to explain. (game)

Reading Skills

A **fact** is something that can be proven to be true. An **opinion** is what a person believes. It may or may not be true. Write **F** before the sentences that are facts. Write **O** before the sentences that are opinions.

1. F Madison's friends are named Drew and Kiona.
2. O Thunderstorms are exciting.
3. F Madison put some popcorn in a bowl.
4. F Drew doesn't know how they will play Mancala without a board.
5. O Drew and Kiona will win the game.
6. O Mancala All-Stars is a great name for the winning team.
7. Check the sentence that best states the main idea of the story.
   ___ Madison gets bored when it rains.
   ✓ On a rainy afternoon, Malaika teaches some friends how to play an African game.
   ___ Malaika tells her friends about her life in Africa.
8. Where did Drew learn how to play Mancala?
   at camp
9. What does the team name the *5Ms* stand for?
   Madison and Malaika the Marvelous Mancala Masters

13

Vocabulary Skills

Write the words from the article that have the meanings below.

1. a quick look
   glimpse Par. 1
2. to seem
   appear Par. 3
3. complicated; not simple
   complex Par. 3
4. as it has been done in the past
   traditionally Par. 4
5. a pleasant way of spending time
   pastime Par. 5

A **synonym** is a word with the same or nearly the same meaning as another word. Find a synonym in the article for each of the words below.

6. easy simple Par. 1
7. goal object Par. 2
8. separated divided Par. 3
9. letting allowing Par. 4

Underline the word with a prefix in each sentence. Then, write the meaning of the underlined word on the line.

10. Do not forget to preheat the oven when you make the pizza.
    to heat before
11. We took a nonstop flight from Cleveland to New York.
    not stop
12. The tickets we bought last week were inexpensive.
    not expensive

Reading Skills

Circle the word that best completes each sentence and write it on the line.

1. The Chinese tangram is harder than it seems.
   easier older (harder)
2. In the past, the *takraw* ball was usually made of rattan.
   plastic rubber (rattan)
3. You cannot use your hands to hit the ball in *takraw*.
   feet shoulders (hands)
4. Check the sentence that best states the main idea of the story.
   ___ *Takraw* is a popular game in Thailand.
   ___ The Chinese tangram puzzle is not as easy as it may seem.
   ✓ It can be fun and interesting to play games from all around the world.
5. How many shapes is the paper divided into in tangram?
   7
6. What rule of the game makes *takraw* difficult to play?
   You can't use your arms or hands.

Write **J** before the words that describe the United State's version of the game of jacks. Write **T** before the words that describe Chinese tangram.

7. J played with metal pieces
8. T possible to make more than 1,500 images
9. T begins with a square divided into seven shapes
10. J exists in many variations

15

Vocabulary Skills

A word that sounds the same as another word but has a different spelling and meaning is a **homophone**. Circle the homophone that correctly completes each sentence below and write it on the line.

1. Madison asks Malaika if she would like to help make breakfast. (would) wood)
2. Dad and Madison think it is hard to break eggs. (brake, (break))
3. Madison uses a flower from the arrangement in the living room. (flour, (flower))

A **compound word** is a word made by combining two smaller words. For example, *lighthouse* is made of the words *light* and *house*. Underline the compound word in each sentence. Then, write the two words that make up each compound.

4. Our dog likes to play in the backyard.
   back yard
5. I would love to own a sailboat one day.
   sail boat
6. Don't forget to bring sunscreen to the beach!
   sun screen
7. I have to do my homework before I can go to the park.
   home work

Reading Skills

Write **T** before the sentences that are true. Write **F** before the sentences that are false.

1. F Madison wakes up Malaika because she is hungry.
2. T Madison's favorite pajamas are pink.
3. T Malaika has not made pancakes before.
4. F Mom helps everyone make pancakes and eggs for breakfast.
5. Do you think Madison will ask Dad and Malaika to help her the next time she wants to plan a surprise? Why or why not?
   Answers will vary.
6. Madison and her dad don't like cracking eggs because they get the shells in the batter.

Circle the word that best completes each sentence and write it on the line.

7. Madison's idea for making a surprise breakfast was a success.
   mistake (success) failure
8. Dad thinks that he, Madison, and Malaika work well as a team.
   (team) business surprise

Study Skills

Circle each word that could be found on a dictionary page having the guide words shown in dark print.

1. **artist—attic**
   anteater argument (ask)
2. **deer—doughnut**
   (distant) deep (dodge)
3. **star—supper**
   soap stand (sunny)
4. **warn—wicker**
   windy (whine) wag

17

Answer Key

19

Vocabulary Skills

Write the words from the recipes that have the meanings below.

1. frying pan
   skillet (Par. 1)
2. damp or slightly wet
   moist (Par. 2)
3. to turn slightly so something slopes or slants
   tilt (Par. 3)
4. a wet mixture used in cooking
   batter (Par. 3)

Underline the prefix in each word for numbers 5–8. Then, complete each sentence with one of the words.

5. misuse
6. preview
7. nonfiction
8. incomplete
9. Kahlil used a nonfiction book about dinosaurs to write his report.
10. My parents wanted to preview the movie before my sister and I watched it.

Reading Skills

1. Check the reason the author probably wrote this story.
   ____ to show you how to become a chef
   ✓ to tell about how to make different types of pancakes
   ____ to explain some important rules to remember when you are cooking
2. Number the sentences below to show the order in which you should do each step when you make banana akara.
   2 Mash the bananas with a fork.
   5 Flip the fritter when the edges turn brown.
   4 Coat the skillet with cooking spray.
   1 Peel the bananas.
   3 Add the nutmeg to the syrup.
3. What will happen if you stir the pancake batter for too long?
   The pancakes will be tough instead of fluffy.

Study Skills

An **index** is located at the end of many nonfiction books. It is an alphabetical listing of all the topics in a book. You can use the index to find out where to look for information about a particular topic. Use the index below to answer the questions.

INDEX

1. On what page can you find a recipe for French toast?
   9
2. How many pancake recipes are there in this book?
   3

21

Vocabulary Skills

Write the words from the story that have the meanings below.

1. in a state of great confusion
   chaotic (Par. 2)
2. something that fits around an animal's upper body
   harness (Par. 5)
3. alert; giving a lot of attention to
   attentive (Par. 7)
4. abruptly; all at once
   suddenly (Par. 10)
5. to train to be well-adjusted and easy to be around
   socialize (Par. 15)

In each row, circle the words that belong together.

6. (tossed) (threw) used (flung)
7. (common) (ordinary) unusual (everyday)
8. wonder (tell) (inform) (explain)
9. (shiny) dry (glossy) (sleek)

When you add an apostrophe (') and the letter **s** to a singular noun, it shows that a person or thing owns something. Write the possessive form of each word in parentheses on the line.

10. Estéban's mother took him to the mall to buy new shoes. (Estéban)
11. A puppy's foster family will keep the puppy for about a year. (puppy)
12. A seeing-eye dog's job is to help a blind person get around more easily. (dog)

Reading Skills

1. Number the events below in the order in which they happened in the story.
   5 Mrs. Ramirez asked Estéban if he would be interested in fostering a puppy.
   4 Estéban said that he missed Sadie.
   1 Mrs. Ramirez looked for her keys in her purse.
   3 Estéban saw a man with a seeing-eye dog at the mall.
   2 Estéban and Mrs. Ramirez went to the mall.
2. Estéban and his mother went to the mall because he needs new shoes.
3. Who is Sadie?
   the mutt the Ramirez family adopted when Estéban was a baby
4. Why would the Ramirez family only have a foster puppy for about a year?
   After a year, they would give the dog back to the agency so it could become a seeing-eye dog.
5. A **summary** is a short sentence that tells the most important facts about a topic. Check the sentence below that is the best summary for paragraph 5.
   ____ The chocolate Labrador wore a red harness.
   ✓ Estéban was interested to see a man and his seeing-eye dog at the mall.
   ____ Estéban found the shoes he wanted.

23

Vocabulary Skills

Write the words from the story that have the meanings below.

1. to take care of temporarily
   foster (Par. 2)
2. fulfilling
   satisfying (Par. 5)
3. to show
   expose (Par. 6)
4. friends
   companions (Par. 11)

A word that sounds the same as another word but has a different spelling and meaning is a **homophone**. Circle the homophone that correctly completes each sentence below.

5. The Ramirez family (made) maid) the decision to foster a puppy.
6. They will (rays (raise)) the puppy for about a year.
7. A puppy will wag its (tale (tail)) to show that it is happy.
8. The teenage girl patted Mitzi on her ((side) sighed).
9. A puppy with large (pause (paws)) will probably grow up to be a big dog.

Underline the compound word in each sentence. Then, write the two words that make up each compound.

10. There is a new playground at the park near my house.
    play ground
11. The small, red farmhouse sat at the edge of the field.
    farm house

Reading Skills

1. Puppies may feel lonely at first because most of them have never been away from the other pups in the litter.
2. Why does a foster family need to expose a puppy to lots of different things?
   so it doesn't grow up to be a dog who gets frightened or startled easily
3. Why does Estéban feel worried about giving up a puppy after a year?
   He thinks the puppy will feel like part of the family.
4. Do you think Mr. Crockett will foster more seeing-eye puppies in the future? Why or why not?
   Answers will vary.
5. Check the words that describe Estéban.
   ✓ responsible
   ✓ kind
   ____ competitive
   ____ funny
   ✓ thoughtful
6. Write **F** before sentences that are facts. Write **O** before sentences that are opinions.
   F About half the people at the meeting are thinking about fostering a puppy.
   O Fostering puppies is an enjoyable way to spend time.
   O Estéban and his parents will be a good foster family.
   F The girl sitting across from Estéban has curly hair.

25

Vocabulary Skills

Check the meaning of the underlined word in each sentence.

1. Helping Hands trains capuchin monkeys.
   ____ groups of railroad cars
   ✓ teaches or instructs
2. A Helping Hands monkey is more than just a pet for its new owner.
   ✓ a tame animal that lives with a person
   ____ to stroke or touch lightly
3. In the wild, capuchin monkeys spend a lot of time playing in the trees.
   ____ out of control
   ✓ a natural area; wilderness

Fill in the blanks below with the possessive form of the word in parentheses.

4. A monkey's opposable thumbs allow it to use its hands for many things. (monkey)
5. The owner's friendship with his or her monkey is often very strong. (owner)
6. People with disabilities are often amused by their companions' actions. (companions)
7. Dr. Willard's experiment was quite a success! (Dr. Willard)

Reading Skills

1. Check the sentence that best states the main idea of the story.
   ____ Monkeys are fun to have as pets.
   ✓ Monkeys can be trained to help people with disabilities.
   ____ Monkeys can be mischievous.
2. Name two reasons why monkeys are good at helping humans.
   they are friendly, intelligent, good with their hands
3. Where is Helping Hands located?
   Cambridge, Massachusetts
4. Where do capuchin monkeys live in the wild?
   South Central America

Write **T** before the sentences that are true. Write **F** before the sentences that are false.

5. F Capuchin monkeys live to be about 20 years old.
6. T Capuchin monkeys can learn to perform many different tasks.
7. F Dr. Willard taught capuchin monkeys to speak.
8. T Most monkey owners form a strong relationship with their companions.

Study Skills

A **table of contents** is one of the first pages in a book. It shows the title and page each chapter begins on. Use the table of contents below to answer the questions.

Monkey Business
Table of Contents

1. What kind of information would you find on page 12?
   Eating Habits
2. On what page does the second chapter begin?
   7

Answer Key

Vocabulary Skills

Write the words from the article that have the meanings below.

1. taught how to behave correctly
   socialized (Par. 2)
2. given something in return for a service or good behavior
   rewarded (Par. 3)
3. an order
   command (Par. 4)
4. to finish
   complete (Par. 4)
5. Write the two words in the first paragraph that are synonyms.
   rare unusual
6. Write the two words in the third paragraph that are antonyms.
   rewarded punished

Find an antonym in the article for each word below.

7. similarity difference (Par. 2)
8. seldom often (Par. 4)
9. simple difficult (Par. 5)

The suffix **-less** can mean *to be without*. For example, *useless* means *to be without use*. Add **less** to each base word below. Then, use each new word in a sentence.

10. worthless Answers will vary.
11. painless Answers will vary.

Reading Skills

1. Does a dog or a monkey have a longer "childhood"?
   a monkey
2. Name two tasks the article says that a monkey can do for a person.
   turn on the lights, pick up something
3. How long do monkeys spend in a foster home before they begin their training?
   4–6 years
4. Why do you think it is more common for people to foster dogs than monkeys?
   Dogs are less work. Dogs do not need to be fostered for as long.
5. Check the phrase that best describes the author's purpose.
   ___ to compare different types of monkeys
   ✓ to share information about how companion monkeys are trained
   ___ to convince the reader to get a monkey as a pet
6. Check the sentence below that is the best summary for paragraph 2.
   ___ Monkeys have a longer life span than dogs.
   ✓ Monkeys need time to grow up before they can be socialized as human helpers.

27

Vocabulary Skills

Write the words from the story that have the meanings below.

1. good at something
   talented (Par. 5)
2. signed-up for
   enrolled (Par. 6)
3. leaders; supervisors at a camp
   counselors (Par. 7)
4. exercises in which you learn by doing something over and over again
   drills (Par. 7)
5. excited and encouraged
   motivated (Par. 8)

Read each word in the column on the left. Then, write the letter of its synonym on the line beside the word.

6. c grin — a. exchange
7. a trade — b. select
8. d notice — c. smile
9. b choose — d. observe

The suffix **-ment** can mean *the act of*. For example, *agreement* means *the act of agreeing*. Add **ment** to each base word below. Then, use each new word in a sentence.

10. excitement Answers will vary.
11. embarrassment Answers will vary.
12. measurement Answers will vary.

Reading Skills

Circle the word that best completes each sentence and write it on the line.

1. Eliza finished each task the counselors assigned.
   (task) conversation team
2. Annie talked to Eliza after the first practice.
   lesson (practice) evening
3. Dad thinks Eliza is a talented soccer player.
   funny (talented) lazy

Write **B** if the sentence describes something that happens before Eliza goes to camp. Write **A** if the sentence describes something that happens after Eliza gets to camp.

4. A Madeline and Eliza are happy to see that two girls they know are enrolled.
5. A Eliza tells Annie she was nervous.
6. B Dad and Eliza set the table for dinner.
7. A Annie thanks Eliza for helping her stay focused.
8. B Dad tells Eliza that she'll do fine at camp.
9. Do you think Eliza will want to go to camp again next summer? Why or why not?
   Answers will vary.
10. Why does Eliza tell Annie that she felt nervous?
    She doesn't know many people, and she thinks she isn't very quick on the field.

29

Vocabulary Skills

Circle the homophone that correctly completes each sentence below and write it on the line.

1. Brazil won three World Cup titles. (one, (won))
2. A ball and some goals are all you need to play a game of soccer. ((ball), bawl)
3. After playing for a long time, the soccer players need to take a break. (brake, (break))

Write a compound word using two words in each sentence.

4. A ball that you kick with your foot is a football.
5. Wood that is used to make a fire is firewood.
6. A yard that is near a barn is called a barnyard.
7. Work that you do at home is homework.
8. A bell that you ring at someone's door is a doorbell.

Reading Skills

1. Number the events below in the order in which they happened in the selection.
   5 More than a billion people watched the World Cup on television.
   4 Pelé was named Soccer Player of the Century.
   2 The first soccer clubs were formed in England.
   1 Games similar to soccer were played in China.
   3 Pelé joined the New York Cosmos.
2. Check the reason the author probably wrote this story.
   ✓ to tell people about the history and popularity of soccer
   ___ to explain how the game of soccer is played
   ___ to show how soccer got its name
3. Name two European countries where soccer is popular.
   Spain, Italy, Germany
4. What do you need to play a game of soccer?
   a ball and two goals
5. In what country was Pelé born?
   Brazil
6. It took longer for soccer to be accepted in the United States because a different kind of football was already being played here and people were not eager to try something new.

Study Skills

Use the chart below to answer the questions that follow.

World Cup Statistics

Country	Number of 1st Place Wins	Number of Games Played	Total Games Won
Brazil	4	80	53
Italy	3	66	38
France	1	41	21

1. Which country has the most first place wins? Brazil
2. Which country has won a total of 21 games? France
3. How many World Cup games has Italy played? 66
4. How many World Cup games has Brazil won? 53

31

Vocabulary Skills

Write the words from the article that have the meanings below.

1. mark of excellence
   honor (Par. 3)
2. of two or more countries
   international (Par. 6)
3. to help or to supply
   support (Par. 7)
4. reach; accomplish
   achieve

Check the meaning of the underlined word in each sentence.

5. Mia has scored many goals in international competition.
   ___ something a person works hard for
   ✓ a score for driving a ball into a certain area
6. When Mia was a teenager, she won a spot on the U. S. National Team.
   ___ a mark or stain
   ✓ a place; a position

The suffix **-able** can mean *capable of*. *Reasonable* means *capable of reason*. Add **able** to each base word below. Then, use each new word in a sentence.

7. affordable Answers will vary.
8. teachable Answers will vary.
9. adjustable Answers will vary.

Reading Skills

Write **T** before the sentences that are true. Write **F** before the sentences that are false.

1. F Mia Hamm was born in Chapel Hill.
2. T Mia's brother's name was Garrett.
3. T Mia is happy to be a role model for young athletes.
4. F Mia wanted to take ballet lessons when she was younger.
5. T Mia helped her team win a gold medal in the 1996 and 2004 Olympics.
6. Why did Mia start the Mia Hamm Foundation?
   to raise money to fight bone marrow disease and to support sports programs for girls
7. Explain why Mia might enjoy being a role model for girls.
   She likes to help other young athletes achieve their goals; there are fewer female athlete role models for girls.
8. Why do you think Mia Hamm has been so successful in her life?
   Answers will vary.
9. Check the sentence that best states the main idea of the selection.
   ___ Mia Hamm liked playing soccer better than taking ballet lessons.
   ✓ Mia Hamm is a talented athlete and a giving person.
   ___ Mia Hamm helped her college team win the national championship four times.

33

Answer Key

Vocabulary Skills

Write the words from the article that have the meanings below.

1. a good set of circumstances; a good chance opportunities (Par. 2)
2. to grow and progress develop (Par. 2)
3. to look up to admire (Par. 6)
4. bravery; courage fearlessness (Par. 6)

Circle the words in each row that belong together.

5. (amazed) worried (surprised) (astonished)
6. (league) (team) (organization) position
7. follow (quick) (speedy) (rapid)
8. (honor) (admire) disappoint (respect)

Underline the suffix in each word. Then, write the meaning of the word on the line next to it.

9. enjoy<u>able</u> capable of enjoying
10. use<u>less</u> to be without use
11. reason<u>able</u> capable of reason
12. amaze<u>ment</u> the act of being amazed

Reading Skills

1. Emelia Adu brought her sons to the United States because she wanted them to have better opportunities for a good education.
2. In what city and state did Freddy live when he first moved to the United States? Potomac, Maryland
3. Why didn't Freddy accept the offer to play for the European soccer league team? He, his coach, and his parents decided that he was too young.
4. Where did Freddy first play soccer? With whom did he play? in his neighborhood in Ghana with older boys and grown men
5. Check the words that describe Freddy.
   - ✓ hardworking
   - ✓ fearless
   - ___ lazy
   - ✓ talented
   - ___ bored

Write **F** before the sentences that are facts. Write **O** before the sentences that are opinions.

6. F Freddy Adu was born in Ghana, Africa.
7. O Emelia Adu made the right choice when she decided to move to America.
8. O Freddy is the nicest young soccer player today.
9. F Freddy trained with the "under-17s" in Florida.

Study Skills

Number the words in each group to put them in alphabetical order.

1. 3 wonder; 1 whisper; 2 whom
2. 2 excited; 3 extreme; 1 exact

35

Vocabulary Skills

Write the words from the story that have the meanings below.

1. a place where fruit trees are grown orchard (Par. 1)
2. window coverings often found on the outside of houses shutters (Par. 1)
3. a sound that is loud and deep booming (Par. 3)
4. kinds or types varieties (Par. 6)
5. to trim or thin out prune (Par. 10)

Circle the homophone that correctly completes each sentence below, and write it on the line.

6. A small creek ran beside the apple orchard. (creak, (creek))
7. Uncle Luis had to hire people to help him pick the fruit. ((hire), higher)
8. There was a tin pail next to the barn door. ((pail), pale)
9. Apple trees need plenty of rain to produce large, sweet fruit. (reign, (rain))

Write the words from the story that match the abbreviations below.

10. Fri. Friday
11. CA California
12. FL Florida

Reading Skills

Circle the word that best completes each sentence, and write it on the line.

1. At the farm, the school bus turned onto the gravel driveway.
   smooth concrete (gravel)
2. Uncle Luis's farm is in Northern California.
   Maine (California) Arkansas
3. Tomás is Ms. Hallowell's student.
   teacher (student) parent
4. Check the phrase that best describes the author's purpose.
   - ___ to convince the reader to buy apples only from California orchards
   - ___ to explain how to buy and run your own orchard
   - ✓ to tell a story about a class trip to an orchard
5. Name two types of apples Uncle Luis grows at Applecreek Orchards. Granny Smith, Braeburn, Pink Lady
6. Do you think Uncle Luis will take a vacation next winter? Why or why not? Answers will vary.

37

Vocabulary Skills

Write the words from the story that have the meanings below.

1. the time of day just as the sun begins to rise dawn (Par. 3)
2. having a pleasant smell fragrant (Par. 4)
3. the son of your brother or sister nephew (Par. 5)
4. twelve dozen
5. people who sell things vendors (Par. 9)

Fill in the blanks below with the possessive form of the word in parentheses.

6. The baker's cinnamon buns were warm and sweet. (baker)
7. Tomás' uncle wanted to sell his apples at the market. (Tomás)
8. Tomás and Uncle Luis drove into the town's small downtown area. (town)
9. The farmers' market offered many different kinds of produce. (farmers)

Reading Skills

1. Why is Tomás spending the weekend with his uncle? to help him set up the fruit stand
2. Do you think Tomás will help Uncle Luis again? Why or why not? Answers will vary.
3. What does Tomás remind his uncle to bring to the farmers' market? money to make change and a scale
4. What does Tomás get for breakfast? What does he plan to exchange for his breakfast? cinnamon buns, apples

Write **T** before the phrases that describe Tomás and **L** before the phrases that describe Uncle Luis.

5. L forgot to load the scale into the truck
6. T traded apples for cinnamon buns
7. L said that your days often start before dawn when you are a farmer
8. T waved to his mom in the driveway

Study Skills

Use the information on the poster to answer the questions below.

Rocky River Organic Farm Produce	
Tomatoes	$1.95 per pound
Peppers	$2.00 per pound
Cucumbers	$1.25 each
Potted Herbs	$2.50 per pot or 5 pots for $10.00
Honey	$2.25 per jar

1. How much would it cost to buy two pounds of peppers? $4.00
2. What costs $2.25 per jar? honey

39

Vocabulary Skills

Write the words from the article that have the meanings below.

1. lose brightness or color fade (Par. 1)
2. to draw to itself; to interest attract (Par. 1)
3. to buy purchase (Par. 2)
4. to let go release (Par. 2)
5. a sweet liquid found in flowers nectar (Par. 3)

In each row, circle the three words that belong together.

6. (bloom) (flower) (blossom) honey
7. (odor) orchard (fragrant) (scent)
8. process (nectar) (pollen) (flower)
9. (twig) (branch) bee (scion)

Fill in the blanks below with the possessive form of the word in parentheses.

10. The apple blossom's color slowly fades to white. (blossom)
11. The bees' wings brush against pollen when they collect nectar. (bees)
12. An apple's seeds might not produce the same type of tree. (apple)
13. The scion's buds will produce new twigs and leaves. (scion)

Reading Skills

Write **T** before the sentences that are true. Write **F** before the sentences that are false.

1. F Most apple tree blossoms are pale yellow.
2. T The sweet smell of the flowers attracts bees.
3. T Bees do not like to be out in bad weather.
4. F A Red Delicious apple seed will always produce a Red Delicious tree.
5. F There are about 3,500 varieties of apples around the world.
6. Why do apple farmers purchase bees? to help pollinate their trees
7. How do bees carry pollen from one flower to another? on their wings
8. What is the name of the process apple farmers use to produce the type of apple tree they want? grafting
9. What is a *scion*? the twig from a parent tree
10. Number the following steps in the order in which they occur.
    - 2 The scent of the flowers attracts bees.
    - 4 The bee carries the pollen to another flower.
    - 3 The bee collects nectar from the flower.
    - 1 The apple tree flowers.

41

Answer Key

43

Vocabulary Skills

Write the words from the selection that have the meanings below.

1. the center parts of things
   cores (Par. 2)
2. to cook at a low boil
   simmer (Par. 3)
3. to take away
   remove (Par. 7)
4. to mix or put together
   combine (Par. 8)
5. a type of apple flavored drink
   cider (Par. 9)

Check the meaning of the underlined word in each sentence.

6. You can buy caramel apples at the fair.
   ✓ an outdoor event with games and exhibits
   ___ equal; just
7. Fresh apples should be firm to the touch.
   ___ a company or organization
   ✓ hard; solid
8. The apple pie took second place in the contest.
   ✓ occurring after the first
   ___ one sixtieth of a minute

Reading Skills

1. Number the directions below from **1** to **5** to show the order in which they are listed in the recipe for baked apples.
   5 Cover the dish with foil.
   1 Preheat the oven.
   4 Top each apple with butter.
   2 Peel the apples.
   3 Spoon the mixture into the hollow core.

Circle the word that best completes each sentence, and write it on the line.

2. You should refrigerate any applesauce you do not eat.
   forget (refrigerate) donate
3. Use a wooden spoon to stir in the sugar.
   whip squeeze (stir)
4. Spoon part of the mixture into the hollow core.
   (mixture) apple cider
5. Why shouldn't you remove the whole core when you make baked apples?
   Leaving a little of the core will hold the juice in.
6. How many ingredients do you need to make baked apples?
   8
7. How long do you need to bake the apples?
   25–30 minutes

45

Vocabulary Skills

Write the words from the story that have the meanings below.

1. a long, deep breath
   sigh (Par. 5)
2. walking for pleasure, usually in a wooded area
   hiking (Par. 7)
3. nation
   country (Par. 8)
4. to wish you hadn't done something
   regret (Par. 10)
5. shows or proves what something is
   identification (Par. 11)

An **antonym** is a word that means the opposite of another word. Find an antonym in the story for each of the words below.

6. last first (Par. 1)
7. far near (Par. 2)
8. finish start (Par. 12)

Write a compound word using two words in each sentence.

9. A pack that you wear on your back is called a backpack.
10. The top of a tree is called a treetop.
11. The days that come at the end of the week are called the weekend.
12. The room where you keep your bed is a bedroom.
13. The head of a trail, or the place where you begin it, is called a trailhead.

Reading Skills

1. Check the reason the author probably wrote this story.
   ✓ to tell a story about a girl and her dad and a hike they went on
   ___ to persuade the reader to hike the Appalachian Trail
   ___ to tell the reader facts about the Appalachian Trail
2. Check the sentence below that is the best summary for paragraph 7.
   ✓ Amira's dad tries to make her feel better about the move to Virginia.
   ___ Amira's dad walked over to the map of Virginia.
3. Do you think Amira will want to go hiking again? Why or why not?
   Answers will vary.
4. Name three things that can be found in Amira's backpack or her dad's backpack.
   Possible answers: bug spray, a water bottle, two granola bars, two oranges, a cell phone, a water bottle, a tree identification guide, sunscreen, a camera.
5. Check the words that you think best describe Amira's dad.
   ✓ athletic
   ✓ cheerful
   ___ angry
   ___ shy
   ✓ caring

47

Vocabulary Skills

Circle the homophone that correctly completes each sentence below, and write it on the line.

1. Many people heard about the Appalachian Trail when it was covered in the news. ((heard), herd)
2. One of the reasons the trail had to be moved was an increase in traffic. (Won, (One))
3. It is not that unusual to see a bear as you hike the Appalachian Trail. (bare, (bear))

Fill in the blanks below with the possessive form of the word in parentheses.

4. Benton MacKaye's plan was a success. (MacKaye)
5. Hikers' families may mail packages to them along the route. (Hikers)
6. The trail's purpose is to give people a place to spend time in nature. (trail)

Reading Skills

1. Where did the first section of the Appalachian Trail open?
   Bear Mountain State Park, New York
2. Why can't people carry all the supplies they need with them on the trail?
   The supplies would be too heavy.
3. About how many people hike the entire trail each year?
   450

Write **T** before the sentences that are true. Write **F** before the sentences that are false.

4. F The Appalachian Trail goes from Georgia to Ohio.
5. F No one has ever hiked the entire trail.
6. T In the 1920s, Myron Avery mapped almost the whole trail.
7. T Part of the original Appalachian Trail had to be moved.
8. Check the sentence that best states the main idea of the selection.
   ___ It takes about six months to hike the entire Appalachian Trail.
   ✓ The Appalachian Trail, built as a natural escape from city life, is the longest trail in the country.
   ___ The Appalachian Trail stretches from Springer Mountain, Georgia, to Mt. Katahdin, Maine.

Study Skills

A **time line** shows the order in which things happened. Use the time line below to answer the questions that follow.

1. What happened in 1925?
   The ATC was founded.
2. When did a hurricane destroy part of the trail?
   1938
3. How many years after the hurricane did Shaffer complete the first thru-hike?
   10 years

49

Vocabulary Skills

Write the words from the article that have the meanings below.

1. feeling afraid of
   apprehensive (Par. 1)
2. forceful; quick to attack
   aggressive (Par. 2)
3. to recognize
   identify (Par. 3)
4. to dig a hole in the ground
   burrow (Par. 4)
5. material that catches the air and slows a fall to the ground
   parachute (Par. 5)

Read each word below. Then, write the letter of its synonym on the line beside the word.

6. b answer — a. find
7. d different — b. reply
8. a locate — c. complete
9. c finish — d. varied

Check the correct meaning of the underlined word.

10. The short story was incomplete.
    ___ complete before
    ✓ not complete
    ___ capable of completing
11. The winner of the spelling bee did not misspell any words.
    ___ spell always
    ___ spell before
    ✓ spell badly
12. We were excited about getting to preview the new movie.
    ✓ view before
    ___ not view
    ___ view badly

Reading Skills

1. Why do you think a hiker might be both excited and apprehensive about seeing a bear?
   It is interesting and unusual to see bears in the wild, but the hiker might be worried about his or her safety.
2. Why is it bad to come between a mother bear and her cubs?
   The mother bear might become aggressive.
3. What are two types of poisonous snakes you might see along the trail?
   copperheads and rattlesnakes
4. What does the name *armadillo* mean in Spanish?
   little man in armor
5. Check the sentence below that is the best summary for paragraph 4.
   ___ The armadillo can swim if it has to.
   ✓ The armadillo is a strange-looking animal that has many ways to protect itself.

Answer Key

51

Vocabulary Skills

Write the words from the article that have the meanings below.

1. left — departed (Par. 1)
2. movement toward a goal — progress (Par. 1)
3. necessary materials — supplies (Par. 2)
4. experienced; ran into — encountered (Par. 5)
5. extremely thirsty — dehydrated (Par. 5)

Write the word or words from the article that match each abbreviation below.

6. GA Georgia
7. AT Appalachian Trail
8. VA Virginia
9. ME Maine

Write a compound word using two words from each sentence.

10. Sarah and Edie visited several rooms where classes were held. classrooms
11. The hikers endured storms during which there was thunder. thunderstorms
12. Hikers can rest at shelters over the period of time when it is night. nighttime

Reading Skills

1. Why did Sarah and Edie plan to post journal entries and photos? so students would be able to check on their progress
2. Do you think Sarah and Edie would recommend this hike to their friends? Why or why not? Answers will vary.
3. Do you think Sarah and Edie will go hiking together again? Why or why not? Answers will vary.
4. How long did it take Sarah and Edie to complete their hike? four and a half months

Check the word that best completes each sentence.

5. Sarah and Edie thought their trip could be a(n) educational experience for students.
   - ✓ educational
   - ___ normal
   - ___ boring
6. Sarah and Edie were grateful for the help of their families and friends.
   - ___ annoyed
   - ___ entertained
   - ✓ grateful
7. Bad weather is one element of the trip that hikers have to plan for.
   - ___ type
   - ✓ element
   - ___ shelter

53

Vocabulary Skills

Write the words from the story that have the meanings below.

1. liked — enjoyed (Par. 1)
2. footprints — tracks (Par. 1)
3. offered an idea — suggested (Par. 2)
4. a part or portion — section (Par. 6)
5. found — located (Par. 10)

In each row, circle the word that does not belong.

6. squirrel chipmunk (tracks) deer
7. photo (detailed) picture camera
8. (rare) common usual ordinary
9. identify (library) match prove

Reading Skills

1. Check the phrase that best describes the author's purpose.
   - ___ to explain where to look for bears on the Appalachian Trail
   - ✓ to tell a story about the tracks a girl and her dad find while hiking
   - ___ to persuade the reader to take photos of animal tracks
2. Who do you think would rather see a bear—Amira or Dad? Why? Amira because Dad doesn't want to get close to a bear.
3. Name two types of tracks Dad and Amira found. Possible answers: chipmunk, raccoon, deer, skunk
4. Why did Dad and Amira bring lunch with them? so they could spend the whole day in the woods
5. How did Amira use the identification guide? She found pictures that looked like the ones she had taken that afternoon.
6. Why does Dad say, "Good eyes!" to Amira? Amira saw some tiny tracks that Dad would have missed.

Study Skills

The bar graph below shows the types and numbers of animal tracks that Amira found during hikes in the fall. Use the graph to answer the questions that follow.

chipmunk
turkey
skunk
deer
raccoon
possum
0 1 2 3 4 5 6 7 8
Sets of tracks

1. How many sets of deer tracks did Amira find? 6
2. Amira found the same number of tracks for two animals. What animals were they? deer and raccoon
3. What type of track did Amira find only one set of? turkey

55

Vocabulary Skills

Write the words from the story that have the meanings below.

1. something said to a large group — announcement (Par. 1)
2. a group of people gathered together — assembly (Par. 1)
3. worried — nervous (Par. 3)
4. eager to learn — curious (Par. 4)
5. said with surprise or excitement — exclaimed (Par. 5)

Find an antonym in the story for each of the words below.

6. part whole (Par. 1)
7. boring interesting (Par. 2)
8. terrible marvelous (Par. 5)
9. remember forget (Par. 5)

Underline the suffix in each word. Then, write the meaning of the word on the line next to it.

10. comfort<u>able</u> capable of comfort
11. develop<u>ment</u> the act of developing
12. thought<u>less</u> without thought

Reading Skills

1. What does the phrase *bon voyage* mean? happy, safe travels
2. Why will the DiSalvos be moving to France for a year? Mr. DiSalvo will be teaching there.
3. Why do you think Jack feels nervous? He will be leaving home and moving to another country where he does not speak the language and he does not know anyone.
4. How will Jack and Hannah send answers to their classmates' questions? by e-mail

Write **T** before the sentences that are true. Write **F** before the sentences that are false.

5. F Hannah and Jack go to Robert Frost Elementary School.
6. F The DiSalvos are moving to France for two years.
7. T Jack doesn't know what *bon voyage* means.
8. F The students are gathered in the gym.

Study Skills

Look at the dictionary entry below. Then, answer the questions that follow.

pen *(noun)* 1. a fenced-in area where animals are kept
2. a tool used for writing

1. What part of speech is the word *pen*? a noun
2. How many definitions of *pen* are listed in the dictionary entry? 2
3. What is the second definition of *pen*? a tool used for writing

57

Vocabulary Skills

Write the words from the article that have the meanings below.

1. marking the date of something that happened 100 years ago — centennial (Par. 1)
2. the date every year that marks a special event — anniversary (Par. 2)
3. a statue or building that helps people remember something important — monument (Par. 2)
4. a raised surface, like a stage — platform (Par. 3)
5. moves back and forth — sways (Par. 4)

Circle the homophone that correctly completes each sentence below, and write it on the line.

6. The Eiffel Tower reaches so high in the sky, it sways back and forth on windy days. (high, hi)
7. You can see 42 miles away from the top of the tower on a clear day. (sea, see)
8. The Eiffel Tower seems as though it would be very solid. (seams, seems)
9. The Eiffel Tower has been one of the most popular spots to visit in France for many years. (been, bin)

Fill in the blanks below with the possessive form of the word in parentheses.

10. France's most well-known monument is the Eiffel Tower. (France)
11. The tower's construction took about two years. (tower)
12. Alexandre-Gustave Eiffel's design was chosen as the best. (Eiffel)
13. The radio's invention saved the tower. (radio)

Reading Skills

1. Number the events below from **1** to **5** to show the order in which they happened.
   - 4 A mountaineer climbed the side of the tower.
   - 3 The Eiffel Tower was almost torn down.
   - 1 Alexandre-Gustave Eiffel's design was chosen.
   - 5 Two people parachuted from the top deck of the tower.
   - 2 France celebrated its centennial.
2. Why was the Eiffel Tower built? to celebrate the centennial of the French Revolution
3. How long did it take to build the Eiffel Tower? two years
4. How far does the tower sway on windy days? up to five inches
5. Do you think the French will want to tear down the Eiffel Tower in the future? Why or why not? Answers will vary.
6. What saved the Eiffel Tower in 1909? the invention of the radio

Answer Key

59

Vocabulary Skills

Write the words from the story that have the meanings below.

1. too much to handle at once
   overwhelming (Par. 1)
2. a pamphlet or booklet
   brochure (Par. 3)
3. had strong, positive feelings about
   impressed (Par. 6)
4. strict; serious
   stern (Par. 10)
5. divided; set apart
   separated (Par. 18)

Check the meaning of the underlined word in each sentence.

6. Jack spotted Hannah in another room.
   ✓ noticed
   ___ covered with spots
7. Hannah's parents seem very patient.
   ___ a person who is receiving medical help
   ✓ calm and understanding
8. The DiSalvos will probably want to rest after their long day.
   ___ the part that is leftover
   ✓ relax; sleep

An **idiom** is a group of words that has a special meaning. For example, the idiom *hit the hay* means *to go to bed*. Write the idiom from paragraph 17 on the line next to its meaning.

9. stay in a group; not get separated
   stick together

Reading Skills

1. Where are the Impressionist paintings located?
   in the Musée d'Orsay
2. What is the name of one of Mom's favorite artists?
   Claude Monet
3. Why does Dad think the family should have a meeting place?
   in case they get separated
4. Do you think Hannah will want to come back to the Louvre on another day? Why or why not?
   Answers will vary.

Write **H** on the line if the phrase describes Hannah. Write **J** if it describes Jack.

5. J recognizes Monet paintings from a calendar at home
6. H meets a French student named Adrienne
7. H tells Mom and Dad where the Impressionist paintings can be found
8. J suggests the café as a meeting place

Underline the word that best completes each sentence, and write it on the line.

9. Hannah and Jack recognize many of the Impressionist paintings.
   (recognize) ignore dislike
10. For a few minutes, Hannah joins a group of French students.
   loses (joins) admires

61

Vocabulary Skills

Write the words from the article that have the meanings below.

1. periods of one hundred years
   centuries (Par. 2)
2. things that someone owns
   possessions (Par. 3)
3. controlled or run by
   operated (Par. 5)
4. to remake something, especially a structure or a building
   remodel (Par. 5)
5. someone who designs buildings
   architect (Par. 6)
6. something created by humans during a certain period of history
   artifacts (Par. 6)

Circle the homophone that correctly completes each sentence below, and write it on the line.

7. During the reign of King Henry IV, a large section was added to the Louvre. (reign, rain)
8. There were so many buildings in the museum, people could not find the entrance. (sew, so)
9. The museum needed a clearly marked entrance. (kneaded, needed)
10. Before 1793, only royalty was allowed to view the art. (allowed, aloud)

Reading Skills

1. What is the name of the river on which the Louvre is located?
   the Seine
2. Do you think the Louvre will grow even larger in the future? Why or why not?
   Answers will vary.
3. Who owns and operates the Louvre today?
   the French government
4. Name one famous piece of art on display at the Louvre.
   Mona Lisa; Winged Victory; Venus de Milo
5. After what major historical event could the public see the art at the Louvre?
   the French Revolution

Write **B** if the sentence describes something that happened before the Louvre opened to the public. Write **A** if the sentence describes something that happened after the Louvre opened to the public.

6. A Mitterand announced a project to expand the Louvre.
7. B The French Revolution began.
8. B One part of the Louvre protected Paris from the Vikings.
9. A I. M. Pei built a glass pyramid for the entrance.
10. B The Louvre was turned into a palace.

63

Vocabulary Skills

Write the words from the article that have the meanings below.

1. stood up against
   challenged (Par. 1)
2. demanding and unchanging
   strict (Par. 2)
3. discouraged; puzzled and helpless
   frustrated (Par. 3)
4. resembling, or looking like, things that are real
   realistic (Par. 4)
5. not being controlled by others
   freedom (Par. 6)

Find an antonym in the article for each of the words below.

6. fearful brave (Par. 1)
7. rejected accepted (Par. 2)
8. boring interesting (Par. 4)
9. complete unfinished (Par. 5)
10. negative positive (Par. 5)

Reading Skills

1. What was the Academy?
   a French government organization with a strict set of rules about art
2. Why didn't Louis Leroy like the paintings of the Impressionists?
   He thought the paintings looked unfinished.
3. Name two Impressionists other than Claude Monet.
   Possible answers: Pierre-Auguste Renoir; Alfred Sisley; Edgar Degas; Mary Cassatt.
4. Which came first—frustrated artists were given their own show by the Academy, or Louis Leroy came up with the name *Impressionists*?
   The frustrated artists were given their own show by the academy.

Write **F** before the sentences that are facts. Write **O** before the sentences that are opinions.

5. F The Impressionists challenged ideas about art.
6. O It is not fair that artists couldn't create the art they wanted to create.
7. F The Impressionists wanted to show movement and light in their paintings.
8. O The paintings of the Impressionists look unfinished.
9. O Artists should be allowed to have the freedom they need to be creative.
10. Check the sentence that is the best summary for paragraph 4.
   ___ The Impressionists did not think that paintings that looked like photographs were very interesting.
   ✓ Instead of painting realistically, the Impressionists wanted to explore light and movement.
   ___ According to the Academy, all art should look realistic.

65

Vocabulary Skills

Write the words from the article that have the meanings below.

1. get used to
   adjust (Par. 1)
2. best parts
   highlights (Par. 1)
3. moved quickly
   sped (Par. 2)
4. people who ride bicycles
   cyclists (Par. 2)
5. sweet-tasting baked goods
   pastries (Par. 3)

Read each word below. Then, write the letter of its synonym on the line beside the word.

6. c	wonderful	a.	section
7. d	famous	b.	chewy
8. a	part	c.	terrific
9. e	answer	d.	well-known
10. b	rubbery	e.	response

Write **S** if the possessive word is singular. Write **P** if it is plural.

11. S Hannah's
12. P classes'
13. S France's
14. S Jack's
15. S photograph's
16. P cyclists'

Reading Skills

1. What French word do Hannah and Jack use in the greeting of their e-mail?
   bonjour
2. What is the Tour de France?
   the most famous bicycle race in the world
3. Do you think Hannah and Jack will try more unfamiliar foods while they are in France? Why or why not?
   Answers will vary.
4. Why didn't Mr. DiSalvo go to the top of the Eiffel Tower with his family?
   He doesn't like heights.
5. Check the phrase that best describes the author's purpose.
   ___ to persuade the reader to try *escargots*
   ✓ to tell a story about a family's experiences in France
   ___ to convince the reader to take a trip to Paris

Circle the word that best completes each sentence, and write it on the line.

6. You can see far into the distance from the top of the Eiffel Tower.
   height miles (distance)
7. Without the butter, the *escargots* would be mostly tasteless.
   (tasteless) rubbery cooked
8. The French have made the DiSalvos feel welcome.
   ignored (welcome) friendly

Answer Key

67

Vocabulary Skills

Write the words from the article that have the meanings below.

1. information to let the public know about something
   publicity (Par. 2)
2. something that happens once a year
   annual (Par. 2)
3. ground; land
   terrain (Par. 4)
4. shirt without a collar
   jersey (Par. 4)
5. a type of award
   trophy (Par. 5)

Check the meaning of the underlined word in each sentence.

6. The racers must be careful not to fall when they are riding at such high speeds.
   ____ autumn; the season that comes after summer
   ✓ to drop or tumble
7. Not every racer can complete the whole course.
   ✓ to be able to
   ____ a metal container
8. Some cyclists like riding because it makes them feel like they can fly.
   ____ an insect
   ✓ to move through the air with wings

Reading Skills

1. Check the phrase that best describes the author's purpose.
   ____ to explain why the Tour de France is the most interesting race in Europe
   ✓ to share some facts about the Tour de France
   ____ to entertain the reader with funny stories about cyclists
2. Check the sentence that best states the main idea of the selection.
   ✓ The Tour de France is the most difficult and popular bicycle race in the world.
   ____ The Tour de France includes different stages so the riders do not have to bike all night.
   ____ The racers may get to wear different colored jerseys throughout the race.
3. How many cyclists begin the race?
   150
4. Why is the yellow jersey the most important?
   It identifies the leader.
5. Who was the first American cyclist to win the Tour de France?
   Greg LeMond
6. What are two historical events that have interrupted the Tour de France?
   World War I and World War II

69

Vocabulary Skills

Write the words from the article that have the meanings below.

1. thought to be
   considered (Par. 1)
2. not professional; a beginner
   amateur (Par. 2)
3. success in hard competitions
   victories (Par. 4)
4. the ability to do something for a long period of time
   endurance (Par. 5)

Write the idiom from paragraph 4 on the line next to its meaning.

5. about to happen; coming up soon ____
   around the corner

Circle the homophone that correctly completes each sentence below, and write it on the line.

6. Lance Armstrong rode two thousand miles in the Tour de France. (**rode**, road)
7. Cyclists in the Tour de France ride through several European countries. (threw, **through**)
8. Armstrong won the race seven times! (one, **won**)
9. Cyclists wear special clothes when they are competing. (**clothes**, close)

Reading Skills

1. Number the events below from **1** to **5** to show the order in which they happened.
   5 Armstrong won the Tour de France for the seventh time.
   4 Armstrong became sick with cancer.
   1 Lance Armstrong was born in Plano, Texas.
   2 Armstrong began to compete in triathlons.
   3 Armstrong won the World Cycling Championship.
2. Check the words that best describe Lance Armstrong.
   ✓ determined
   ____ lazy
   ✓ athletic
   ____ scientific
   ✓ strong-willed

Circle the word that best completes each sentence, and write it on the line.

3. One of Armstrong's greatest influences is his mother.
   influences regrets reasons
4. Armstrong did not allow cancer to stand in his way.
   prove consider **allow**
5. Armstrong's biggest accomplishment is winning the Tour de France seven times.
   goal **accomplishment** future
6. What is the Tour DuPont?
   one of the most important bicycle races in the United States

71

Vocabulary Skills

Write the words from the story that have the meanings below.

1. a party for a special occasion
   celebration (Par. 1)
2. give or offer
   contribute (Par. 1)
3. sadly
   glumly (Par. 4)
4. mixed-up; puzzled
   confused (Par. 6)
5. creative; first of its kind
   original (Par. 10)

Write the idiom from paragraph 3 on the line next to its meaning.

6. to think about something sleep on it

In each row, circle the word that does not belong.

7. bird falcon **protect** nests
8. recycle **litter** reuse environment
9. **extinct** cities skyscrapers bridges
10. original **weird** unique creative

Fill in the blanks below with the possessive form of the word in parentheses.

11. Akiko's expression was confused. (Akiko)
12. Akiko liked Ben's idea. (Ben)
13. The falcons' nests were located in New York City. (falcons)
14. The students' tables would have many different themes. (students)

Reading Skills

1. On what day is Earth Day celebrated?
   April 22
2. Why do you think it is more dangerous for peregrine falcons to live in cities?
   There are more cars and more places for them to get hurt in cities.
3. What is Ben's perfect idea?
   to have a computer that displays the Web cam image of the falcon nest
4. Why does Akiko say that Earth Day seems far away all of a sudden?
   because she is excited about their idea for a table
5. Check the words that describe Ben.
   ____ lonely
   ✓ excited
   ✓ enthusiastic
   ____ boring
   ____ hilarious
   ✓ creative
6. On the lines below, write a summary for paragraph 1.
   Ben and Akiko's school was having an Earth Day celebration.

73

Vocabulary Skills

Write the words from the article that have the meanings below.

1. having babies; reproducing
   breeding (Par. 1)
2. in danger of becoming extinct
   endangered (Par. 1)
3. not in the wild; under someone's control
   captivity (Par. 2)
4. become used to
   adapted (Par. 3)
5. watch closely
   monitor (Par. 5)

Write the words from the article that match the abbreviations below.

6. m.p.h. miles per hour
7. NY New York
8. U.S. United States
9. CA California
10. ft. feet

Reading Skills

1. What caused the falcons' eggshells to become too thin?
   the use of the pesticide DDT
2. How high in the air do falcons make their nests?
   50 to 200 feet in the air
3. How are the places that peregrine falcons nest in the wild similar to the places they nest in cities?
   They are both in high places.
4. Do you think people will continue to help protect peregrine falcons in the future? Why or why not?
   Answers will vary.

Write **T** before the sentences that are true. Write **F** before the sentences that are false.

5. F Only the mother raises the peregrine falcon babies.
6. F DDT is harmless to peregrine falcons.
7. T Peregrine falcons usually mate for life.
8. T Some peregrine falcons are bred in captivity.
9. T Peregrine falcons can fly almost 200 miles per hour.

Study Skills

The graph below shows the fastest speed at which each person or animal can move. Use the graph to answer the questions that follow.

Speed of Movement (in m.p.h.)

peregrine falcon
coyote
deer
dragonfly
average child
0 30 60 90 120 150 180

1. Which two animals travel at about the same speed?
   a deer and a dragonfly
2. Which can move more quickly, a coyote or a deer?
   a coyote

Answer Key

Vocabulary Skills

Check the meaning of the underlined word in each sentence.

1. The volunteers stored their supplies in the trunk of the car.
   - ✓ the back of an automobile, often used for storage
   - ____ the long nose of an elephant
2. Their goal was to save the young birds.
   - ✓ something a person works hard for
   - ____ a score for driving a ball into a certain area
3. It does not take long for the fledglings to learn to fly.
   - ____ to wish for something
   - ✓ having a great length

Reading Skills

Circle the word that best completes each sentence, and write it on the line.

1. It is not as dangerous to learn to fly in natural areas.
   fun (dangerous) interesting
2. Young falcons in urban areas can run into buildings or get hit by cars.
   (urban) country mountain
3. A fledgling is a bird that is learning how to fly.
   falcon (fledgling) volunteer
4. Name one thing for which Salt Lake City is famous.
   the Great Salt Lake; hosting the Olympics
5. How old are the peregrine falcon babies when they begin learning how to fly?
   five or six weeks old
6. Why do the volunteers wear bright orange vests?
   to protect themselves; so they can be easily seen
7. Why do the volunteers work such long hours to help save the young peregrine falcons?
   They know that the work they are doing makes a difference.
8. Check the phrase that best describes the author's purpose.
   - ____ to explain why peregrine falcons don't take good care of their babies
   - ____ to entertain the reader with a funny story
   - ✓ to tell about a group of volunteers who saved some young peregrine falcons

Study Skills

Use the schedule of volunteer hours to answer the questions below.

Volunteer Schedule

Name	Mon.	Tues.	Wed.	Thurs.	Fri.
Margaret	8–12		8–12		
Omar	4–6	4–6	4–6	4–6	
Maria			1–5		1–5
Sam	12–4	12–4	12–4		12–4
Dennis		8–12		8–12	
Linh				12–6	12–6

1. Which day is Sam not scheduled to work?
   Thursday
2. How many days a week does Maria work?
   2

75

Vocabulary Skills

Write the words from the story that have the meanings below.

1. easy to break
   brittle (Par. 1)
2. to hold in place
   anchor (Par. 3)
3. a solid geometric shape that looks like a globe
   sphere (Par. 3)
4. the use of scientific knowledge to make new things
   technology (Par. 7)
5. pointing; motioning toward
   gesturing (Par. 10)

A **word family** is a group of words that have the same letter combinations. For example, the words *could*, *would*, and *should* are in the same word family because they all contain the *-ould* combination. Circle the words in each row that are part of the word family in parentheses.

6. (*-ight*) write (delight) (tight) tiger
7. (*-ought*) (fought) our (brought) broke
8. (*-ight*) (night) (right) rice (sight)

Fill in the blanks below with the possessive form of the word in parentheses.

9. Grandpa's memories of the fair make good stories. (Grandpa)
10. Grandpa went to the World's Fair in 1939. (World)
11. The poster's purpose was to advertise the fair. (poster)
12. Henry remembers eating pastries called elephants' ears at a fair. (elephants)

Reading Skills

1. Number the events below from **1** to **5** to show the order in which they happened.
   - 3 Grandpa tells Henry that the fair was about technology and things that were new.
   - 1 Grandpa is pricing things to sell at a yard sale.
   - 2 Grandpa and Henry unroll the poster.
   - 5 Henry says the fair is not like the ones he has visited.
   - 4 Grandpa remembers seeing a television for the first time.
2. What major event in history did the 1939–40 World's Fair follow?
   the Great Depression
3. Why did Americans want something that could give them hope?
   They had been through some hard times.
4. What were the biggest attractions at the fair?
   the Trylon and the Perisphere
5. Why do you think Grandpa says the fair was "a once-in-a-lifetime kind of experience"?
   Answers will vary.

Circle the word that best completes each sentence, and write it on the line.

6. Grandpa attended the 1939 World's Fair in New York.
   forgot (attended) disliked
7. People wanted to see the latest technology at the fair.
   (latest) oldest strangest

77

Vocabulary Skills

Words that have two middle consonants are divided into syllables between the consonants, for example, *pic/ture* or *bas/ket*. Divide the words below into syllables using a slash (/).

1. p u r/p o s e
2. b u r/g e r
3. t a r/g e t
4. c o m/p a r e

Underline the compound word in each sentence. Then, write the two words that make up each compound.

5. The 1904 Olympics were held at the fairgrounds.
   fair grounds
6. The Montreal Expos are a baseball team.
   base ball
7. Ask your grandparents if they ever went to a World's Fair when they were young.
   grand parents
8. Maria won a goldfish at her town's summer fair.
   gold fish

Reading Skills

1. Why were World's Fairs first begun?
   to show all of the latest technology in one place
2. Why was it important for Chicago to host the World's Fair in 1893?
   to show the world that Chicago had recovered from the Great Chicago Fire
3. Name two structures that were built for a World's Fair but still exist today.
   Answers will vary.
4. How many countries were part of the largest fair in Missouri?
   62
5. Why did people need to be cheered up during the Great Depression?
   Life had been hard for people during the Depression.

Write **F** before the sentences that are facts. Write **O** before the sentences that are opinions.

6. F The Museum of Science and Industry was built in Chicago.
7. F About 50 million people came to see Expo '67.
8. O The St. Louis World's Fair was the most exciting fair.
9. F The 1939 World's Fair had a time capsule.
10. O It is more fun to ride the Ferris wheel than any other amusement park ride.
11. Check the line beside the word that tells what type of selection this is.
    - ____ fiction
    - ____ fantasy
    - ✓ nonfiction

79

Vocabulary Skills

Write the words from the article that have the meanings below.

1. sudden and exciting
   thrill (Par. 1)
2. people who write or study about history.
   historians (Par. 1)
3. well-liked
   popular (Par. 2)
4. no longer used
   abandoned (Par. 3)
5. success and wealth
   prosperity (Par. 3)

Read each word below. Then, write the letter of its synonym on the line beside the word.

6. c during		a. demonstrate
7. a show		b. stay
8. e constructed		c. while
9. b remain		d. attempt
10. d try		e. built

Write **S** if the possessive word is singular. Write **P** if it is plural.

11. S coaster's	12. S park's
13. P Russians'	14. P rides'
15. S mountain's	16. P tracks'

Reading Skills

1. Which country had the first thrill ride that looped upside down?
   France
2. How many people rode the Mauch Chunk Railway every year?
   35,000
3. What was the name of the first roller coaster in an amusement park?
   Switchback Railway
4. Why were old roller coasters torn down during World War II?
   so the wood and steel could be reused in new ways to help fight the war
5. Many amusement parks closed during the Great Depression because people did not have enough money to go to them.
6. Number the events below from **1** to **5** to show the order in which they happened.
   - 2 A coal-mining company built a tunnel through a mountain.
   - 3 The Switchback Railway opened at Coney Island.
   - 1 The Russians built wooden slides and covered them with ice.
   - 5 Amusement parks in Ohio and California have the most roller coasters.
   - 4 Many amusement parks closed during the Great Depression.
7. Check the sentence that best states the main idea of the selection.
   - ____ Roller coasters are popular again, and you do not have to travel far to find one.
   - ✓ People around the world have loved thrill rides for many years and still do today.
   - ____ People wanted to have fun and enjoy themselves during the "Roaring Twenties."

81

Answer Key

Vocabulary Skills

Write the words from the story that have the meanings below.

1. not bought at a store
homemade (Par. 2)
2. not calmly
impatiently (Par. 2)
3. hung
draped (Par. 3)
4. desire for food
appetite (Par. 5)
5. a piece of cloth that protects the clothes you wear beneath it
apron (Par. 13)

Write the idiom from paragraph 3 on the line next to its meaning.

6. not feeling well under the weather
7. Find a homophone in paragraph 13 for the word *peace*.
piece

Write a compound word using two words from each sentence.

8. Tess was tired of being in the room where her bed was kept.
bedroom
9. Tess had an ache in her head.
headache
10. Because she was sick, Tess was wearing the gown that she usually wore at night.
nightgown

Reading Skills

1. Do you think Tess will ask Nonnie to tell her more stories from the quilt? Why or why not?
Answers will vary.
2. Which piece of the quilt does Tess like best?
the red flowered block
3. What does Nonnie mean when she says, "This quilt has seen a lot of things"?
The quilt has been there for many events in her life.
4. How did Nonnie's mother tear her apron?
rescuing Nonnie's brother from the creek
5. What problem does Tess have at the beginning of the story?
She is bored because she has been sick for a week.
6. **Dialogue** is what a character says. The words in dialogue are always in quotation marks. On the line below, write the words that are dialogue in paragraph 12.
"What about this one?"
7. Check the phrase that best describes the author's purpose.
✓ to entertain the reader with a story about a girl who learns about her grandma's quilt
___ to explain how to make a quilt at home
___ to tell the reader facts about Nonnie's childhood

83

Vocabulary Skills

Write the words from the article that have the meanings below.

1. small pieces
scraps (Par. 3)
2. useful; having a purpose
practical (Par. 3)
3. different types
variety (Par. 3)
4. ability to make original or artistic things
creativity (Par. 4)
5. to talk and spend time with friends
socialize (Par. 4)

In each row, circle the word that does not belong.

6. (colonial) practical useful sensible
7. stitch sew (express) weave
8. pattern design decoration (scrap)

Divide the words below into syllables using a slash (/).

9. p r a c/t i c e
10. f a b/r i c
11. l a r/g e r

Circle the homophone that correctly completes each sentence below, and write it on the line.

12. It takes many days to sew a quilt by hand. (days) daze)
13. Today, some quilts are made using a machine. (maid (made)
14. A decorative border is often sewn around the edge of a quilt. (border) boarder)
15. It is not difficult for a quilter to fix a small hole in a quilt. (hole) whole)

Reading Skills

1. How did Turkish soldiers use quilted material?
They wore it under their armor.
2. What is a patchwork quilt?
a quilt made of many tiny pieces of fabric sewn together in pretty patterns
3. What is a quilting bee?
a gathering of women who help each other with their quilts
4. Why were quilts practical?
They used up scraps of material. They kept people warm.
5. What historical event was Susan B. Anthony a part of?
women's right to vote
6. How can a quilt tell a story?
It can have images of a family. It might be made up of pieces of clothing that have stories behind them.
7. Check the sentence that best states the main idea of the selection.
___ A quilt is made of two pieces of fabric with a layer of batting sewn in between.
___ Quilting bees were a good place for women to socialize while they were still doing useful work.
✓ Quilts, which are both beautiful and practical, were a way for women throughout history to reuse scraps of material to make something useful.

85

Vocabulary Skills

Find a synonym in the article for each of the words below.

1. colorful decorative (Par. 1)
2. journey trip (Par. 2)
3. captured caught (Par. 2)
4. relatives ancestors (Par. 3)

Circle the words in each row that are part of the same word family.

5. (*-ight*) (moonlight) (fright) excite frost
6. (*-ought*) (fought) (bought) fox boot
7. (*-ould*) (should) cold (could) wood

Reading Skills

1. Check the sentence below that is the best summary for paragraph 4.
✓ Some people think that patterns like the log cabin, the wagon wheel, the bear's paw, and the star were used to tell secret codes.
___ The bear's paw told the slaves to walk north over the mountains.
2. What was the Underground Railroad?
It was the name used for the route that slaves took north.
3. What did a star pattern on a quilt mean?
It meant the slaves should follow the North Star.
4. Why did the slaves want to travel north?
They wanted to live in freedom.
5. Why don't historians know for certain whether the quilts were used by slaves to communicate information about escaping?
None of the quilts have survived long enough to prove the stories. The stories were not written down.
6. Do you think the mystery of the slave quilts will be solved in the future? Why or why not?
Answers will vary.

Circle the word that best completes each sentence, and write it on the line.

7. Quilts may have been used to pass information to other slaves.
(information) generations patterns
8. None of the quilts survived long enough for historians to study.
agreed (survived) proved
9. Some historians have different ideas about the purpose of the quilts.
few studied (different)

Study Skills

Guide words are printed at the top of each page in a dictionary. The guide word at the left is the first word on the page. The guide word at the right is the last word on the page. Check each word that could be found on a page having the guide words shown in dark print.

1. **answer—appear**
✓ anteater ___ apple ___ annex
2. **wheel—wing**
✓ wind ___ wax ✓ where
3. **ridge—roar**
✓ rind ___ reality ___ route

87

Vocabulary Skills

Write the words from the article that have the meanings below.

1. to happen in turns; every other one
alternate (Step 1)
2. full of importance
meaningful (Step 2)
3. place in a particular order
arrange (Step 3)
4. figure out; decide
determine (Step 5)

Check the meaning of the underlined word in each sentence.

5. Sewing with a machine can make quite a racket.
✓ a loud noise
___ a paddle used to hit a ball
6. Even a scrap of material can be used in a quilt.
___ an argument
✓ a small piece

Reading Skills

1. Check the phrase that best describes the author's purpose.
___ to persuade the reader that quilts are difficult to make
✓ to explain how to make a paper quilt
___ to tell about the history of quilts
2. Name two ideas of pictures you could include in your quilt.
Answers will vary.
3. How big should the squares of paper be?
4-inch squares
4. What information should people be able to get by looking at your quilt?
the story your quilt tells about you
5. Number the steps below from **1** to **5** to show the order in which they appear in the selection.
3 Decorate your squares of paper.
2 Decide what type of quilt to make.
5 Attach the rows of squares using tape or glue.
4 Arrange the squares on a table.
1 Gather the materials you will need.
6. Check the line beside the word or words that tell what type of nonfiction selection this is.
___ biography
✓ how-to text
___ history

Study Skills

Use the index below to answer the questions that follow.

Index

Fabrics 17–24
History of Quilts 2–8
Patterns 36–42
Quilting with a Machine 25–35

1. On what pages can you find information about patterns?
36–42
2. Which topic is covered on the greatest number of pages?
Quilting with a Machine

89

Answer Key

Vocabulary Skills

Write the words from the story that have the meanings below.

1. built up over time — accumulated (Par. 2)
2. lost color or brightness — faded (Par. 4)
3. a look that shows a mood — expression (Par. 10)
4. a group of four people — quartet (Par. 13)
5. signatures of a famous person — autographs (Par. 13)
6. Find the simile in paragraph 11, and write it on the lines below. — as smooth as honey
7. Write the idiom from paragraph 14 on the line next to its meaning. something extra; a bonus — icing on the cake

Divide the words below into syllables using a slash (/).

8. i/t e m
9. r e/c o r d
10. r e/l a x

Reading Skills

Write **F** before the sentences that are facts. Write **O** before the sentences that are opinions.

1. O Uncle Frank's band was the best jazz band of the last 50 years.
2. F Devon is helping Uncle Frank clean the attic.
3. O Devon should learn how to play the trumpet.
4. F Uncle Frank's band played at Missouri jazz clubs.
5. F Aunt Clara was in the same band as Uncle Frank.

Write **D** before the phrases that describe Devon and **F** before the phrases that describe Uncle Frank.

6. D sneezes because of the dust in the attic
7. D has never played the trumpet before
8. F thinks Aunt Clara had a beautiful voice
9. F has not played the trumpet in many years
10. D holds up a stack of records
11. What do you think Uncle Frank means when he says, "Once the jazz bug bites you, there's no going back"? — Once you like listening to or playing jazz music, you will always like it.
12. What does Devon want to do when he hears the music on the records? — tap his toes or drum his fingers on the coffee table
13. Do you think Devon will learn to play the trumpet in the future? Why or why not? — Answers will vary.

91

Vocabulary Skills

Write the words from the article that have the meanings below.

1. different forms of something — versions (Par. 1)
2. twisted into a spiral — coiled (Par. 2)
3. the Middle Ages in Europe, around A.D. 500 to 1450 — medieval (Par. 3)
4. something that blocks an opening but can be opened or closed — valves (Par. 5)

Find an antonym in the article for each of the words below.

5. latest — earliest (Par. 1)
6. modern — ancient (Par. 2)
7. lowest — highest (Par. 6)
8. wider — narrower (Par. 7)

Write a compound word using two words in each sentence.

9. The trumpeter puts his or her mouth on the piece shaped like a cup. — mouthpiece
10. A shell that was found near the sea was one early version of a trumpet. — seashell
11. The members of the band boarded a plane that would fly through the air. — airplane
12. The band had to be in St. Louis by the end of the week. — weekend

Reading Skills

Circle the word that best completes each sentence below, and write it on the line.

1. In a horn, the longer the sound has to go, the lower the note will be. — higher louder (lower)
2. Wider bells produce a softer sound. — (Wider) Narrower Older
3. The trumpeter has to vibrate his or her lips in the mouthpiece. — place (vibrate) stop
4. In what way did people in medieval times use the trumpet to communicate? — Different sections of the army would use the trumpet to tell each other important information.
5. Why do some trumpeters use a mute? — to make the sound muffled
6. What kind of sound will a trumpet make if the trumpeter does not push down any valves? — a higher sound
7. What was one reason the trumpet became recognized as an important musical instrument? — Valves were introduced, and the trumpet could make a greater variety of sounds.
8. On the lines below, write a summary for paragraphs 2 and 3. — Trumpets have been used to communicate since ancient times.

93

Vocabulary Skills

Write the words from the article that have the meanings below.

1. doing something in front of an audience — performing (Par. 1)
2. a name that is used instead of a given name — nickname (Par. 1)
3. not following a usual pattern — irregular (Par. 3)
4. easy to remember — memorable (Par. 4)
5. fun and interesting; amusing — entertaining (Par. 4)

Read each word below. Then, write the letter of its antonym on the line beside the word.

6. a unusual	a. regular
7. b purposely	b. accidentally
8. d united	c. stingy
9. c generous	d. divided

Divide the words below into syllables using a slash (/).

10. n i c k/n a m e
11. l i f e/t i m e
12. k e y/b o a r d

Write **S** if the possessive word is singular. Write **P** if it is plural.

13. S Dizzy's
14. S band's
15. P musicians'
16. P records'

Reading Skills

1. How many children were there in Dizzy Gillespie's family? — 9
2. What instrument did Charlie Parker play? — saxophone
3. Name one thing that was different about bebop. — Possible answer: It moved more quickly; the notes flowed with an irregular pattern.
4. Why was Dizzy's trumpet bent? — Someone had once accidentally fallen on it.
5. How do we know that Dizzy cared about social causes? — He did some work for the United Nations. He was a civil rights activist.

Read the phrases below. Write **D** next to the phrase if it describes Dizzy, write **C** if it describes Charlie, and write **B** if it describes them both.

6. D born in South Carolina
7. C played the saxophone
8. B made bebop popular
9. D played a bent trumpet
10. Check the sentence that best states the main idea of the selection.
    - ✓ Dizzy Gillespie was a talented musician and a caring person.
    - Dizzy Gillespie was the youngest of nine children.
    - Dizzy Gillespie played with saxophonist Charlie Parker.

95

Vocabulary Skills

In each row, circle the words that belong together.

1. (music) (jazz) railroad (blues)
2. (different) similar (variety) (diverse)
3. popular (words) (lyrics) (singing)
4. records (train) (railroad) (sleeper car)

Underline the compound word in each sentence. Then, write the two words that make up each compound.

5. The railroad tracks run near my apartment building. — rail, road
6. The afternoon train will arrive at 3:00. — after, noon
7. Louis Armstrong was an outstanding musician. — out, standing
8. Without jazz, the world of music would be very different. — with, out

Reading Skills

1. Why is America called "a great melting pot"? — Different cultures of America's citizens combine to make one diverse culture.
2. What are two adjectives the author uses to describe the blues? — sad, hopeful
3. What two things helped jazz become known around the country? — railroads, phonographs
4. What sorts of sounds does a singer who is scatting make? — nonsense sounds that are like the music an instrument would make
5. How did jazz help end segregation? — The white bandleader Benny Goodman hired an African American pianist and guitarist.

Write **T** before the sentences that are true. Write **F** before the sentences that are false.

6. F The blues are a type of railroad car.
7. F The 1940s were known as the Jazz Age.
8. T Many African American men worked for the Pullman Company.
9. F At first, jazz was mostly played in Georgia.
10. T Ella Fitzgerald was a famous scat singer.

Study Skills

You can use a computer's reference system to help you find a book you want in a library. Use the information below to answer the questions that follow.

Call No:	667.42 HO
Author:	Hoffman, William C.
Title:	Jazz Through the Years
Publisher:	Avondale Press

1. What is the title of the book? — Jazz Through the Years
2. What is the author's last name? — Hoffman
3. What is the book's call number? — 667.42 HO

97

Answer Key

Vocabulary Skills

Write the words from the story that have the meanings below.

1. an event that celebrates something
festival Par. 2
2. became aware of; figured out
realized Par. 7
3. having all around
surrounded Par. 7
4. getting ready
preparing Par. 9
5. a time in an older person's life when he or she stops working
retirement Par. 10
6. a regular beat or sound
rhythm Par. 11

Circle the homophone that correctly completes each sentence below, and write it on the line.

7. Devon's mom packed a lunch to eat at the festival. (packed, pact)
8. Uncle Frank blew into the mouthpiece of the trumpet. (blue, blew)
9. Uncle Frank and Aunt Clara made a wonderful pair. (pear, pair)
10. Mom heard Uncle Frank's band play in Missouri. (heard, herd)

Underline the prefix in each word. Then, write the meaning of the word.

11. impolite not polite
12. nonidentical not identical
13. redeliver deliver again

Reading Skills

1. Check the phrase that best describes the author's purpose.
___ to persuade the reader to learn how to play a musical instrument
✓ to entertain the reader with a story about a boy watching his uncle perform
___ to explain how to play the trumpet
2. Name two things that were in the picnic lunch Mom packed.
Answers will vary.
3. Why does Will think Uncle Frank might be nervous?
He has not played in public in a long time.
4. Why has Uncle Frank started playing the trumpet again?
He missed playing music and being surrounded by people who love it.
5. Why do you think Devon grins at his mom and Will at the end of the story?
He felt happy to see his uncle play the trumpet, and he couldn't wait to learn to play like his uncle.
6. Check the words that you think describe Devon.
✓ curious
✓ excited
___ stingy
✓ supportive
___ angry
___ impatient

99

Vocabulary Skills

Write the words from the story that have the meanings below.

1. a greenhouse where plants are grown and displayed
conservatory Par. 1
2. rose very high in the air
towered Par. 3
3. easily affected by something
sensitive Par. 6
4. responds
reacts Par. 8
5. from a particular place
native Par. 11

Read each pair of words listed below. If the words are synonyms, write **S** on the line. If the words are antonyms, write **A** on the line.

6. S enormous huge
7. A gently harshly
8. A unusual common
9. S traps captures
10. S smiling grinning

Write the possessive form of the word in parentheses on the line below.

11. Mrs. Singh's class visited a conservatory. (Singh)
12. The palm tree's leaves were green and spiky. (tree)
13. The class laughed at Terrell's joke. (Terrell)
14. The students' assignment was to choose a favorite plant. (students)

Reading Skills

1. What happens if a person touches the leaves of the sensitive plant?
The leaves fold up.
2. What is another name for the sensitive plant?
mimosa
3. Where does the Venus flytrap grow in the wild?
in North and South Carolina
4. How does the Venus flytrap know that an insect has landed on it?
It uses its trigger hairs.
5. Do you think Beatriz and Abby will visit the conservatory again? Why or why not?
Answers will vary.
6. Check the sentence below that is the best summary for paragraph 11.
___ The Venus flytrap lives in the Carolinas.
✓ The Venus flytrap attracts and captures insects and small animals.
___ The Venus flytrap has sensitive trigger hairs.

Read the sentences below. Write **A** next to the sentence if it describes Abby. Write **B** if it describes Beatriz.

7. A Her brother had a Venus flytrap.
8. B She didn't know that plants could move.
9. B The Venus flytrap is her favorite.
10. A The sensitive plant is her favorite.

101

Vocabulary Skills

In each row, circle the word that does not belong.

1. (light) moss fern violet
2. pebbles gravel (jar) stones
3. moist damp (dry) wet
4. total (part) complete entire

Check the meaning of the underlined word in each sentence.

5. A fern has many small leaves.
___ to go away
✓ the flat green part of a plant
6. A terrarium does not need much light.
✓ a form of energy from the sun
___ not heavy
7. If there is not room in the yard for a garden, make a terrarium.
✓ the area around a house
___ 36 inches

Reading Skills

1. Check the phrase that best describes the author's purpose.
___ to show that terrariums are the best type of gardens to have
___ to tell the history of terrariums
✓ to explain how to assemble and care for a terrarium
2. What kind of a container can you use to make a terrarium?
a large glass or plastic jar with a lid; a fish bowl covered with plastic wrap
3. Why don't you have to water the plants in a terrarium very often?
The lid keeps moisture from escaping. The water gets recycled.
4. Name two types of plants that do well in terrariums.
Possible answers: small ferns; moss; violets; baby tears; begonias
5. What kind of light will your terrarium need?
a bit of sunlight, but not direct sun or complete shade
6. What can happen if you put too much water in a terrarium, and you do not take off the lid to let some of the water evaporate?
The plants can rot.

Study Skills

A table of contents is one of the first pages in a book. It shows the chapters that are in a book. It also shows the page on which each chapter begins. Use the table of contents below to answer the questions.

Table of Contents

1. What is the title of Chapter 3?
Large Terrariums
2. On what page does Chapter 5 begin?
48
3. What chapter would you use if you wanted some information about terrarium animals?
Chapter 4

103

Vocabulary Skills

Write the words from the article that have the meanings below.

1. to be careful not to use up
conserve Par. 2
2. a journey that is made for a specific purpose
expedition Par. 3
3. created or established
founded Par. 3
4. threatened; exposed to danger
endangered Par. 5
5. people who work to preserve and protect something
conservationists Par. 5

Write the idiom from paragraph 6 on the line next to its meaning, and write it on the line.

6. have the solution hold the key

Circle the homophone that correctly completes each sentence below.

7. The bloom of the plant beside you is a beautiful pale yellow. (pail, pale)
8. I passed the Orchid House without going inside. (past, passed)
9. There is a large pane of stained glass in the window of the conservatory. (pane, pain)

Reading Skills

1. Where is the United States Botanic Garden located?
in Washington, D.C.
2. Name two things plants provide for people.
Possible answers: food; shelter; medicine; fuels
3. Who was Admiral Wilkes?
He led the expedition to the South Seas.
4. Why do you think that different categories of plants are located in different areas at the U.S. Botanic Garden?
They need to have different types of environments.
5. How can plants help save people's lives?
Some plants are used to make life-saving medicines.
6. Do you think the U.S. Botanic Garden will continue to grow and preserve new kinds of plants? Why or why not?
Answers will vary.

Write **F** before the sentences that are facts. Write **O** before the sentences that are opinions.

7. F Plants provide the oxygen we breathe.
8. O The most interesting plants are the ones in the Desert House.
9. F Admiral Wilkes led the expedition to the South Seas.
10. F The *Brighamia insignis* grows in Hawaii.
11. O The orchid is the most beautiful type of plant at the U.S. Botanic Garden.

105

Answer Key

107

Vocabulary Skills

Write the words from the article that have the meanings below.

1. come in contact with
   encountered (Par. 1)
2. a smell
   odor (Par. 2)
3. a sample that is used for scientific study
   specimen (Par. 3)
4. sometime in the future
   eventually (Par. 4)
5. can be found
   exist (Par. 5)

Find a synonym in the story for each of the words below.

6. unusual rare (Par. 5)
7. moment second (Par. 6)
8. often frequent (Par. 6)
9. chance opportunity (Par. 7)

Underline the compound word in each sentence. Then, write the two words that make up each compound.

10. Some plants are raised in greenhouses.
    green houses
11. People like to have frequent updates when the titan arum is blooming.
    up dates
12. Everyone seems to be interested in this enormous, stinky plant!
    every one
13. Television stations videotape the plant while it is in bloom.
    video tape

Reading Skills

1. For what is the titan arum best known?
   for having the smelliest flower
2. Where does the titan arum grow in the wild?
   Sumatra, Indonesia
3. Why do you think people are so eager to see the titan arum?
   It is very rare and unusual.
4. The next time a titan arum blooms in the United States, do you think people will line up to see it? Why or why not?
   Answers will vary.
5. Why does the titan arum smell so awful?
   It has to attract the insects that will pollinate it.
6. Check the sentence that best states the main idea of the selection.
   ___ The bloom of the titan arum lasts only one or two days.
   ___ The titan arum grows in the rain forests of Sumatra, Indonesia.
   ✓ The titan arum is fascinating because it is rare, and it is the largest and smelliest flower in the world.

Write T before the sentences that are true. Write F before the sentences that are false.

7. F The titan arum can be found growing in the wild all around the United States.
8. T Both male and female flowers exist in the center spike of the titan arum.
9. T The titan arum has an awful odor.
10. F The bloom of the titan arum can last for two to three weeks.

109

Vocabulary Skills

Write the words from the story that have the meanings below.

1. thinking of ideas
   brainstorming (Par. 1)
2. an idea
   suggestion (Par. 7)
3. hot springs that spray steam and water into the air
   geysers (Par. 10)
4. to make a decision that pleases everyone
   compromise (Par. 11)
5. complete agreement
   unanimous (Par. 14)

Circle the homophone that correctly completes each sentence below, and write it on the line.

6. Maria hopes to see a bear and other animals at Yellowstone National Park. (bare, **bear**)
7. Mom knew that the family could reach a compromise. (**knew**, new)
8. The Garzas will meet many friendly people on their trip. (meat, **meet**)

Underline the suffix in each word. Then, write the meaning of the word.

9. thoughtless without thought
10. government the act of governing
11. fearless without fear
12. comfortable capable of comfort

Reading Skills

Circle the word that best completes each sentence below, and write it on the line.

1. Dad gathers the family for a meeting.
   gathers commands requests
2. Mom records everyone's vacation ideas.
   changes **records** ignores
3. Dad thinks that going someplace new would be a(n) adventure.
   journey **adventure** mistake
4. Name two things Dad says the family could do in Florida.
   Possible answers: swim in the ocean; eat fresh seafood; collect shells
5. Do you think the Garzas will be happy with their decision to camp at Yellowstone? Why or why not?
   Answers will vary.
6. How can you tell that Dad wants to go to the beach?
   He is wearing a sun visor, sunglasses, flip-flops, and a Hawaiian shirt.
7. What problem are the Garzas trying to solve in the story?
   where they should go on their vacation

Read the phrases below. Write M if it describes Maria. Write J if it describes Juan.

8. J has a friend named Sophie who went camping
9. M guesses that Dad wants to go to the beach

111

Vocabulary Skills

Find a synonym in the story for each of the words below.

1. responded replied (Par. 5)
2. choose select (Par. 6)
3. separates divides (Par. 9)

Fill in the blanks below with the possessive form of the word in parentheses.

4. The Garzas' vacation was going to be in Wyoming. (Garzas)
5. The library's selection of books was very helpful. (library)
6. It was Maria's idea to go to Yellowstone. (Maria)
7. Sophie's family was going to lend the Garzas a tent. (Sophie)
8. Mom thought the book's list would be useful. (book)

Reading Skills

Write B next to the sentence if it happened before the Garzas had chosen their books and met at the table. Write A if it happened afterward.

1. A The Garzas left the library.
2. B Mom and Juan made a list of call numbers.
3. B Dad scanned books about Wyoming and national parks.
4. B Mom and Juan spread out books on a table.
5. A Maria said that they should bring layers of clothes to wear.

Circle the word that best completes each sentence below, and write it on the line.

6. Sophie's family would loan the Garzas a tent.
   loan borrow sell
7. The materials were divided into categories.
   removed explained **divided**
8. Check the sentence that best states the main idea of the selection.
   ✓ The Garzas go to the library to find out how to prepare for their trip to Yellowstone.
   ___ The Garzas agree to meet by the reference desk.
   ___ Juan finds a helpful book that includes different types of checklists.

Study Skills

Use the information below to answer the questions that follow.

Call No:	462.65 KE
Author:	Kean, Maggie
Title:	Visiting the National Parks
Publisher:	Merli & Ball Publishing

1. Circle the call number of the book that would be closest on the shelf to the book listed above.
   462.65 PO 464.45 KA 460.65 MI
2. What is the book's title?
   Visiting the National Parks

113

Vocabulary Skills

Write the words from the article that have the meanings below.

1. not controlled by anyone else
   independent (Par. 1)
2. let go
   released (Par. 2)
3. animals that hunt and kill other animals
   predators (Par. 3)
4. got in the way
   interfered (Par. 3)
5. all sides are equal
   balanced (Par. 3)

Check the meaning of the underlined word in each sentence.

6. If you camp at Yellowstone, you might hear a wolf bay at night.
   ___ part of a sea
   ✓ howl
7. Wolves usually travel in a pack.
   ___ to fill with things
   ✓ a group

Write a compound word using two words in each sentence.

8. Antoine will carry a pack on his back when he hikes at the park.
   backpack
9. The family will bring some trail mix they made at home.
   homemade

Reading Skills

Write F before the sentences that are facts. Write O before the sentences that are opinions.

1. O Wolves are beautiful creatures.
2. F Yellowstone currently has the major predators it had throughout history.
3. O Wolves are an annoyance.
4. F Wolves mostly hunt elk and deer.
5. F More than 250 wolves live in Yellowstone today.
6. What caused the "see-saw" to become unbalanced at Yellowstone?
   Humans interfered with nature.
7. If another species disappears at Yellowstone in the future, what do you think scientists might do?
   Answers will vary.
8. What is a keystone species?
   a species upon which many other plants and animals depend
9. Did the environment at Yellowstone begin to change right before or right after the wolves were brought back?
   right after
10. What problem did some people have with wolves in Yellowstone?
    They thought the wolves were a dangerous annoyance.

Answer Key

115

Vocabulary Skills

Write the words from the article that have the meanings below.

1. suddenly bursts out

erupts (Par. 1)

2. water in the form of a gas

steam (Par. 1)

3. all together

combined (Par. 2)

4. a strong force

pressure (Par. 4)

5. said that something would happen in the future

predicted (Par. 5)

Check the correct meaning of the underlined word in each sentence.

6. Old Faithful is the most famous geyser.

____ capable of fame
✓ has much fame
____ to be without fame

7. Kyra was speechless the first time she saw a geyser.

✓ without speech
____ capable of speech
____ the act of speech

8. I just read an excellent nonfiction book about Yellowstone.

____ the act of fiction
____ before fiction
✓ not fiction

Reading Skills

1. Why do geysers erupt?

Heated water is trapped deep underground. Eventually the pressure from the hot water underground becomes stronger than the weight of cold water.

2. About how often does Old Faithful erupt?

every 30 to 90 minutes

3. Name two places other than Yellowstone where geysers can be found.

Possible answers: New Zealand; Japan; Iceland

4. How far into the air can Steamboat Geyser shoot water?

350 feet

5. What happens when the pressure of the hot water underground is greater than the cold water on top?

The geyser erupts.

6. Check the sentence below that is the best summary for paragraph 4.

____ The steam in a geyser has nowhere to go.
✓ Boiling water and steam build up below the cold water until the pressure is too great and the geyser erupts.
____ When a pot boils on a stove, the steam can evaporate.

Write **T** before the sentences that are true. Write **F** before the sentences that are false.

7. T There are almost 400 geysers at Yellowstone.
8. T After all the pressure is released, the eruption ends.
9. F All geysers shoot water into the air at the same height.

117

Vocabulary Skills

Write the words from the article that have the meanings below.

1. protect; make something last a long time

preserve (Par. 1)

2. worried

concerned (Par. 1)

3. someone who travels to different places for fun

tourist (Par. 2)

4. became bigger

expanded (Par. 3)

5. buildings or statues that help remind people of something

monuments (Par. 3)

Read each sentence below. Then, write a word from the **-ought** word family that best completes the sentence.

6. Who thought of creating national parks?
7. Throughout history, many people have fought to preserve natural areas.
8. Some wealthy Americans have bought land and donated it to the national parks.

Reading Skills

1. Why were the railroad companies happy about the creation of the national parks?

They wanted more people to travel greater distances so they could make more money.

2. How tall can redwoods grow to be?

more than 300 feet tall

3. Name one of the national monuments that was created while Theodore Roosevelt was President.

Petrified Forest; the Grand Canyon

4. Do you think more national parks will be founded in the future? Why or why not?

Answers will vary.

5. Number the events below from **1** to **4** to show the order in which they happened.

1 George Catlin was concerned about people moving westward.
4 The National Park Service was given the War Department's monuments.
2 Yellowstone National Park was created.
3 Congress passed the Antiquities Act.

Study Skills

A **time line** shows the order in which things happened. Use the time line below to answer the questions that follow.

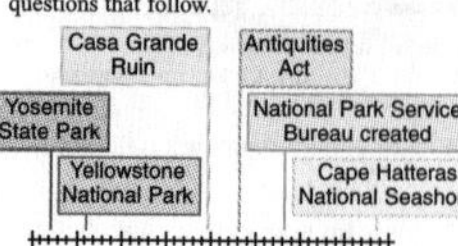

1. What year was the Antiquities Act passed?

1906

2. Which park was created in 1872?

Yellowstone National Park

3. Was Yosemite or Yellowstone created first?

Yosemite

119

Vocabulary Skills

Write the words from the story that have the meanings below.

1. large and oddly shaped

bulky (Par. 1)

2. the use of math to figure out or estimate something

calculations (Par. 3)

3. getting closer to

approaching (Par. 5)

4. a small round window, usually on the side of a ship

porthole (Par. 6)

5. enormous; very large

massive (Par. 6)

Write the idiom from paragraph 4 on the line next to its meaning.

6. getting nervous getting cold feet

Read each pair of words listed below. If the words are synonyms, write **S** on the line. If the words are antonyms, write **A** on the line.

7. A correct — wrong
8. S massive — enormous
9. S nervous — worried
10. A calm — excited
11. S rapidly — quickly
12. A remember — forget

Reading Skills

1. Check the words that describe Max.

____ competitive
✓ adventurous
✓ curious
✓ imaginative
____ shy

2. Why was Max glad to have Winnie with him on the spacecraft?

He would feel lonely without her company.

3. What was Max trying to take a picture of when he woke up?

a massive crater

4. In his dream, Max thinks he is bobbing up and down in the air as he is trying to snap a photo. What is happening in real life that makes him think this?

Winnie is prancing around on his waterbed.

5. On the line below, write the words that are dialogue in paragraph 5.

"Prepare for landing!"

If the event described takes place in reality, write **R** on the line. If it takes place in Max's fantasy, write **F** on the line.

6. R Winnie was trying to let Max know it was time for her breakfast.
7. F Max took a picture from the porthole of the spaceship.
8. F Max unsnapped parts of his spacesuit.
9. R Max got out of bed.
10. F Max told Winnie her picture would be in a history book.

121

Vocabulary Skills

Write the words from the article that have the meanings below.

1. an expert in the study of the universe

astronomer (Par. 2)

2. watching closely

observing (Par. 2)

3. ahead of its time

advanced (Par. 3)

4. to send upward with great force

launched (Par. 4)

5. prepared with things that are necessary

equipped (Par. 6)

Circle the homophone that correctly completes each sentence below, and write it on the line.

6. Our planet may not be the only one that has ever supported life. (Hour, (Our))
7. They made an amazing discovery. ((made), maid)
8. Sending spacecrafts to Mars was quite a feat. (feet, (feat))
9. NASA's space program has grown over the years. ((grown), groan)

Write **S** if the possessive word is singular. Write **P** if it is plural.

10. P astronomers'
11. S Mars's
12. S spacecraft's
13. S NASA's
14. P newspapers'
15. P scientists'

Reading Skills

1. What did Percival Lowell think Schiaparelli saw on the surface of Mars?

canals

2. What was the name of the American spacecraft that was sent to Mars in 1965?

Mariner 4

3. Do you think that scientists will continue to look for life on Mars? Why or why not?

Answers will vary.

4. In the passage, what problem did Percival Lowell have? Lowell began the theory that an advanced civilization on Mars had built canals all over the planet. He was wrong because Schiaparelli said there were channels, not canals, on Mars.

5. Does this selection take place in reality, or is it a fantasy? How can you tell?

The selection takes places in reality. You can tell because the author writes about things that actually happened in history.

6. Check the phrase that best describes the author's purpose.

____ to explain why there is no life on Mars
✓ to tell about the search for life on Mars
____ to persuade the reader to visit Mars someday

Read each sentence below. If the event took place before 1965, write **B** on the line. If it took place after 1965, write **A** on the line.

7. A *Spirit* and *Opportunity* landed on Mars.
8. B Schiaparelli noticed lines that ran across the surface of the planet.
9. B Lowell created the theory about canals and civilization on Mars.

Answer Key

Vocabulary Skills

Check the word that is a synonym for each word listed below.

1. brave
   ✓ courageous ____ afraid ____ thoughtful
2. goal
   ____ effort ✓ purpose ____ idea
3. strength
   ____ attitude ____ weakness ✓ power

Underline the word with a prefix in each sentence. Then, write the meaning of the word on the line.

4. The astronaut's children love it when she retells the story of her flight into space.
   tells again
5. Astronauts do things people once thought would be impossible.
   not possible
6. An astronaut should not be a dishonest person.
   not honest
7. It is important that an astronaut does not misunderstand directions he or she is given.
   understand badly

Reading Skills

1. What is the first thing you need to do if you want to become an astronaut?
   get a college education
2. What was the profession of most of the first astronauts?
   pilot
3. Why do you need to be in good shape to be an astronaut?
   Space flight is hard on the human body.
4. Why do you think astronauts need to be good communicators?
   Possible answers: They work in teams. It is important for reasons of safety.
5. What is a simulator?
   a computer game that looks and feels like the inside of the shuttle
6. On the lines below, write a summary for paragraph 4.
   To be an astronaut, you should be educated in the sciences, be in good physical shape, and be a trustworthy person.
7. Write **T** before the sentences that are true. Write **F** before the sentences that are false.
   F New astronauts can fly as soon as they have finished their training.
   T Today, astronauts need to be able to perform many tasks.
   F Alan Shepard was the oldest astronaut to go into space.
   F If you fly 40 miles above Earth, you are officially in space.
   T You need to have good eyesight to be a shuttle pilot.

Study Skills

Use a dictionary to help you divide these words into syllables.

1. astronaut as/tro/naut
2. orbit or/bit
3. scientist sci/en/tist
4. engineer en/gi/neer

123

Vocabulary Skills

Write the words from the story that have the meanings below.

1. hanging down
   dangling Par. 1
2. looking forward to something
   anticipating Par. 1
3. feeling pleased about something that you or someone else has done
   proud Par. 8
4. a measurement from side to side
   width Par. 9
5. showed
   demonstrated Par. 10

Find the simile in paragraph 4, and write it on the line below.

6. swims like a dolphin

Find an antonym in the story for each of the words below.

7. everything nothing Par. 3
8. depressed cheerful Par. 5
9. disappointed proud Par. 8

Divide the words below into syllables using a slash (/).

10. k i c k/b o a r d
11. b a r e/f o o t
12. l i f e/g u a r d

Circle the word in each row that does not belong.

13. happy (glum) excited cheerful
14. (brave) teach instruct show
15. swim kick (sit) paddle

Reading Skills

1. Check the words that describe Amelia.
   ____ funny
   ✓ brave
   ✓ determined
   ____ suspicious
   ✓ proud

Circle the word that best completes each sentence, and write it on the line.

2. Mom and Maggie helped Amelia overcome her fear of the water.
   ignore (overcome) explain
3. Maggie enjoys Amelia's company.
   (enjoys) dislikes forgets
4. Amelia's dad had not expected her to learn so much in one afternoon.
   wanted (expected) selected
5. Why does Maggie feel sad at the beginning of the story?
   She doesn't think Amelia will come over to swim, and nothing is as much fun without Amelia.
6. What does Dad mean when he says, "I'm going to have a prune for a daughter all summer"?
   He thinks Amelia will be in the water so much that her skin will be wrinkled for much of the summer.
7. Why does Amelia want to learn how to swim?
   She is tired of being scared of the water, and she doesn't want to miss a whole summer of swimming with Maggie.
8. Why does Amelia say that she wants to come back tomorrow?
   She is excited that she is learning how to swim.

125

Vocabulary Skills

Write the words from the article that have the meanings below.

1. packed tightly together; heavy
   dense Par. 2
2. able to float
   buoyant Par. 4
3. melts; turns from a solid into a liquid
   dissolves Par. 5
4. the amount of space something takes up
   volume Par. 6

Check the meaning of the underlined word in each sentence.

5. The carrot should sink in the first experiment.
   ✓ go below the surface
   ____ a container with faucets and a drain
6. Please turn down the volume on your stereo.
   ✓ the degree of loudness
   ____ the amount of space something takes up
7. The grape will float in fresh water but not in salt water.
   ____ a large exhibit in a parade
   ✓ to stay above the surface

Fill in the blanks below with the possessive form of the word in parentheses.

8. A carrot's cells are packed together more tightly. (carrot)
9. The Dead Sea's water is much saltier than the water of other oceans or seas. (Sea)

Reading Skills

Circle the word that best completes each sentence, and write it on the line.

1. Salt water is denser than freshwater.
   (denser) colder deeper
2. Something that is heavier than the same volume of water will sink.
   older (heavier) stronger
3. The Dead Sea is saltier than the oceans of the world.
   lighter fresher (saltier)
4. Check the phrase that best describes the author's purpose.
   ✓ to explain how to conduct two experiments about floating
   ____ to persuade the reader to become a scientist
   ____ to show why the water in the Dead Sea is so salty
5. Why do you think you need to use warm water in the second experiment?
   so the salt will dissolve
6. Why does the apple float while the carrot sinks?
   The cells of the apple are not packed as tightly. Because they have more air, they are lighter and float better.
7. What do you think would happen if you used an egg instead of a grape in the second experiment?
   the same thing
8. Where is the Dead Sea located?
   near Israel

127

Vocabulary Skills

Write the words from the story that have the meanings below.

1. without stopping
   steadily Par. 1
2. flowed over the top of
   overflowed Par. 3
3. equipment for a particular activity
   gear Par. 9
4. flowed in a thin stream
   trickled Par. 9
5. to cover one thing with part of another thing
   overlap Par. 12

Underline the word with a suffix in each sentence. Then, write the meaning of the word on the line below it.

6. This was the closest the Lopez family had been to having their house flooded.
   most close
7. The members of the family gave each other a lot of encouragement as they worked.
   the act of encouraging
8. Mom and Dad carried the heaviest bags.
   most heavy

Reading Skills

1. Name two rainy day activities Teresa and Manuel did.
   Possible answers: played games, painted, made cookies, watched movies, helped their mom clean out closets
2. Why did the grass squish beneath their feet as they walked across it?
   The ground was full of water.
3. Where did Mrs. Lopez hear the news that Sawmill Creek was flooding?
   on the radio
4. If the story continued, what do you think would happen next?
   Answers will vary.
5. Name one way that Teresa and Manuel are similar.
   Possible answers: They are both bored; they both want to play outside; they both think that sandbagging the house is exciting.

Write **F** before the sentences that are facts. Write **O** before the sentences that are opinions.

6. F At the beginning of the story, Teresa and Manuel are bored.
7. O Keeping the basement from flooding is exciting.
8. F Sawmill Creek is rising quickly.
9. F Mom and Dad overlap the sandbags so there are not gaps between them.
10. O Rainy days are boring.

Study Skills

Check each word that could be found on a page having the guide words shown in dark print.

1. **bread—broccoli**
   ✓ brick ____ brush ✓ brittle
2. **wallow—water ski**
   ✓ walrus ✓ wasp ____ web
3. **hoax—hooked**
   ____ hoarse ✓ homestead ✓ honk

129

Answer Key

131

Vocabulary Skills

Read each word below. Then, write the letter of its antonym on the line beside the word.

1. b closer — a. destroyed
2. d mountain — b. farther
3. a created — c. wonderful
4. c terrible — d. valley

Circle the words in each row that are part of the same word family.

5. (-ought) (thought) thank (sought) thump
6. (-ight) (sunlight) sundae fling (flight)
7. (-ould) wonder (would) (could) wound

Underline the compound word in each sentence. Then, write the two words that make up each compound.

8. The city was built on a floodplain in Pennsylvania.
flood plain
9. South Fork Dam was 14 miles upstream.
up stream
10. People received help from places that were far from southwestern Pennsylvania.
south western

Reading Skills

1. Who owned South Fork Dam at the time of the flood?
South Fork Fishing and Hunting Club
2. Why does the author say that the fact that Johnstown exists today shows the strength of people in that town?
They didn't let the flood destroy them or their town. They were able to recover from the tragedy.
3. What problem did the people of Johnstown have in the selection?
The dam burst and water destroyed much of the town and took many lives.
4. Number the events below from 1 to 5 in the order in which they happened.
2 Some people were worried that the dam might not hold.
3 The dam sent 20 million tons of water rushing down the Little Conemaugh River.
5 The Johnstown Flood National Memorial was founded.
1 The South Fork Fishing and Hunting Club bought the South Fork Dam.
4 The people of the town were caught by surprise.
5. Check the sentence that best states the main idea of the selection.
___ The water flooded Johnstown at speeds of about 40 miles per hour.
___ The city of Johnstown is located in southwestern Pennsylvania.
✓ The Johnstown Flood in 1889 was one of the worst disasters in American history.
6. Check the line beside the word or words that tell what type of nonfiction selection this is.
___ biography
✓ history
___ how-to text
7. Does this story take place in reality, or is it a fantasy? How can you tell?
The selection takes places in reality. You can tell because the author writes about things that actually happened in history.

133

Vocabulary Skills

Write the words from the story that have the meanings below.

1. a job or profession
career (Par. 1)
2. practical; similar to the way things are in real life
realistic (Par. 2)
3. someone who designs buildings
architect (Par. 3)
4. someone who studies oceans and ocean life
oceanographer (Par. 4)
5. the story of someone's life
biography (Par. 8)

Write the idiom from paragraph 2 on the line next to its meaning.

6. something that is not likely a long shot

In each row, circle the words that belong together.

7. (ocean) (underwater) career amazing
8. biography (career) (job) (profession)
9. (structure) information (building) forest

Write S if the possessive word is singular. Write P if it is plural.

10. S Saki's
11. P ballplayers'
12. S Hiroshi's
13. P firefighters'
14. S house's
15. S apple's

Reading Skills

1. What is Hiroshi's homework assignment?
to decide what kind of career he wanted and to research it
2. What did Hiroshi like about Fallingwater?
He felt like the house was part of the forest and the waterfall was part of the house.
3. How does Saki tease her brother at the end of the story?
She reminds him that he wanted to be a clown when he was little.
4. What made Hiroshi want to be an oceanographer?
He likes that there are so many things humans don't know about the ocean yet.
5. On the line below, write the words that are dialogue in paragraph 4.
"What are you doing?"

Read the sentences below. Write H next to the sentence if it describes Hiroshi. Write S if it describes Saki.

6. S eats a green apple
7. H wanted to be a firefighter
8. S has a good memory
9. H likes the mystery of the ocean
10. H makes a list of career ideas

Study Skills

Use a dictionary to help you divide these words into syllables.

1. information in/for/ma/tion
2. professional pro/fess/io/nal
3. oceanographer o/cea/nog/ra/pher
4. assignment a/ssign/ment

135

Vocabulary Skills

Write the words from the article that have the meanings below.

1. natural; made of living things
organic (Par. 2)
2. copied
imitated (Par. 4)
3. able to be seen
visible (Par. 5)
4. something that creates new ideas
inspiration (Par. 6)
5. an artist's greatest work
masterpiece (Par. 7)

Write the words from the article that match the abbreviations below.

6. WI Wisconsin
7. IL Illinois
8. PA Pennsylvania

Reading Skills

1. How were the prairie houses similar to the landscape of the Midwest?
Both are flat and spread out.
2. How do you think Fallingwater got its name?
There are waterfalls nearby.
3. What is the shape of the Guggenheim Museum in New York City?
a spiral
4. What do you think Wright's feelings about the natural world were?
He probably had an interest in and respect for the natural world.
5. Check the sentence below that is the best summary for paragraph 4.
✓ One of Wright's most popular designs was the prairie house, which imitated the Midwest landscape.
___ The Midwest contains many areas of flat farmland.
6. Check the words that describe Wright.
✓ imaginative ✓ unique
___ talkative ___ rude
✓ creative
7. Check the line beside the word or words that tell what type of selection this is.
✓ biography ___ myth
___ how-to

Study Skills

Use the table below to answer the questions that follow.

Frank Lloyd Wright Buildings		
1909	Robie House	Chicago, IL
1911	Taliesin	Spring Green, WI
1915	Imperial Hotel	Tokyo, Japan
1936	Johnson Wax Headquarters	Racine, WI

1. Which building was built in 1915?
Imperial Hotel
2. In what year was the Robie House built?
1909
3. Which building is located in Spring Green, Wisconsin?
Taliesin

137

Vocabulary Skills

Write the words from the article that have the meanings below.

1. very interested in
fascinated (Par. 1)
2. making a map of
mapping (Par. 3)
3. any living creatures
organisms (Par. 4)
4. something expensive and pleasurable that isn't really necessary
luxury (Par. 6)
5. first or earliest
maiden (Par. 7)
6. a device that uses sound waves to find underwater objects
sonar (Par. 7)

Check the correct meaning of the underlined word.

7. The ocean is a mysterious place.
___ capable of mystery
___ without mystery
✓ full of mystery
8. Ballard's enjoyment of the ocean makes his hard work worthwhile.
___ full of enjoying
✓ the act of enjoying
___ without enjoying

Reading Skills

Write F before the sentences that are facts. Write O before the sentences that are opinions.

1. O Robert Ballard is the greatest living scientist today.
2. F Ballard grew up in San Diego.
3. O More money should be spent on space exploration than on ocean exploration.
4. F The *Titanic* sank on her maiden voyage in 1912.
5. F Ballard discovered tubeworms near the Galápagos Islands.
6. What is one way in which outer space and the oceans are similar?
There are mysteries about both that humans have not discovered yet.
7. Why was Ballard's discovery of deepwater tubeworms so important?
It showed that a form of life could survive without the sun. This changed the way scientists thought about the possibility of life on other planets.
8. What did *Argo* send back to the surface from deep underwater?
photographs
9. Why did Ballard have to wait a year before exploring the *Titanic*?
He had to wait for good weather conditions.
10. Who is the author of the novel *20,000 Leagues Under the Sea*?
Jules Verne

Answer Key

Vocabulary Skills

Write the words from the story that have the meanings below.

1. satisfying rewarding (Par. 4)
2. to express in a different language or a different way translate (Par. 4)
3. built or put together constructed (Par. 6)
4. to follow shadow (Par. 8)

Circle the homophone that correctly completes each sentence below, and write it on the line.

5. Hiroshi's aunt told Mr. Daley to expect an e-mail from her nephew. (**aunt**, ant)
6. The greeting Hiroshi uses in his e-mail is "dear." (**dear**, deer)
7. The architect does not actually build the structure. (billed, **build**)
8. A person who plans to buy a house might meet with an architect. (bye, **buy**)

Fill in the blanks below with the possessive form of the word in parentheses.

9. Hiroshi's aunt is Mr. Daley's friend. (Hiroshi)
10. An architect's job is to make a building interesting, safe, and easy to use. (architect)
11. Schools' designs are created by architects. (Schools)

Reading Skills

1. How do you think Hiroshi was introduced to Mr. Daley?
   His aunt probably introduced him.
2. Why does Mr. Daley say that architecture is unusual?
   It is a blend of both art and science.
3. What is Mr. Daley's favorite part of being an architect?
   seeing the idea that he had in his mind become an actual building
4. Name four types of buildings an architect might design.
   Possible answers: houses, apartments, schools, office buildings, grocery stores, churches, malls, hotels, factories, gymnasiums, airports, hospitals
5. Do you think that Hiroshi and Mr. Daley will ever meet in person? Why or why not?
   Answers will vary.
6. Check the phrase that best describes the author's purpose.
   - ✓ to entertain the reader with a story about how a boy learns what an architect does
   - ___ to persuade the reader to become an architect
   - ___ to describe the schooling an architect needs
7. Check the words that describe Mr. Daley.
   - ✓ helpful
   - ✓ kind
   - ___ unpredictable
   - ✓ intelligent
   - ___ stingy

139

Vocabulary Skills

Write the words from the article that have the meanings below.

1. the place someone or something is going destination (Par. 1)
2. a way of sending messages by wire to a receiving station telegraph (Par. 2)
3. to move from one place to another transfer (Par. 4)
4. occurred; was real existed (Par. 6)
5. warned; let someone know alerted (Par. 6)

Circle the homophone that correctly completes each sentence below and write it on the line.

6. The Pony Express riders rode many miles to deliver the mail. (road, **rode**)
7. A rider's weight was important because it could affect how fast a horse could travel. (wait, **weight**)
8. The Pony Express route was so dangerous that the owners suggested the riders be orphans. (**so**, sew)
9. A rider got a new horse every 10 to 15 miles. (**horse**, hoarse)

Find the compound words from the selection that contain the words below.

10. parent grandparent
11. mail mailbox
12. air airplane

Reading Skills

1. What is a *mochila*?
   a saddlebag that was used to carry mail
2. Why was the Pony Express originally needed?
   to get mail from the Midwest to California
3. Name one important message that was carried to California by the Pony Express.
   Possible answers: Abraham Lincoln was elected president; the Civil War began.
4. Why did Pony Express riders have to be small and light?
   so their horses could go farther and move faster
5. About how long was the route between St. Joseph, Missouri, and San Francisco, California?
   about 2,000 miles
6. Check the line beside the word or words that tell what type of selection this is.
   - ___ fiction
   - ✓ historical nonfiction
   - ___ fantasy
7. Number the events below in the order in which they happened in the selection.
   - 2 The Pony Express was founded.
   - 3 The first rider left St. Joseph on horseback.
   - 5 The Pacific Telegraph Company completed its line to San Francisco.
   - 1 People began moving to the American West.
   - 4 Abraham Lincoln was elected President.

141

Vocabulary Skills

Find an antonym in the story for each of the words below.

1. less more (Par. 1)
2. shortest longest (Par. 8)
3. closing opening (Par. 10)
4. different same (Par. 12)

Write **S** if the possessive word is singular. Write **P** if it is plural.

5. P riders'
6. S Kenji's
7. S schedule's
8. P friends'
9. S Alexi's
10. P books'

Reading Skills

1. Where did Kenji and Alexi's class go on their field trip?
   Pony Express National Museum
2. Which state does Kenji say has rough terrain?
   Wyoming
3. How often do the members of the National Pony Express Association do a reenactment?
   once a year
4. What is one difference between the reenactors and the original Pony Express riders?
   Possible answers: They use their own horses; they only ride about five miles.
5. Check the line beside theword or words that tell what type of selection this is.
   - ___ biography
   - ✓ fiction
   - ___ historical nonfiction

Read the sentences below. Write **K** next to the phrase if it describes Kenji. Write **A** if it describes Alexi. Write **B** if it describes both Kenji and Alexi.

6. K says that the trip through Wyoming must have been difficult
7. B lives in St. Joseph, Missouri
8. B visited the Pony Express Museum the day before
9. A wants to cheer on the reenactors as they ride through St. Joseph

Study Skills

Use the information below to answer the questions that follow.

Pony Express Museum Information

Tickets:

Adults	$4.00	Students (7–18)	$2.00
Seniors	$3.00	Kids 6 and under	Free

Hours:
Mon.–Sat.: 9–5
Sun.: 1–5

1. How much is admission for a student?
   $2.00
2. What are the museum's hours on Sunday?
   1–5
3. Who can get into the museum for free?
   kids 6 and under
4. Which type of ticket is most expensive?
   adult tickets

143

Vocabulary Skills

Write the words from the article that have the meanings below.

1. hard to tell what is coming unpredictable (Par. 1)
2. impossible to be crossed or traveled past impassable (Par. 1)
3. versions of a story accounts (Par. 5)
4. something that people tell each other instead of writing down word-of-mouth (Par. 6)
5. said to be bigger or more interesting than it actually is exaggerated (Par. 6)

Check the correct meaning of the underlined word.

6. Riders on the Pony Express were <u>courageous</u> young men.
   - ___ capable of courage
   - ✓ full of courage
   - ___ without courage
7. The stories about Buffalo Bill Cody say that he was <u>fearless</u>.
   - ✓ without fear
   - ___ full of fear
   - ___ fear again

Reading Skills

1. Who was Johnny Fry?
   He was probably the first westbound Pony Express rider.
2. What sorts of difficulties did riders face on the trail?
   Possible answers: bad weather; rough terrain, conflict with bandits or Native Americans
3. About how much were the Pony Express riders paid?
   one hundred dollars a month
4. Who did Johnny Fry fight for during the Civil War?
   the Union
5. Why aren't historians sure who made the longest ride on the Pony Express?
   There were few written records. Information was passed along by word-of-mouth.

Write **T** before the sentences that are true. Write **F** before the sentences that are false.

6. F Buffalo Bill Cody started riding for the Pony Express when he was 11 years old.
7. T Johnny Fry rode from St. Joseph, Missouri, to Seneca, Kansas.
8. T There was the frequent threat of bad weather on the route.
9. T Johnny Fry was killed during the Civil War.
10. F Most of the Pony Express riders weighed more than 150 pounds.

Study Skills

Use a dictionary to help you divide these words into syllables.

1. courageous cour/a/geous
2. Americans A/mer/i/cans
3. experienced ex/per/i/enced
4. dangerous dan/ger/ous
5. information in/for/ma/tion

145

Answer Key

147

Vocabulary Skills

Write the words from the article that have the meanings below.

1. stored food and supplies provisions (Par. 2)
2. extremely happy overjoyed (Par. 5)
3. nervous; easily frightened skittish (Par. 6)
4. able to be proven true confirmed (Par. 8)
5. faraway; hard to reach remote (Par. 8)

Write the words from the story that match the abbreviations below.

6. TX Texas
7. CO Colorado
8. NV Nevada
9. ID Idaho

Divide the words below into syllables using a slash (/).

10. t h e m/s e l v e s
11. o/v e r/j o y e d
12. s o u t h/w e s t

Write S if the possessive word is singular. Write P if it is plural.

13. S military's
14. P camels'
15. S Congress's
16. P animals'

Reading Skills

1. What kinds of problems was the U.S. military having with the camels?
   Some soldiers did not like the camels. Also, the Camel Corps still was not used very often.
2. Do you think there are any camels still living in the U.S. deserts today? Explain your answer.
   Answers will vary.
3. Check the line beside the word or words that tell what type of selection this is.
   ____ fairy tale
   ✓ nonfiction
   ____ biography
4. How did the camels help the people when the expedition became lost?
   They led the people to water.
5. Why did some soldiers dislike the camels?
   They thought the animals were bad tempered and had a strong odor.
6. Number the events below in the order in which they happened in the selection.
   4 The U.S. Camel Corps no longer existed.
   1 Jefferson Davis recommended that the army try using camels for transporting things in the desert.
   5 The last confirmed camel sighting happened in the American desert.
   2 Members of the U.S. military went to North Africa to look for camels to purchase.
   3 Another 41 camels arrived in the United States.

149

Vocabulary Skills

Write the words from the article that have the meanings below.

1. moved from one country or area to another migrated (Par. 1)
2. turned into; became developed (Par. 1)
3. trained; used by human beings domesticated (Par. 2)
4. features or qualities characteristics (Par. 3)

Circle the words in each row that are part of the same word family.

5. (-ought) (bought) sigh sing (brought)
6. (-ight) (fight) (right) ton (tonight)
7. (-ought) trout (fought) (thought) thimble

Underline the word with a suffix or a prefix in each sentence. Then, write the meaning of the word on the line.

8. The camel is one of the <u>strangest</u> animals alive today. most strange
9. It is <u>incorrect</u> to believe that camels store extra water in their humps. not correct
10. Camels do not show a great <u>enjoyment</u> of the work they do. the act of enjoying
11. Sarah felt like the <u>luckiest</u> girl in the world when she got to ride a camel on her trip to Egypt. most lucky

Reading Skills

Write F before the sentences that are facts. Write O before the sentences that are opinions.

1. F There are two types of camels.
2. F Camels can go without water for long periods of time.
3. O Camels are more interesting than horses or mules.
4. F A camel's body temperature can vary by 11 degrees.
5. O Camels are very strange-looking animals.
6. How did camels travel from North America to Asia millions of years ago?
   on a bridge of land over the Bering Strait
7. Name one way the dromedary and the Bactrian camel are alike.
   Possible answers: They run the same way; they both will eat almost anything; both can carry large loads and go for long periods without water.
8. Name one way the dromedary and the Bactrian camel are different.
   Possible answers: number of humps; where they are found; body shape and weight; pads on the feet
9. What is a camel's hump made of?
   fat and muscle
10. Why does a camel rock from side to side when it runs?
    It lifts both feet on one side at the same time.

151

Vocabulary Skills

Write the words from the story that have the meanings below.

1. not enough of something that is needed scarce (Par. 6)
2. change in order to survive in different conditions adapt (Par. 6)
3. not active for a period of time dormant (Par. 8)
4. active only at night nocturnal (Par. 10)
5. to dig a hole in the ground burrow (Par. 10)

Check the meaning of the underlined word in each sentence.

6. Mr. Patel turned around to <u>face</u> the class.
   ✓ to look at
   ____ the front part of the head
7. Mr. Patel discussed three <u>major</u> types of desert plants.
   ____ an officer in the military
   ✓ important; basic
8. The cactus is one <u>type</u> of desert plant.
   ✓ a group that has common characteristics
   ____ to write using a computer

Find the compound words from the selection that contain the words below.

9. ground underground
10. skate skateboard
11. after afternoon

Reading Skills

1. What is one way the cactus has adapted to life in the desert?
   Possible answers: It stores water so that it can go for long periods of time without rain. The stem is thick and has a waxy skin. Its spines give it some shade from the hot desert sun.
2. How are a dormant plant and a hibernating animal similar?
   They both go through a period where they are in a type of deep sleep.
3. What do nocturnal desert animals do during the day?
   sleep
4. How do the long roots of some desert plants help them survive?
   They can reach water that is far below the surface of the desert.
5. About how much of the human body is made of water?
   more than half
6. On the line below, write the words that are dialogue in paragraph 3.
   "Is it water?"
7. Check the sentence that best states the main idea of the selection.
   ____ Some desert animals are nocturnal and avoid the most extreme heat of the day.
   ✓ Mr. Patel's class learns about how plants and animals survive in the desert.
   ____ Water is necessary to all forms of life.

Notes

Notes

Notes

Notes